PREPARED AND RESOLVED

The Strategic Agenda for
Growth, Performance and Change

PREPARED AND RESOLVED

The Strategic Agenda for
Growth, Performance and Change

Daniel Wolf

Dewar Sloan
Consultants & Advisors to Management
dwolf@dewarsloan.com

dsb

Published by dsb Publishing
Administrative Offices
29 Pearl St. NW
Suite 227
Grand Rapids, MI 49503

ISBN 13:978-0-9791300-0-7
ISBN 10:9791300-0-X
Library of Congress Control Number: 2006910135
Printed in Canada
10 9 8 7 6 5 4 3 2 1
Development by Team Einstein.
Design elements by Saxon Design.

Several dsb Publishing books are available for executive development, management
education or board development on a special program basis. Special excerpt materials
and monographs can be developed from this book as well as others published by dsb
Publishing. For details, contact the dsb Special Markets Group at 231-929-1667.
See also www.preparedandresolved.com.

CONTENTS

PART TWO
Strategy Direction, Integration and Execution

PART THREE
The Purpose and Practice of Strategy

CONTENTS

FOREWORD

The way leaders have made organizations successful has been of profound interest to people for centuries. In business, government, the arts and other fields, we have focused on answering one fundamental question: "What really makes a difference?" The basic issues transcend every discipline, for a business trying to compete and serve its markets, or an organization striving to uphold its public obligations. Since everyone has a stake in finding the answer to this question, we owe it to ourselves to embrace new and practical ideas on strategy, along with a new kind of leadership.

> *"So there are five things leaders must treat carefully:*
> *order, preparedness, resoluteness, discipline, simplicity."*
> —*Wu Qi, circa 400 BC*

This quote came to mind when I read the first manuscript for this book. When we think of business success, we usually consider things like management depth, business strategy and communication skills. But these considerations constitute only a fraction of what is really needed to lead a successful company. If organizations attempt to compete without first mastering the foundations for success, they will always fall short of their potential. Leading and managing the agenda for business success is indeed harder than it looks, and it's tough to sustain. Business success is an evolutionary objective in an uncertain world that is influenced by many forces.

Wolf strikes a chord in *Prepared and Resolved* that is powerful and opens the mind to the real issues that shape business success. He gets at the gut-level issues that leaders must address in order to do their very best, to deliver results with enduring impact. He is one of a few authorities who have been able to approach the subject of business success from so many perspectives: practitioner, consultant, studied observer, and thought leader.

Dan Wolf has been my consultant, counselor and confidant for more than 25 years. I was very pleased when he told me he was writing this book. After reading *Prepared and Resolved*, I am hopeful that he will write more, sharing his insights on business growth, performance and change.

Steven P. Krakoff
Chief Executive Officer, Medical Center of Newark

PREFACE

My intent with this book is to share a point of view on business, one that provides a practical agenda for growth, performance and change.

My approach is anchored by the idea that successful companies are more prepared and resolved than their peers, and here is what I mean:

Prepared – they are focused and ready to conduct business in a world that is dynamic and complex.

Resolved – they are committed to think and behave in ways that deliver results and evolve the business.

This book presents a focused point of view about business strategy and company success. Pioneers including Lèon Danco and others have taught us to consider the bridges between the *strategy of the business* and the *success of the company*. My framework extends that idea further.

It helps redefine the practice of strategy in terms that are meaningful and relevant to the organization.

It helps recast the work of leadership and management in every corner of the organization, focusing on results.

It helps settle the common disconnects that lurk in the work of strategy direction, integration and execution.

It helps recharge the people of the organization on the road of business growth, performance and change.

It helps build sound disciplines and principles that engage strategic thought and behavior for everyone.

My sense is that most people in most organizations can benefit from *Prepared and Resolved* as a natural set of ideas and principles. This is not a formula, but a foundation for business thought and behavior. It represents a progressive approach to company growth, performance and change.

My inspiration for this book and its subject matter comes from more than 25 years of direct experience with companies facing issues in business growth, performance and change. My team has researched business practices, and we have evaluated the common barriers to business success. We have concluded that the *best opportunities come to those organizations whose people are prepared and resolved for business success*, in the most complete and confident manner, in the face of today's challenges as well as tomorrow's frontiers. These organizations are ready and resilient and focused.

My approach is structured, and my basic framework is suitable for any business, regardless of scale or scope. The ingredients of this approach include several closely-related subjects:

Strategy as a Disciplined and Evolving Process...
Our research and experience suggest that strategy in everyday practice can be more effective, always improving, evolving.

The Development of Leadership and Management Practices...
Our research and experience indicate that people can be more effective in the management and leadership of every aspect of growth, performance and change, at every level of the company.

Communication that Engages Human Performance...
Our research and experience suggest that the right kind and form of communication can power the broader engagement of people.

From my point of view, a company's agenda for success starts with a commonsense base – being prepared and resolved. How people direct and connect that agenda makes all the difference. My task is to clarify the strategic agenda for people in every corner of the company. Building the company's agenda for business growth, performance and change is the outcome we intend to frame as you read through the pages of *Prepared and Resolved*. The agenda for business success starts now, not with some new theory, but with a more prospective and focused mindset.

My apologies to all the original thinkers in philosophy, economics, leadership, organization, behavior, religion, design and management. My purpose is to put the work of effective leadership and management in perspective. The strategic agenda of *Prepared and Resolved* is my vehicle for getting these ideas on the ground. This approach is catalytic and practical and targeted.

3okdonego OKok

There are many different ways to approach the subject of strategy, and the concerns of management and leadership in the practice of strategy. My path is one that many people find useful as they break out of the many confounded ruts of conventional strategic planning procedures and exercises.

Abraham Lincoln, remarking on some of his early writings suggested that *...People who like this sort of thing will find this the sort of thing they like...*or something to that effect. This book is not about parables, case studies, check lists or hero worship. Instead it tackles business strategy in a way that works, by common sense. That's my approach and I believe it will work for you. Cases are perishable. Hero worship can be misleading and harmful. Cultures cannot be transferred from one company to another; recipes are nice, but they don't inspire. I deal with the realities and nuances of business.

My intent here is to encourage people to appreciate what is really involved in this "sort of thing" we call *Prepared and Resolved*. We are living in an age with great opportunities and challenges, and as we move along our strategic journeys, the way we approach business strategy demands a new kind of leadership and management. We require a better way, with new vision.

Getting prepared is no mean task or feat. Becoming resolved is a personal charge. This "sort of thing" is not for the meek, and it's not part of some easy shortcut to sustainable business performance. This "sort of thing" is a cultural foundation of successful companies. Faced with the many challenges of business evolution, this "sort of thing" is what really makes the difference between success and degradation. Successful companies have near-term and long-term goals, anchored in the agenda for growth, performance and change. We put those goals in context with *Prepared and Resolved.*

My passion for this "sort of thing" is lifelong. My worldview has been shaped by experiences with technical, social, and economic change. My compass has some deeply personal settings that reflect upon the greater need for thoughtful, prepared and resolved behavior. This "sort of thing" can make a huge difference in the life of a company. That is my simple proposition.

Daniel Wolf
September 30, 2006

DEDICATION

Arthur Landon Sloan
[1899–1988]

Make them evermore aware. Help them share in understanding.
Engage them in their very best thoughts and behaviors.

Many people have contributed to the premises and ideas that form the backbone of this book, *Prepared and Resolved*. Executives, advisors, educators, trustees, adversaries, friends and enemies have shaped what has become our platform for strategy management and leadership. Naturally, I am indebted to many people for the good stuff that flows into our way of thinking. I take full credit for the ideas that may have less merit and value, along with any aspects of this work that don't make sense. My family is blessed in many ways; it shows in their patience. My friends and colleagues are a solid bunch, never bashful with their thoughts and never lacking in their integrity. My teachers are faithful in their roles and their engagement. Thanks to all of you, who inspire us to be prepared and resolved. And thanks most of all to my trusted advisor, first mate and confidant, JW.

PROLOGUE

My colleagues asked me to write this book to help people manage and lead the evolution of their organizations. The strategic agenda for growth, performance and change is important. However, this world is complex and dynamic. Framing the *strategic agenda* and making it happen are real challenges. This practice is harder than it looks.

These issues are relevant to people at every level of the company, from governance to operating management, and from tactical teams to senior leadership. Everywhere in today's business organization is the need for a business agenda that helps people get prepared and resolved for success. This relates to near-term and long-term business plans.

The meaning of business success has been studied and preached by many experts and many business leaders. My approach to defining business success is very simple. It's what you do to drive results, and what you do to evolve with a responsible approach to change, and how you engage your people with a cause-and-effect strategic agenda.

COMMON CONCERNS ABOUT STRATEGY

Large and small companies alike share a number of common concerns regarding their business agenda, plans, actions and results. Our research and experience over the past 25 years sets up three areas of concern:

Strategic Direction and Purpose
Concern about the company's goals, intentions, focus and values. Concern about the principles and choices of the company, and the communication of these ideas to every level and every corner of the organization.

Planning and Resource Integration
Concern about the company's structure, resources and mechanisms for driving the company's strategic agenda. Concern about the integration of people, ideas, processes, assets, relationships and systems, as conditions change.

Execution Sense and Capacity
Concern about the company's ability to execute plans and ideas in a business environment that is both complex and dynamic. Concern about the energy required, judgment and resolute courage to get things done, regardless.

In our experience, most organizations share these concerns and most organizations face serious barriers to success due to the nature of these issues. We will address these concerns. However, the answers begin with a commitment to a better approach to managing and leading the company's strategic agenda. That is our purpose in this book, and it's the opportunity platform we use in guiding companies today.

As you continue reading, the familiar challenges of management and leadership will unfold. The consequences of miscues and obstacles in strategy direction, integration and execution will be put into context. The agenda for business growth, performance and change will become clear for your company, and clear to everyone who works with you. The thought and behavior that help strategy mesh will be revealed. *Prepared and Resolved* provides a framework for leading and managing the strategic agenda and it presents critical questions that every company must answer.

2

THOUGHTS ABOUT BUSINESS SUCCESS

Roughly 25 years ago, we suggested an idea – *the natural goals of business.* This is an idea that often appears in mission statements and corporate vision documents. In addition, these are frequently stated as themes that appear in company performance measures, and as parts of so-called scorecards.

Natural goals are a meaningful starting point for the discussion about business success. Here is my condensed version of natural goals and the important areas that are shaped by the natural goals of business in most companies.

NATURAL GOALS OF BUSINESS

Financial Performance
Creating New Economic Value; Balancing Risks

Competitive Advantage
Category Position and Differentiation, Market Edge

Customer Connection
Attracting, Managing and Sustaining Customers

Corporate Stewardship
Social Responsibility to Key Stakeholder Groups

Source: Exploring The Four Natural Goals of Business: Principles that Shape Strategic and Economic Value for Companies. Revised 2004, Dewar Sloan White Paper, part of ongoing research program in Boards and Strategy, 2004-2006.

Business success is often measured in these terms. However, business success is driven by other factors. Those include innovative goods and services, the tangible and intangible resources that are managed by people, the culture and structure of the business organization, and the leadership of thought, behavior and action of the company. These and other factors are part of the success formula in most business sectors. They are often tallied in notes that are off-balance sheet, and they may be undeveloped or unexploited as success engines. These factors will be addressed in Chapters 04, 05, and 06.

GETTING FOCUSED ON BUSINESS RESULTS

At the highest level, most company executives define their business agenda around the idea of creating new strategic and economic value. The value creation formula is unique to each business entity, but for most companies, value creation tends to be something that has mixed meaning for customers, investors, suppliers, partners and employees.

My thoughts on value creation have been shaped over the years by experience in product development, business alliances, marketing management, operating partnerships and new ventures. What really drives value creation? Good people working with effective processes and proper resources are surely part of the equation. When everything is said and done, however, the most successful companies are simply more focused on business results, measured in value terms. They create new strategic and economic value through their agenda. The strategic agenda connects people, ideas, actions and results at every level of the business enterprise.

BUSINESS PRINCIPLES AND OBJECTIVES

Focus is something that reflects established principles and objectives. Principles are extensions of what a company stands for, and where it's headed. Principles are normally embedded in company culture and structure. Objectives represent a company's targeted, measured ideas. They are things to accomplish, guides of meaningful action and impact.

Frequently missing in management and leadership effort is the credibility of business principles and objectives. When stakeholders are unclear about the company's principles and objectives, there is less energy for getting focused on business results. When the management team "declares" strategy without substantive reflections on business principles and objectives, the task has only just begun and success is probably a long way down a frustrating, messy and conflicted road. *Espoused strategy* can differ greatly from a company's everyday strategic behavior. That may reflect a problem of principle.

When I examine a company's focus, I consider the language and symbols used to express strategic direction, integration and execution. I look at the passion that surrounds big ideas. I look at the priorities that are more or less clear to everyone. Focus is the start of everything and the spark of success.

THE MEANING OF STRATEGY

The theory and practice of business strategy has been emerging for decades, blending economic, social and technical themes. This book is dedicated to a redefinition of strategy that is relevant in terms of organizational thought, behavior and action. Strategy is not an abstract set of ideas hatched in some dark room, although a lot of companies appear to favor such an approach. Instead, strategy is a thoughtful and behavioral practice that helps a company advance its business agenda. **Strategy is essentially an agenda for driving business success.** It's an agenda that brings meaning and purpose, which in turn, inspires the thought and behavior of the organization.

Our approach to strategy combines sound theory and practice with three elements that frame business growth, performance and change...

This general approach connects essential "who-what-how-when" ideas in strategy management and leadership. When these ideas are connected and communicated throughout the organization, the odds of business success are greatly enhanced. When blocks and disconnects exist and when communication efforts are ineffective, barriers to business growth, performance and change are likely to mount, constraining success. Strategy direction, integration and execution must be linked and supported.

Strategy takes on new issues and new meaning in a world that is shaped by 21st century realities in technology, competition, market relationships and social change. Strategy is all about your agenda for driving business success and evolution, both near-term and long-term. Further, it embraces the realities of a networked, broadly connected business world.

This view is a critical departure from conventional strategic planning and conventional wisdom regarding management and leadership. My framework conveys a different kind of thinking about strategy and business success. This book helps set the stage for getting a company prepared and resolved to succeed in a changing, turbulent, sometimes ambiguous world.

RELEVANCE TO PERFORMERS

Making business principles, strategy and objectives more relevant to people in every area of a company is increasingly important. People are performers on the proverbial stage of business. They drive success, and they provide ideas and energy that fuel business evolution.

Strategy has to make sense if people are going to put their energy into the cause. That simple truth is a trouble spot for many companies, large and small. How do we ensure that our business stakeholders are on the same page with respect to principles, strategy and objectives? How do we ensure that they're engaged in the natural goals and intentions of the company? How do we ensure that they're moving forward in thought, behavior and action? These are foundation questions for management and leadership.

The answers reside in effective communication about business strategy. My framework for effective management and leadership communication reflects a scheme of individual learning about the ideas in strategy direction, integration and execution throughout the organization. Our people need to be aware, they need to engage; and then, they can focus on business results.

COMMUNICATION AND THE STRATEGY AGENDA

Strategy AWARENESS in the Organization	Strategy UNDERSTANDING in the Organization	Strategy ENGAGEMENT in the Organization
Subjects	Relevance	Priorities
Activities	Key Roles	Results

Source: Dewar Sloan research on strategic and operational communication in conventional and collaborative organizations; 2004-2006 Collaboration and Entreship Project and the Front Line/First Level [FL/FL] Leadership Program research.

Moving people from a sense of strategic awareness through strategic understanding and strategic engagement is part of the natural path to business success. In our experience, most communication breakdowns occur somewhere on this journey, causing the strategic agenda to decompose. We clearly must address these strategic communication problems, or the company's prospects for near-term and long-term success will be dashed.

THEMES AND ORIENTATION

My business and personal thoughts on strategy stem from two very simple themes – being prepared and resolved. For me, these are at the very heart of getting companies focused on business results. They are the oxygen for growth, performance and change. They form the basic differences between success and struggle. They sustain the company, and they sustain the people whose efforts help make the company work every day.

Getting any company prepared for success today requires anticipation, prospective and true readiness. Preparation is a fundamental principle in corporate life, government, warfighting, sports, the arts, education and the basic endeavors of human affairs. When we prepare in business, we get ready to succeed in a world that can be uncertain and complicated. When we work to prepare an organization for growth, performance and change, we get people ready to think, behave and take action wisely. When we prepare in business, we work to get our enterprise ready to prosper, survive, change and sustain in a world of challenges and opportunities. Good fortune goes to the prepared. Luck helps, especially if we're prepared.

To become resolved is to draw from the energy, courage, inspiration and abilities of the organization – to press on, regardless. Resolution is a key principle in every field of human endeavor. When we resolve to move forward onto new business frontiers, we marshal people and ideas that are critical to success. When we resolve to improve our business performance, we get focused on the priorities that can make a real difference. When we resolve to change, we fix our sights on the ways and means that are necessary to escort our companies into better, smarter, faster arenas for creating new, sustainable business value. We depend on resolve to secure our compasses when times are tough. Resolve carries people forward.

The utility of these ideas – being prepared and resolved – is simple and obvious in companies with good strategy elements in place. However, when we ask executives and corporate directors to comment on the degree to which their companies are truly prepared and resolved, most respond with a portfolio of strategic concerns. There is room for improvement in every organization. Every company faces strategic challenges, and every employee owns a piece of those challenges. Ideas and challenges present themselves in ways that *engage people in everyday strategic thought and behavior*.

PRACTICAL AGENDA FOR EVOLVING BUSINESS

Building a sound management and leadership agenda that drives the evolution of a business is a function of discipline and practice. It requires strategic thought and behavior. It requires foresight and perspective. It requires principle, character, purpose and maturity. Constructing an effective and practical agenda takes foresight and discipline. The agenda takes balanced management and leadership. My intent is to tackle what this means in terms of strategy, and the management and leadership of the strategic agenda.

Framing an effective agenda for growth, performance and change is served by management that is focused on business results. The effective agenda for evolving business is served by the kind of leadership that inspires people to move the organization along the pathways toward the natural goals of the company. My intent is to connect the strategic elements of the agenda for growth, performance and change with the everyday roles of management and leadership in your organization, and specifically to the people whose roles and practices guide the business. That, I believe, is the main task in play.

DEALING WITH THE REALITIES OF THE BUSINESS

The context of strategy includes the realities that exist in the business environment, as well as issues that exist in the business enterprise. These realities are complex and dynamic. They shape challenges and opportunities, and they keep wise managers and leaders on guard.

These realities represent a source of energy in some organizations. They present situations for action and impact, and they inspire the best efforts of people to tackle serious challenges. These realities can also hobble a company and block its resolve. Realities block innovation, constrain decisions and otherwise undercut the company's ability to evolve. They can get in the way of the best intentions. Realities can also open great options and choices for growth, performance and change.

We want to help build an agenda for growth, performance and change that is practical, realistic and always focused on business results. The strategic agenda is a platform. It guides the way people think and how they act. The agenda frames expectations, and it guides choices. It provides meaning and relevance, and it frames cultural systems and subcultures.

BOOK ORGANIZATION – OUTLINE OF APPROACH

This book is presented in three parts. My intent is to set the stage with material that shapes an appreciation for a better, more pragmatic approach to strategy management and leadership. Each part ties back to the agenda for business growth, performance and change. Each part provides concepts and context for strategy, and in the scheme of things, these elements tie back together to frame the strategic agenda.

In *Part One*, we provide a basic foundation for strategic assessment and understanding. There are three chapters devoted to this starting tack.

> **Chapter 01 Challenges in Strategy** deals with the
> many realities of modern business and the challenges
> that companies face on the road to success. The strategic
> themes of growth, performance and change are defined in
> the context of everyday problems and opportunities. Basic
> concerns about running the company are addressed.

> **Chapter 02 The Framework for Strategy** begins
> with a primer on the relevance of strategy, its cause
> and effect connections with business conditions and
> business results. The framework for strategy leadership
> and management is presented with a series of definitions
> and ideas that are key to building a company's agenda for
> business growth, performance and change.

> **Chapter 03 Business Consequences** presents the litany
> of practical issues, metrics and concerns that relate to
> effectiveness of strategy leadership and management that
> serves the company and its stakeholders. From a sense of
> entreship and venture to the realities of troubled business
> recovery, dealing with consequences is part of strategy.

These chapters provide important definitions and assumptions for managing and leading business strategy. They are prospective; they encourage foresight and reality checking and honest appraisal. And, they provide the essentials for developing the right kind of strategic agenda for evolving companies.

In *Part Two,* we explore the components and details of strategy and the nuances of strategy management and leadership in three areas:

Chapter 04 Strategy Direction presents ideas and issues that provide for business model definition, intention and discovery. Direction is the part of strategy management and leadership that sets the evolutionary course in play for a company, reflecting choices in business focus and purpose. Direction can be concise or general in nature.

Chapter 05 Strategy Integration deals with the critical mechanics and practices of strategy deployment through the resources, processes and networks of assets available to the company. Integration is the part of strategy management and leadership that provides the ways and means for making strategy happen as the business evolves.

Chapter 06 Strategy Execution examines the technical and behavioral aspects of implementing and assuring strategy at the everyday action plan and impact level. Execution is the part of strategy management and leadership that engages accountability for results as well as personal responsibility for adaptive efforts to succeed in the strategic agenda.

These chapters provide the essential components of what strategy is, what it does, how it works, who makes it happen and how it shapes the success of the company. These chapters also speak to the common barriers to strategy leadership and management. By reframing the elements of strategy in this way, we can better define the ideas and practices that shape strategic and economic value. How strategy leadership and management shape the agenda is manifested in these three elements. These elements have to be developed and balanced and discharged in order to engage and inspire employees, customers, suppliers and investors. They frame the agenda for business success in the context of choice-making, asset deployment and action management. People operate in this commonsense scheme of strategy.

In *Part Three*, we examine the major issues that connect strategy, culture, structure and resources in effective business organizations. This is where the impact elements of *Prepared and Resolved* come together:

> **Chapter 07 Creating New Value** introduces a series of definitions that explain how the creation of new strategic and economic value takes place, how it's measured and why it really matters to the organization. Value creation is powerful and evolutionary stuff, and this chapter makes it the purpose of everyone in the organization.

> **Chapter 08 Energy and Impact** provides a review of what it really means to be resolved to succeed in a business world that has more than a few uncertainties and no shortage of risks. The energy of strategy leadership and management is a huge engine, if it remains positive. If that energy dissipates, the company may be toast.

> **Chapter 09 Major Applications** presents a series of ideas and application models that connect the specific issues of your business. We use these application tools in our education and consulting work. The subjects included in this section of this book reflect on:

> > Quality and Lean Management

> > Category Management and Change

> > Product and Service Development

> > Mergers, Acquisitions and Ventures

> > Business Scale and Scope Change

Throughout this book, I have attempted to focus on the key issues of business success in practical, bare-knuckle terms. The examples I have used are targeted; the reader is spared the hype and blather of shopworn stories about excellent companies and super star executives. *I want to focus on your company's agenda for success, as that is what really counts.*

RESETTING THE STAGE FOR STRATEGY

The issues and ideas presented in Part One may resonate with you in a number of ways. Most of us have confronted tough strategic issues. Most of us have struggled with change and barriers to change. Most of us have wrestled with ideas that could make a big difference in our companies.

From the Pentagon to the smallest company, and from the successful practices of the most mature organization to the stumbles of the most emergent new venture, people face many challenges. They seek direction and ground rules for planning and execution. They seek order and balance, even in the midst of chaos. We need to reset the stage for strategy management and leadership for their success. Let's begin with a realistic set of perspectives.

01

THE CHALLENGES OF STRATEGY

Challenges...calling into question the key
strategic issues and realities that determine
business survival and success...

One of the most basic concerns in business is the selection of the right
business model, the right place, form and frame to be as a company. For
most companies, this is a matter of setting **strategy direction** for the
organization. How can a company position and sustain itself in attractive
market categories, with good prospects for creating strategic and economic
value? Clearly, this is a key question in every company.

Another common business concern is the coordination of plans, people,
resources and ideas across the organization. This becomes a matter of
strategy integration. How can a company develop and connect the right
assets and actions to be successful? Yet another key strategic question, and
the source of a great many challenges and opportunities.

Even companies with sound direction and capabilities have issues with their
sequences of thought, behavior, action and results. For most companies, this
is a matter of **strategy execution**. Execution is what delivers on the intent
of strategy. Execution is what successful companies must do every day in the
context of dynamic business conditions. How do we frame and engage the
disciplines of execution? Are we effective in our execution?

These questions are part and parcel of the series of issues to be addressed in
strategy. They are the essence of strategy, and the heart of the challenges that
shape the success and sustenance of every company.

LOOK AHEAD, PLAN AHEAD, MOVE AHEAD

The success frontiers of a company are dotted with many concerns and options. The business environment of the early 21st century is truly a wondrous puzzle of technical, social, market and economic forces. Complex patterns of globalization, demographic change, technological advances, business innovation and social development have put us on the edge of many things. The challenges to management and leadership have been, and continue to be, quite expansive. They are exciting and often crazy for the people who work in our companies. They can also be quite gloomy. That is, perhaps, a matter of worldview, purpose and personal take.

To *look ahead* for most companies means to anticipate the issues that will shape their business destiny. This look ahead takes curiosity and perspective, foresight and knowledge. It takes judgment, creativity, analytics and a sense of adventure. To look ahead is to search and learn, wonder and dream.

When we *plan ahead,* we ask the entire organization to get with the charter and the agenda. We ask them to assemble ideas and processes that will enable success. We ask them to secure the priorities of the business with plans that make sense. We ask for readiness, and more.

The evolving focus, however, is *how to move ahead.* When the broader organization is focused on business results, people are geared to move ahead. This takes action sense and action edge. It takes energy and persistence. To move ahead is also to face departures from the past, and that can be tough.

Historians argue the importance of understanding the technical, social, political and economic patterns of our world. Futurists argue the importance of understanding the predictable and unknowable issues that are shaping the future conditions of business. We support a studied approach to understanding the environment of your business as the basis for looking, planning and moving ahead. This is a challenge for most organizations – a fundamental challenge. It calls for a kind of *practical contemplation* that is incumbent in very few organizations. Executives, managers and directors may not take time to wrestle with strategic issues and options. We need to set *better disciplines for engaging strategic thought and behavior.* Too often, we shortchange this effort, distracting our people.

BUSINESS SUCCESS THEMES IN STRATEGY

We tend to consider a company's success in terms that frame business growth, performance and change. In fact, this book is influenced by the nearly universal themes defined in the vocabulary of growth, performance and change. We can break these success themes down further as foundation goals. These are critical themes, everywhere, in every company.

Business Growth: Common Success Themes

The main growth ideas on a company's strategic agenda are often posed in revenue and portfolio terms; we want to grow revenue in order to enhance economic and strategic value, pure and simple. Or, in some companies, the agenda calls for changes in growth patterns and business models. These growth themes wear many colors. Business growth has many facets.

Revenue growth that is truly value-enhancing must also address profitability and capital considerations. We are reminded of the challenges that companies face in mapping out profitable growth strategies and their implications for *margins*. Margin enhancement versus margin degradation is a very common challenge in the context of profitable, capital-efficient growth and, some may argue that growth may not be a good prescription.

Capital efficiency is another real and common challenge in managing growth. Working capital is but one aspect of the revenue growth challenge, and working capital is commonly miscued in growth plans, even in the best companies. Other resources, including HR, systems and operating capital are also part of the growth formula. We see examples every day where capital resources are not in sync with business growth plans and intentions.

The financial effects of revenue growth need to be fully understood in margin and capital management terms. This is a challenge, because growth plans are typically based on plan premises and assumptions that may or may not materialize. Risk factors surround business growth plans. The realities of business are not static or fixed. Growth is part of the basic thought and behavior scheme of successful companies. The kind of growth, the risks of growth and the means of growth are all key issues. Revenue and income leverage help assure a company's perpetuation.

A company's **business portfolio** tends to reflect its core collection of product and service positions, expressed in terms of the targeted solutions it offers to customers. A company's business portfolio also reflects how its resources and capital are allocated and managed.

The portfolio issues for business growth are related to the purpose, focus and impact of the specific growth strategy. Most often, these portfolio issues can be cast in the context of market and category conditions. Here are some of the most common portfolio and growth considerations we see in practice today as practical **areas of growth intent:**

> Competing within a market category
>
> Expanding the boundaries of a category
>
> Enhancing the position of a product
>
> Altering the approach to customers
>
> Resetting the resources of the company
>
> Expanding into adjacent market areas
>
> Exploring new profit opportunities
>
> Resetting parts of the business model
>
> Developing new markets via innovation
>
> Enhancing the company's stewardship
>
> Recasting the business model

These ten areas of growth intent have many facets and many nuances. They provide the promise and rationale for revenue growth. They frame the challenges of growth in ways that can confuse and entangle the organization. Growth is a hopeful idea for most companies. It's also an idea that introduces **creative and analytic tension.** The challenge is to manage that tension in a manner that drives the creation of new strategic and economic value.

Organic growth evolves from ideas and methods that are unique to each company. The foundations for organic growth depend on capabilities, entreship, resources, structure and no small amount of adaptive readiness and resolve. These foundations are born of intent and purpose, and they are powered by a mindset of internal resourcefulness, invention and resolve.

Business Performance: Common Success Themes

When we ask people about business performance issues, we usually get a range of responses that tie into things related to what we can express in terms of the *natural goals of business.* These include:

Financial Performance –
Revenue, margins and capital

Competitive Advantage –
Foundations and sustainability

Customer Connections –
Relationships and development

Corporate Stewardship –
Purpose, ideology and practice

For the most part, these are external performance issues that reflect how well a company is doing in its markets. Financial measures, market share, customer relationships, reputation, market systems, product edge, operating edge, expense management, quality edge and position with stakeholders are common indicators of business and company performance.

Several internal performance issues are also germane to a company's health. These include technical resources, human capital, market assets, culture and subcultures, knowledge, leadership, process and systems assets, knack, alliances, supply chains, demand chains and a host of other measures we often associate with strategic assets.

How is the company doing? The answer to that colloquial question depends on your perspective. A truthful answer is usually one that has many parts. That's because there are different ways to gauge performance. Near-term and long-term success. Turnaround. Transformative success. Sustainable success. Performance measures indicate what a company has achieved, and how it manages and leads success. They may track business performance cause-and-effect. Really, how is the company doing? The simple dashboard answer to that question should reflect upon the natural goals of business. The appropriate answer may be set in evolutionary terms.

The patterns of company performance we have experienced tend to demonstrate themselves in four ways. Over the course of time, most companies will have the opportunity to manage and lead strategy in one or more patterns, gauged by circumstances and performance.

PATTERNS OF BUSINESS PERFORMANCE

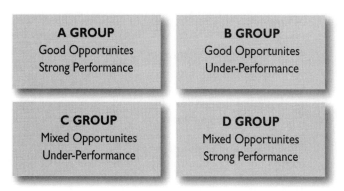

A GROUP Good Opportunites Strong Performance	**B GROUP** Good Opportunites Under-Performance
C GROUP Mixed Opportunites Under-Performance	**D GROUP** Mixed Opportunites Strong Performance

Notes: Companies with strong performance and prospects are the subject of many studies and articles. A 05/2005 article in Wired presents a good overview of performance variables, including themes like relentless innovation, technology leverage, strategy adaptation, global sense and reach and networked business model/structure integration. www.wired.com

A Group Companies

Typically, companies with *good opportunities and strong performance* are likely to operate in market categories that are attractive. That is, they play in markets that have some inherent growth and competitive balance. But, this is not the result of fate or luck. Sustained strong performance accrues mainly to those organizations with strategic management and leadership that is prepared and resolved to succeed with a business agenda that is focused on business results. Stryker Corporation, a leading player in the medical products sector, is a good example of a company with sustained strong performance. They're blessed with attractive markets and they have very strong performance cultures. There are many other examples... Toyota, FedEx, Cisco, Schlage, Samsung and Intel.

Companies with sustained, positive performance take advantage of their business opportunities, and they address business challenges better than their market sector peers. *They're consistent and they're persistent.* They're focused on results; they're often obsessive about results measures.

B Group Companies

Companies with *good opportunities and business under-performance* are likely to operate in market positions that are unworkable with respect to attainable margins. In other words, they operate in ways that lack the foundations for positive near-term or long-term business success. Under-performance is common with undermanaged companies, where human capital, systems and processes are simply not in sync with the realities of the organization. These players are simply not as good as their peers. They need to change, and they need to reset their respective business models.

Under-performance may be a harsh reality for companies with relatively low market shares, in sectors with excess capacity and market system imbalance. The economics of business and competitive structure are what they are. Companies that lack efficiency and differentiation in the categories they serve face challenges with sustainability. Their destiny may be marginal. Competitive and industry structure pose economic realities.

Chronic underperformance seems to be acceptable for many companies. Perhaps they are resigned to their status as troubled companies. Perhaps the energy that's required to enhance performance is just too great a challenge. Some business development planners and a growing number of private equity players look at these companies as latent opportunities for:

Takeover and Turnaround Strategies –
Based on better resource platforms

Consolidation and Domination Strategies –
Based on strategic assets, leverage ideas

Competitive Repartitioning Strategies –
Based on changing market structure

The strategic challenge with sustained under-performance companies is really two-fold. First, many lack the capital to support an agenda for business enhancement. Second, many face limited choices for driving better performance. This is a tough place to be, a real strategic challenge zone. These companies can be resettled in different ways, but not without a serious check on performance realities. Significant evolution must be an option, and the contemporary prospects for turnaround and structural change are a part of the strategic agenda.

C Group Companies

Companies with *mixed opportunities and business under-performance* have some risk. They're in a position to emerge toward a level of success on the basis of some competitive edge or some set of circumstances that opens a door with a combination of imperatives, perhaps with:

Meaningful New Products or Services –
Something to shift revenue and margins

Different Segmentation or Approach to Customers –
Something to build new business platforms

Enhancements in Operating Platforms –
Something to shift margins and capital

Such a company may or may not emerge fully from its status as a chronic under-performer. Often these emergent business opportunities fail to materialize. The initiatives in place don't get the needed traction, or they don't get the time and quality of management they need to succeed. Key elements of emerging opportunity may go unnoticed, and the efforts mounted to drive change may simply be inadequate.

The challenges of some emergent under-performance companies relate to moving strategy, culture, structure and resources toward new levels. How do people lead and manage this idea of emergence? How do they tackle the obstacles and constraints of new strategy emergence? How do they nourish the disparate pieces and parts of their strategy? What do you expect of governance and management? These are significant questions that demand some honest soul-searching. They force the change card.

The answers here are not simple. Emergent under-performing companies have patterns of inconsistency that threaten the ways and means of the organization. These patterns are often baked into corporate culture and subcultures, and they're tough to break. One could argue that emergent underperforming companies are the clear norm in business today. One could also argue that these settings are superb grounds for talent development. An interesting paradox to be sure; how can managers and leaders break through this paradox? What does it take? What are the rewards and the risks?

D Group Companies

Companies with *mixed opportunities and strong business performance* may have a working pipeline of business development options, and enough capital to manage their strategic agenda. The main differences between a company that exploits its changes and prospects for success and a company that is consistently less fortunate include:

Their Core Business Assets and Scope –
Differences in focus and attention

Their Management Disciplines in Place –
Differences in practice and process

Their Leadership Benchstrength in Place –
Differences in human capital, talent

Their Business Definition and Stance –
Differences in clarity and intention

Their Approach to Performance Plans –
Differences in managing for results

Opportunistic business performance situations arise and open unique and profitable doors for these companies. If the company is prepared to take advantage of these opportunities, good things are bound to happen. Lacking the preparation, the company may fail to get any kind of traction with the opportunities at hand, not to mention the opportunities ahead.

The challenge in these situations is to recognize, early and often, the performance options available to the business. Hence, a simple maxim:

> Chance favors the prepared. Results go to the resolved.

The challenge in creating strategic and economic value on a more consistent basis is what this is all about. Most companies live with the realities of occasional, sporadic performance spurts. This is the way in almost every market sector, and in every technical area, and it's reality. Research and common sense dictate that we reset the strategic performance agenda in a better, more focused manner, to be more ready and to be more engaged.

Business Change: Common Success Themes

The need for change is a prime strategic issue every company must address. Change management and leadership is part of what companies do to survive, prosper and sustain. Companies are naturally evolving entities. They change in ways that enable or constrain the creation of strategic and economic value. They can change in radical ways, or they can change in very gradual, almost glacial ways. The readiness and capacity for change amount to a company's systemic and cultural assets for survival and success. We can approach the subject of business change in the context of three general types of adaptation. These reflect three critical frames of business evolution.

BUSINESS CHANGE AND ADAPTATION

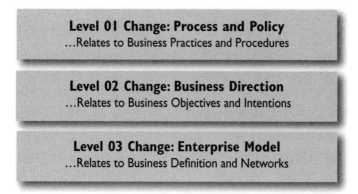

Level 01 Change: Process and Policy
...Relates to Business Practices and Procedures

Level 02 Change: Business Direction
...Relates to Business Objectives and Intentions

Level 03 Change: Enterprise Model
...Relates to Business Definition and Networks

Notes: The change management domain is rich with ideas about the need for change, the structures and behaviors that influence change, and the practices of change. *Breaking the Code of Change* [2002] by Beer, et al, is an excellent reference on change management. See dewarsloan.com/research. The essence of organizational change is infused with technical, behavioral and economic realities. A company's appetite and capacity for change can be a curse or a blessing, and as contemporary business researchers have noted, change capacity is a strategic competence.

Generally speaking, Level 01 changes are modest in scope and implications. They deal with business practices that guide thought, behavior and action on routine matters. Level 02 changes deal with the strategic and operational intentions of the company. These changes can be disruptive if they involve significant new learning and shifts in principles. Level 03 changes are geared to transforming the company and its purpose in business. Level 03 changes are often radical and sweeping in nature, and they involve the entire business model framework. Every company should examine these change avenues.

BUSINESS ADAPTATION ISSUES

The action challenges associated with change relate to the dynamics of the change adventure itself. What are the barriers to change? What are the incentives for change? What are the intervening, mitigating ingredients of change management? When we look at change management and leadership from a distance, there are two implications we need to examine. First, a company's ability to change can have an important bearing on its ability to realize its natural goals and objectives:

> Can the company address the conditions for reaching its goals in financial performance? Change issues?

> Can the company adapt and respond to the issues that shape competitive advantage? Change issues?

> Can the company continue to connect with customers in a manner that is effective? Change issues?

> Can the company adapt and respond to the shifting sands of corporate stewardship? Change issues?

These are important questions. Every company faces a certain amount of jeopardy and risk in each of these areas. Building a sense of these risks is a management and leadership task. We look at strategic risk in terms of shifts in the technical, social and economic environment that could upset the order of a company. We look at strategic risk in organizational terms as well; how well does the enterprise serve its purpose and its stakeholders, and are its basic capabilities at risk of devolution? Strategic risks can paralyze or inspire an organization. They can engage innovative thought and behavior, and they can also freeze people in their tracks. There is a big difference.

The second consideration is risk factors and the approach to change. Dealing with the possibilities of technical, social, market and economic change is part of sound planning. The alternative is risky business. The alternative is to take a more passive, reactive stance on change management. That stance may put strategic and economic value creation at great risk. This more passive/reactive approach can threaten the attainment of natural goals and business evolution, and it can confuse the organization.

The second implication of a company's ability to change is even more significant. Our research suggests that change management and leadership can be a major strategic asset in companies with strong patterns of business growth and performance. By itself, this is really not very surprising, but the underlying components of change mangement are more complex. Can a company shape its own destiny, as well as its category?

What is most relevant here is the more intriguing issue of a company's capacity to change its category – to alter the business environment in which it competes. This reflects upon a set of challenges that present themselves in a wide range of companies and in a wide range of industry settings. These challenges can manifest themselves in a number of ways, including:

> Product innovation; Service innovation
>
> Customer and channel resegmentation
>
> Operational innovation and restructuring
>
> Technical and operational realignment
>
> Marketing system and network innovation
>
> Solution customization and deployment
>
> Category boundary and frontier change
>
> Trade model disruption and evolution
>
> Disruptive business practices, processes

The ongoing evolution of e-business economics fuels some of this adventure in category-changing strategy. A strategic agenda that anticipates the risks and options for Level 03 change – changes in the basic enterprise model – will be informed by the conditions for business evolution. This is a significant value creation frontier. *Change management* is part of a practice of sensing and acting upon just the right issues at just the right time with just the right assets. Patience is part of the practice. So is readiness and perspective. So is capacity for change. Some advisors have addressed the merits and value of patience and strategy pacing as foundations for strategic change. Frankly, patience and urgency are in a dance that shapes the setting for wise decisions, in the context of specific trade sectors.

CHANGE ENGINES IN CONTEXT

Managing and leading the change process draws on the best abilities of people at every level of a company. The general pathways of change management are recognized in terms of preparing and planning for change, and executing. This seems quite straight-forward, and in many ways it is. However, the experiences of change management bring to bear a few very important lessons in strategy. These can be very tough lessons indeed.

In preparing for change, we are gauging the realities that surround our current status, our environment and the need for change. We are also gauging the conditions of the place we're headed and the emerging realities and key success factors. What lies ahead, and how do we change to accept and accomodate the next realities of the business?

In planning for change, we are preparing the company for the strategic, cultural, resource and structural issues that will be recast and reframed in the business model. *We are building new strategic thought and behavior patterns.* We're making the organization ready for action in a new setting that is different than the old setting. We are putting into practice new ideas and ground rules, new systems and precepts, new standards and principles. The way people think about change and the way they react to change says a lot about the prospects for company success and evolution.

The execution of change requires engaging the organization to move ahead, and to take charge of new issues. We are managing and leading people to approach an agenda of change, and to take responsibility for making it happen. We are putting change into the everyday measure of business thought and behavior, for everyone in the company. People and groups play out these roles on the sometimes fuzzy frontiers of the business.

Change management is a facet of *Prepared and Resolved,* and a theme in strategy management and leadership. Change management is a principal engine of business success, and clearly a primary challenge in the continuous evolution of the successful company. The change engine must be fully engaged, or the strategic prospects of most companies cannot be tapped to their full potential. *A positive approach to change is critical.*

WHERE THE GOING GETS TOUGH

The challenges that companies face reflect on the many unbounded trends in the business environment, as well as concerns that are internal to the organization. Our experience with companies, large and small, reveals a number of internal issues that can either block or support the advance of its strategic agenda. Some of these business concerns include:

> Focus and Definition
>
> Integration and Collaboration
>
> Action and Execution

Management and leadership abilities are at the heart of these challenges. Miscues, upheaval, degradation, arrogance, bad habits and planning glitches are common issues in troubled organizations. Again, strategy management and leadership is harder than it looks. It takes good people with courage and foresight, purpose and energy. The business literature is growing rich and deep with research on effective leadership and management, or the lack thereof. When we examine the conditions for business success and/or failure, human capital at every level is perhaps the most critical indicator.

Getting prepared and resolved for growth, performance and change is dependent on effective learning and communication. Managers and leaders at every level are called upon to take responsibility. There are very few magical pathways to business success. This is serious work, and the pathways are complex and dynamic. No company is blessed with a strategy so grand or a culture so great that it can transcend the messiness of these particular human challenges. This is business, and the laws of gravity suggest that greatness is a fleeting idea in a world that is subject to shifting technical, social and economic sands. Managers and leaders must be cognizant of and committed to dynamic conditions and business realities. This is true at GE and Acme Dynamite. It's true at Dell and Starbucks and DuPont.

At the same time, managers and leaders with the right kind of discipline and orientation can take even the most troubled company to success. It's important to make the complex more simple, but it's also important to frame the challenges. Look at the evolution of Google, or Tyco.

STRATEGIC THOUGHT AND BEHAVIOR

The days of grand strategy flowing forth from some inspired senior leader are long over. Strategic thought and behavior is something that must pervade the entire organization. It must reflect the knowledge, culture, networks and communication of a company's people and processes. Here are a few indicators that suggest the prevalence and interactions of strategic thought and behavior across an enterprise:

Strategic ideas are managed at every level of the organization, and across the boundaries, from basement to boardroom.

Subcultures of the organization are recognized for their technical, social and operational ideas, and their everyday actions.

People in the very deepest reaches of the organization take responsibility for moving key ideas forward in the company.

Conversations take place, and they shape ideas and encourage actions on a self-organizing, free stage, open source basis.

Principles support a creative and analytic setting for entreship, business improvement and company evolution.

Strategic thought and behavior in most successful companies is a powerful and valuable asset. Everyday thought and behavior in these settings is cognizant of cause-and-effect in the business – what must happen to drive results. The challenge in all of this is obvious. How do we disperse the intellectual and behavioral responsibility for strategic thought? How do we recognize and cultivate the behaviors that go with the adventure? How do we manage and lead strategy so that more people have a personal piece of the agenda? How do we connect everyday strategic thought and behavior?

All of this requires that senior executives open themselves and the organization to the *extended responsibility for strategy*. For some, that really means letting go. For most, it means better learning, communicating and discerning. For every company it means, we think, the ***encouragement of strategic engagement of people*** at every level of the organization, with fully ***prepared and resolved*** intentions that infuse real meaning.

CHALLENGES ON THE FRONTIER

Our business environment today is stocked with many issues that pose uncertainties for companies. Some would argue that we live in a period of great dynamics, and that seems true. Some would argue that business and society are moving on constantly changing frontiers, ones that have been shaped by many forces over time, since the beginning of time. Changes in technical, social and economic frontiers reflect on:

The human condition

Forms of technology

The balance of power

Economic standards

Business organization

Business practices

Business networks

Social expectations

Workforce values

Political economics

Market trade patterns

Our friends with a disciplined sense of economic and business history tend to have a more discerning sense of these changes in the context of their own particular business environment. This should not come as a surprise to seasoned observers and investors. Emotional and intellectual balance is one of those intangibles that shapes successful business cultures and their incumbent thought and behavior patterns. Some call this wisdom.

A combination of maturity, judgment and humility seems to be part of the *healthy paranoia* in successful organizations as they define and confront the challenges on these frontiers. Companies find ways to draw energy from the adventures they are living, as they are moving onto and across frontiers. Where some companies are constrained by the issues and uncertainties in the business environment, our friends in successful companies are motivated, inspired and engaged by the challenges they face. They feed off change and they are powered by a special kind of discretionary effort.

COMMUNICATION AND CONVERSATION

Much has been said about communication as an organizational process. However, when everything is said and done, too often, more is said than done. Or so it is said by those who ponder such things.

Here is the essential challenge. There is a communication structure in most organizations, and it comprises three levels of strategic interaction:

> **Awareness...**at this level, people are aware of the strategic intentions, principles and agenda of the organization, and their general roles in the strategy.

> **Understanding...**at this level, people comprehend the nature of cause-and-effect considerations that go into the company's strategic agenda and plans.

> **Engagement...**at this level, people take raw energy from the strategic agenda; they find ways to assure their roles and personal responsibilities for results.

Our research and experience suggests that while most companies have strategic plans in place, they have trouble communicating their plans beyond the awareness level. In other words, most organizations suffer from a lack of understanding and engagement in their strategy agenda. This is a cultural phenomenon, and a reflection of management and leadership. This is what Judy Pelham of Trinity Health refers to with her call for greater discernment in company mission and strategy. Others look to the cultural practice of *fierce conversations*, as defined by Susan Scott in her book by the same name. This is part of cultural openness to big ideas.

Communication is wonderfully simple and complex at the same time. In strategy conversations, the simple stuff is about purpose and intention and realities that impact the business. The more complex stuff is all about the discernment, contemplation, conversation and assessment haze that hangs over and around strategy. The complex stuff ranges from efforts to argue the best strategy, to efforts that get people engaged in organized, adaptive and meaningful action. Sure, a key part of strategic success is communication. The challenge is huge, however, and it's part of the broader practice of strategy in the everyday world of business.

ESSENTIAL CONNECTIONS IN STRATEGY

Another challenge in business is matching the company's plans to all the facets of the organization and its resources. Organizations are complexes of people and processes. How do we get everything in sync? How do we encourage the proper cadence, pace and rhythm of the organization? How do we disperse the responsibility for coordination? How do we engage true and effective collaboration of people and ideas? These questions are at the heart of the internal challenge. They are essential connections. They really communicate.

The external aspects of this challenge are no less important, and no less perplexing. How do we get company plans in sync with the technical, market and economic environment? How do we pace our plans and actions to gain strategic advantage? How do we advance the rationale for decision making and action planning? How do we gauge near-term and long-term results? Our sense of these strategic connections is forged by experience with companies whose people are more discerning in their approach to organizational communication. Strong companies are committed to open, energetic debate and heartful contemplation.

THE SEQUENCE OF STRATEGIC THOUGHT AND BEHAVIOR

From these essential connections in strategy, we see a very basic *sequence of organizational thought and behavior* that frames and reframes the intentions and activities of a business. The company sets expectations, which influence relevant behaviors, which under the right conditions should drive success. This is how it works, and how it shapes business success.

Expectations ·······▶ Relevant Behaviors ·······▶ Performance

The challenge in this context derives from a few practical concerns and facts. First, expectations are often ambiguous. Ambiguity, in turn, can lead to confusion. Second, many different behaviors in an organization are relevant. Matching the right behaviors with the strategic agenda is critical. And third, performance is known by many different measures. Measurement can be a muddy practice. The sequence of success is not as simple as it looks, and the links that connect to performance are quite often constrained.

FROM FORMULA TO DISCOVERY

For most of the last century in business, executives have sought the general formula for corporate performance. From methods developed in scientific management and practice, to concepts spawned by academics in the post-war environment, to emergent ideas promoted by new economy types more recently, there are many ingredients in the success formula, many pieces of the *strategy-results puzzle.* There is plenty to discover in this arena.

Part of the challenge for today's organization is a sorting process in strategy management and leadership. The proliferation of business cookbooks and fad surfing only clouds the picture. We see growing skepticism when managers pull yet another concept off the shelf, or after the latest consulting brigade has done its dance and left its stuff on the table for others to implement.

The knowledge available to companies is daunting. How can busy people grasp everything that is necessary to produce the right products and services for the right markets, in the right system of capital and resources, while focusing on business results? This challenge is dynamic. Success depends on continuous *discovery and entreship* at every level. Entreship is the discipline, craft, art and practice of creating new strategic and economic entities. Entreship means entering the new space of some market, changing the scheme of business in that space. Entreship is powered by discovery, in different forms and modes. Entreship is a corporate discipline which is further defined in our research on *Collaboration and Entreship*, and this is a critical domain for large and small companies alike.

THE CONDITIONS OF ADVENTURE

Adventure involves the vast unknown. Surprises, risk, energy, rewards, excitement, curiosity, direction, awareness and some amount of change go with adventure. These are the conditions of adventure. They are not necessarily rooted in clearly mapped, concise targets, or *unambiguous expectations.* Things were not always orderly on the Lewis and Clark trail. The challenge of being prepared and resolved is always relative to the conditions of the adventure, and those conditions are dynamic in many ways. Organizations need to be more open to discovery and supportive of discovery risks and realities. Strategy is a dynamic journey of value creation and destruction, a journey that passes many signals, and many forks in the road.

AGENDA RESET

Most of the good research on strategy and performance suggests that successful companies earn their marks with strong competitive positions in attractive markets. The dynamics of market categories and the evolving nature of competition make this a game of good moves. The premise of a strategic agenda for growth, performance and change is essentially one of movement and evolution in the position of the company.

In their 2006 book, *Competition Demystified,* the authors Judd Kahn and Bruce Greenwald reflect on the relevance of industry structure, customer captivity and certain operational strategy elements. They conclude that business success and advantage has a lot to do with taking and holding critical ground in capacity that is bunkered by certain barriers to market entry. This is a good and basic economic reference point for the assessment and evolution of a company's strategic agenda. More and more companies are facing the realities of capacity and customer captivity as Kahn and Greenwald have framed them. Research on *The Long Tail* by Chris Anderson, 2006, and others suggests that certain economic rules and commercial systems are changing in ways that redefine markets. The emergence of web-centric business models shapes a less certain realm for growth, performance and change.

Scoping and engaging a strategic agenda that is based on movement and evolution is both powerful and problematic. Leaders may be confident in the "growth and change" pitch at their strategic off-site meetings, only to return to business as usual on Monday with all the obvious disconnects in strategic thought and behavior. On the other hand, the strategic agenda can enrich the purpose of an organization as people sense the relevance and meaning a strategy holds for them at the personal level.

People are challenged at every level by the nature of the strategic agenda for growth, performance and change. Powerful shifts in global trade, supply chains, demand bases and infotech are just some of the forces that reframe the structure of industries and the behavior of customers. The strategic agenda for most companies can be reset to a more evolutionary mode, one that draws upon the collective thought and behavior of the people who shape the vision, craft the value and focus on results. The conception and conveyance of the reset agenda is a process that deserves more attention and discernment. Focus on the realities of business change.

SUMMARY NOTES AND THOUGHTS

Successful companies tend to address their challenges in creative and effective ways. They confront the same uncertain business world that management advocate Peter Drucker framed over the past half century. In his 1980 book, *Managing in Turbulent Times*, Drucker suggested that managing and leading effectively was all about the actions taken by companies to adapt and prosper, and the effective discharge of business directions, plans and priorities. Some companies draw new energy from these so-called turbulent times. Others manage and lead as though they are victims of the times. The *social ecology* later framed by Drucker shapes our view of strategy.

A company's perspectives and inclinations are shaped by its views of the future, its principles and its sense of opportunity. These things are tempered by many challenges, or the perceptions formed by those challenges. We are optimistic about the capacity of organizations, and their approach to getting prepared and resolved. Every company faces internal and external challenges. Strategic management and leadership builds from that premise, and from those evolving business realities. Successful companies reshape their strategic agenda to address those challenges. That is our starting point, and our platform for framing and guiding the proper strategic agenda.

02

THE FRAMEWORK OF STRATEGY

Framework...a set of basic assumptions,
concepts, values, themes and practices that
constitute a way of viewing reality...

Successful companies are blessed with an effective concoction of thought,
behavior, action and results. In this chapter, we define a framework that
examines the practical strategy elements which enable individuals and
organizations to focus on and achieve their intentions. This is a practical
and commonsense business approach that respects the dynamics of market
environments and the nuances of organizations.

Growth, performance and change are the result of many separate and
collective causes. We need to understand these causes along with the who,
what, how and when drivers of success. We need to respect the realities of
the business environment as part of the success formula. And, we need to
recognize how priorities make sense, what is actionable and how plans and
people drive the creation of new strategic and economic value. This is all
about *cause-and-effect*, those dynamic forces and the quest for impact.

What is the context for becoming more prepared and resolved as a company?
The answer to that question lies in this basic framework, we believe. It's an
approach, a thought process and to some degree, an attitude about focusing
on business results. This framework is also the keyhole and pathway for
engaging the best thought, behavior and action of people at every level, in
every corner of the organization. Companies are evolving entities. This is a
framework for business evolution – growth, performance and change.

COMMENTS ON RELEVANCE

An important parameter of any business plan or policy argument is relevance. What is the strategic and economic relevance of the choices we make in business direction or capital management? What about the relevance of how we develop people as resources, or customers as assets, or networks as business model platforms? Relevance is really a restatement of things in a way that is meaningful and valuable to those who really care about the success of the business. The key question is: Who really cares? Several groups of stakeholders care a great deal.

> **Investors care** about the relevance of plans and actions as they are drivers of strategic and economic value, and risk.

> **Employees care** about the relevance of plans, because they are part of the action, cause and effect process of the company.

> **Suppliers and other partners care** about relevance, as they are also part of the performance process, and they share risks.

> **Customers care** about the relevance of plans, because they are beneficiaries as well as partners in the value stream.

Why is this so important? It's important for two reasons. First, people are most inclined to engage in thought, behavior and action when a subject is meaningful and valuable to them. From a personal and individual point of view they ask, *what's in it for me?* Our intent with this framework is to make the work of getting a business prepared and resolved for success meaningful to everybody, at every level of the enterprise, in every corner of the organization. Relevance becomes power. Relevance becomes memory. Relevance becomes truth. Relevance makes strategy meaningful to the enterprise. When strategy is relevant, people engage, they become part of the agenda for growth, performance and change. When strategy is relevant to people, they engage in the work of making it happen.

Second, individuals and groups create value through their everyday thoughts, behaviors and actions. We want people to take charge, be responsible and do what needs to be done, within the principles and boundaries of the enterprise. This is something that lies in the culture and structure of every company; *we need to disperse responsibility for actions and results.*

RELEVANCE AND BEHAVIOR

When people throughout a company sense the strategic and economic relevance of its plans, they're more likely to contribute their best efforts. This may seem like a simple point. To some, it may seem like academic noise. However, one of the most important business indicators in companies that are fumbling with objectives is relevance. They've lost relevance with customers. Their plans and priorities are disconnected and irrelevant to their employees, channel partners and supplier partners. Their own investors wonder about their relevance as a business entity. Strategic and economic relevance is a key facet of success planning, and when it goes missing, there will be problems. Effective behavior starts with relevance. Make strategy meaningful to people and they will engage. It can emerge as a most powerful motivation agent for people at every level.

CAUSE AND EFFECT THEMES IN STRATEGY

Over the past 50 years, leading business schools and consultants have advanced many explanations and theories on success. Manager's bookshelves are populated with plenty of ideas that shape business growth, performance and change. Today, we have no shortage of precepts and concepts for managing and leading strategy. In fact, we probably have too many ideas, an impression profoundly captured by Eileen Shapiro in her 1995 book, *Fad Surfing in the Boardroom*. Organizations may be nearing the end of their promiscuity with business concepts. However, that prediction could be too hopeful. The broader appeals for greater accountability in business and society reflect unmet needs and problems in strategy leadership and management practice. Too much blather, not enough success.

Our intention with this framework is to break things down to the basics of strategy management and leadership. We believe that companies can deal effectively with the cause-and-effect constructs that enable them to be successful. In Exhibit 02.A, we have a very basic outline of this cause-and-effect puzzle. This is our way of unwinding the hype that so often accompanies the business strategy exercise. Successful companies tend to focus on their most essential cause-and-effect constructs, and this emerges as a critical core of their business agenda. ***Success is a cause-and-effect adventure, an adventure that is dynamic, uncertain and emergent.***

Exhibit 02.A

CAUSE-AND-EFFECT THEMES IN STRATEGY

Cause Factors	Effect Factors
A. Consistent Focus on Key Objectives Organization-Wide Engagement	A. Targeted Financial Measures Revenue, Margins and Capital
B. Strategic Assets and Orientation Management of Strategic Resources	B. Customer Management Measures Relationships and Profitability
C. Reputation with Key Stakeholders Relationships and Credibility	C. Competitive Advantage Measures Positioning and Capabilities
D. Balanced Structure and Leadership Leadership in Every Dimension	D. Business Relationship Measures Stakeholder Value and Leverage
E. Innovative Systems and Resources Capabilities, Entreship Networks	E. Change Management Measures Capacity for Business Evolution

Notes: This outline has evolved with experience in hundreds of business settings where strategy management and leadership concerns have been debated, framed, reframed and settled. Effects are measures of relevant business impact and business results. Causes are the ideas and assets that drive opportunities, intentions, and under the right set of circumstances, they drive business success. Sorting strategic cause-and-effect is critical work. As companies construct and engage their performance scorecards and dashboards, the nature of cause-and-effect relationships is often confused. This is one of the common traps of business measurement, and one that will be addressed in later sections of this book.

GETTING BEYOND SWOT REVIEWS

The conventional approach to strategic planning would have us comment on the *strengths, weaknesses, opportunities and threats* of the business. As an alternative, we begin with the premise that cause-and-effect dynamics lie at the heart of business strategy. This really speaks more clearly to the natural goals of business and the agenda to create new strategic and economic value. Sure, every company has strengths and weaknesses, opportunities and threats. But the very meaning and relevance of these ideas is really more about cause-and-effect than the issues themselves. We need to approach strategic issues through the analytic and creative lenses of cause-and-effect. We need to treat these cause-and-effect topics with absolutely brutal truth and reality tests. It's important to understand the requisites of strategy.

POINTS OF ORIGIN

Every company is a unique enterprise. We can't simply transfer the strategic ideas and patterns from one company to another. It does not work that way. The intentions, cultures, challenges and realities of companies are singular and dynamic in their own way. This is an important point of origin. Sure, you can attempt to be innovative like 3M, or maybe evolutionary like GE, or perhaps integrative like BP. However, you are your own dog in this world of planning for growth, performance and change. Companies must start everything with the premise of unique cause-and-effect interests, in unique business settings, with unique conditions for success. This is the foundation for everything, and the essential strategic idea for going forward.

THE WHO AND THE WHAT

We ask people to pause and reflect upon their company as an entity, a dynamic and living enterprise. Who are they and what are they? Who are the people that populate the company and what can be said about their purpose? Who has shaped the company's existence and what has it become? Who is responsible for its principles and direction and do people demonstrate their commitment? Who provides the foresight and vision of the organization, and what does that mean for people in the organization? Who are the performers and what is the essential performance plan in which they're engaged? Who is responsible for results and what are the gauges and markers for measuring success? Who lives with business results and consequences?

These questions and their many variations are basic to business **thought, behavior, action and results**. They provide identity. They produce energy. They encourage new ideas. They help set the stage for getting prepared and resolved for business success. They define the things that count the most and provide meaning. In the work of strategy management and leadership, nothing is more important than defining the business agenda in simple terms that frame "Who we are, and what we stand for" as a company. These are foundation ideas and cultural themes that shape the opportunities and orientations of the entire organization. The who and the what provide a launch pad for exploring the challenges, orientation, ideology, opportunities, needs and choices of the company: **who we are, and what we stand for.** This goes beyond the normal hype of vision and mission.

SUSTAINABILITY

Much is said about sustainability in business. It is a very hopeful concept. We want to help sustain the world's resources. We want to sustain what we have that is good in society. We want to sustain business success. It's tough to argue with the very concept of sustainability, but the real issue is bigger than it appears. There is a lot more to business sustainability than meets the eye.

Companies exist in a world that is quite dynamic and complex. Technical, social, market and economic order evolves in many ways. Radical shifts in technology and emergent patterns in demographics can crush a business. So, one must ask, what should we attempt with regard to sustainability in the contemporary world of business development? Our answer on these matters reflects three basic sustainable business guidelines:

Expect to Evolve

If your organization can expect to evolve in a way that makes business sense, you have a key part of the agenda for success in place. Expectations drive behavior.

Sense Your Natural Goals

If your organization sees its evolution in terms of natural goals – financial, competitive, customer and stewardship interests, you are on track with a sense of success.

Be Responsible

If your organization takes its proper place at the table of society, it will be responsible for business results and its impact on the world it serves, today and tomorrow.

This book is about modern capitalism. Unless companies create strategic and economic value, societies cannot prosper. For those who embrace this ideology, sustainability is really about the evolution of companies for the creation of strategic and economic value, under conditions that are dynamic and complex, and sometimes ambiguous. Sustainability today is a matter of responsibility and stewardship—and performance. Business can and does make the world a much better place, serving customers, managing assets, creating value, engaging people and making innovation happen.

STRATEGY DEFINED AND REDEFINED

There are volumes of material that attempt to define strategy. They borrow from every discipline and philosophy. They bring together economic and social themes. They reflect upon the human condition and the talents of people. We believe that strategy means different things to different groups. We are comfortable with the collections of theories about strategy and the concoctions of strategic practice in business. We find that most organizations are not so comfortable in their approach to balancing strategy discipline and practice. Strategy remains elusive as a concept, a disjointed practice.

The matter comes down to this, however. Business research shows that there is little relationship between strategy and performance. That is troubling, if taken at face value. It surely bothers academics like McGill Professor Henry Mintzberg, as he expressed in his 1994 book, *The Rise and Fall of Strategic Planning*. We think this challenge begs another view of what strategy really means, and what it's all about. A better, more useful definition of strategy is surely in order, and taking a broader approach to strategy is a start.

Strategy is something that can be described in many ways. We can look at strategy as a set of ideas that give meaning to a business. Strategy supports *meaning and purpose*. Strategy frames enterprise intention, identity and ideology. Strategy shapes what a company stands for, what it's all about in the world, what it has evolved from, and what it intends to become. Strategy is a company's rationale for existence. ***Strategy is the agenda for growth, performance and change, and we use that as the fundamental premise of this book, and our work.*** The strategic agenda is the big idea here.

We can also look at strategy as an ***intellectual process***. It's how we learn, and it's how we go about the engagement of learning in the business. What we see in the business and how we process our thoughts about the business are sometimes the exclusive domain of our so-called "strategic thinkers" in the organization. In successful companies, we're convinced that strategic thought, behavior and action are the province of people at every level, in every corner of the organization. We need to disperse the processes of strategy, so that we get the right people engaged in the right manner, in the right mode. This is too important to be left to a few strategy wonks.

Strategy is a *cultural component* in organizations, reflecting the company's values, tendencies, ethos and principles. Some companies have cultures that are curious and discerning in their strategic behaviors. Some companies are seemingly oblivious to the linkages between culture and strategy. Some blend perspective, discovery and adventure in their strategy. Some adhere to strong and steady principles. Strategy is manifested, more or less, in company cultures. This is a part of the reason why strategic change can be tough. The attitudes of stakeholders toward strategy are important as change catalysts. Many people have a stake in the strategy.

Strategy is a *mechanistic process* as well. It's used to gauge decisions and direction. It connects analytic and creative activity. It provides order. It sets the context for action through pathways and processes. It helps define and engage priorities. Strategy organizes ideas and people. It seeds a company's agenda, and in that context, it puts boundaries around what could be done, and what should be done to drive business success. Strategy is really a prime collaborative device, connecting business thought and behavior.

Above all, strategy is what *informs business evolution*. Strategy nags us to transform our business models and our business intentions. It provokes us to consider our challenges and our opportunities. It forces us to ask the most difficult questions about direction and execution. It sometimes tests our values and principles. It introduces ideas that disturb our status quo, our comfort levels. It encourages risk and it mitigates risk. Strategy makes us think hard about where we've been and where we're headed, and the reasons for our business existence. It challenges who we are.

In summary, strategy is something that deals with meaning and purpose, intellectual practice, culture, planning, mechanics and the essence of business evolution. We need a pragmatic framework that encompasses each of these ideas. We need a framework that is more relevant to everybody responsible in the business. Such a framework would help us think about the business in evolutionary terms. It would provoke what some refer to as fierce conversation about the key issues that shape the key choices of the company. Strategy is all of these things. Strategy is everything that goes into the agenda for growth, performance and change, and it sets the way we think and act. As such, strategy is a broad and dynamic responsibility, one that may extend well beyond orthodox planning practices.

STRATEGY AND VALUE CREATION

At the highest level, the intention of most companies is to create new value. New value is generally measured and coded in economic and strategic terms. It may be considered and measured in terms of broader mission or relevance, and in the context of a company's principles. It may be addressed in the natural goals of business as they are gauged across the organization. Companies exist to create new economic and strategic value, and for the most part, they do that by serving the interests of stakeholders. Once again, we define these stakeholders as customers, employers, suppliers and investors; more broadly, we would include society in general as a stakeholder.

Investors and employees should desire a more valuable company because it serves their interests. Value creation is clearly a part of the business sustainability equation. Companies that create new economic and strategic value contribute taxes to the public sector and grants to the projects that society desires. *That is enlightened capitalism at work.* The strategic and economic value created by an enterprise serves what the late Drucker called *social ecology,* and similar themes are on the agenda of most companies.

Customers and suppliers should desire more valuable companies because these companies would be better in terms of:

> Goods and Services
>
> Community Assets
>
> Sources of Innovation
>
> Partners in Trust
>
> Employment Bases
>
> Growth Opportunities

Think about how companies create new economic and strategic value in different industries. Think about the relevance of value creation to social development and culture. People who take responsibility for business strategy are really taking on something much larger – the creation of value that shapes everything from social health to public assets. Enlightened self-interest drives the creation of strategic and economic value, and new value creation really must be at the heart of the strategic agenda.

FOCUSED ON BUSINESS RESULTS

Strategy is the agenda for driving business results. It respects the realities of the business. It's evolutionary by its very nature, and it's based on thought processes and action plans. It reflects the economic, cultural and technical nuances of the company and its business values. Strategy mixes principles, resources, capability and direction, and in the process, it provides four essential ideas for the evolution of an organization:

> A sense of what the company stands for and a platform for discerning its real business purpose.

> A sense of where the company is headed and a general roadmap for the journey into the future.

> A sense of cause-and-effect factors that influence the drivers and achievement of business success.

> A sense of evolution and the mindset that engages the company in work that drives meaningful change.

When all the clatter ceases, strategy is about purpose, direction and process, and the focus on business results. The framework we propose is an agenda for driving business results. The goal is the creation of new strategic and economic value for the company and its various stakeholders. The task is to frame the whole of strategy management and leadership as a discipline. This discipline sets the agenda for successful business growth, performance and change in environments which are constantly changing and evolving.

FRAMEWORK AND PERSPECTIVE

How can we begin to approach strategy management and leadership as a practice that makes sense and fuels impact? Our answer to that question is in the framework defined in Exhibit 02.B on the following page.

This framework represents the essential working elements of strategy management and leadership, and it deals with the issues of the most complex enterprise, as well as the challenges of the smallest niche business. It also provides basic constructs for corporate governance, a theme that is increasingly important to every organization large and small.

At the heart of this framework is the orientation of strategy itself, the ingredients of **direction, integration and execution**. These are engines of strategy management and leadership. They house the basic ideas and the plan levers we pull to succeed with the strategic agenda. Conditions of the business environment set many of the ground rules for strategy. Revenue and resource leverage are outcome factors, as are the natural goals of business, and the company's value creation themes.

Exhibit 02.B

STRATEGY MANAGEMENT AND LEADERSHIP FRAMEWORK

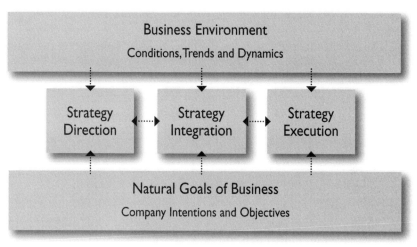

Chapter 04 is dedicated to the elements of strategy direction. Chapter 05 is dedicated to matters of strategy integration and Chapter 06 deals with strategy execution. Chapter 09, Major Applications presents a series of five of the most important challenges for strategic leadership and management, complete with the context of strategy direction, integration and execution as practice elements. This framework is a simple, adaptive model that drives strategic perspective. It anticipates change in the business environment as well as shifts in company goals and intentions, near-term and long-term.

When successful companies reflect on their strategic agenda along with the management and leadership of the agenda, they can explain things in terms of these simple, common sense business systems themes. These frame how the organization becomes aware of strategic issues and the strategic agenda. They frame how well people understand the cause-and-effect ingredients of the strategy, and how they engage at a personal level in the journey that is defined by the nature of the company's strategic agenda. This framework ties conditions, company purpose and objectives together in a practical way.

COMMON LOGJAMS AND MISCUES

Our strategy research suggests that successful companies get things right in *direction, integration and execution*. Their less fortunate peers suffer in different ways, but here are the most common patterns of strategic miscue and failure from our broad-based research and experience:

> **Miscues in strategic direction.** We estimate that no less than 30% to 40% of companies pursue directions that are unlikely to succeed in creating new value, near-term or long-term. Some of these organizations are really quite sophisticated, but their strategic compass is broken. They have fundamental problems with strategic direction.

> **Miscues in strategy integration.** Most companies face basic challenges in the integration of strategy, resources, process and structure. We estimate that 50% to 60% of companies experience significant problems with regard to strategy integration, and these present major barriers to the creation of new business value. Strategy integration problems can render any company into mincemeat.

> **Miscues in strategy execution.** These are legendary, but the reality here will surprise many business observers. We estimate that of those companies with sound, realistic foundations in strategy direction, fewer than 20% to 30% experience significant problems in strategy execution. The foundation of sound direction serves good execution.

What does all this really mean? One assessment you can take away relates to the true scope of strategy management and leadership. That scope must include direction, integration and execution. Strategy, in its purest form, connects and discerns these elements. Another assessment is that execution is a common and frequently voiced challenge, but half of all companies are probably pounding away on a strategic agenda that has flawed direction and integration elements. For executives, this explains why people might not be willing to engage in the process, and why they are just a little skeptical of the latest program and the latest appeal to play in the new business plan. Credibility depends on the alignment of direction, integration and execution. This reflects on the relevance of strategy to employees.

NATURAL GOALS AND LEVERAGE

Another part of this strategy management and leadership framework is the body of natural goals. Again, companies discern their natural goals in the context of financial performance, competitive advantage, customer connections and corporate stewardship. These goals are focal points and success measures. They are the terms through which we define business results. They are the gauges of growth, performance and change. They translate mission into results. While there are many things to consider in this assessment of natural goals, we believe it's helpful to focus on three themes:

> **Revenue leverage,** and the company's agenda for revenue growth and revenue/margin enhancement.
>
> **Network leverage,** and the company's agenda for linking supply and demand chain assets.
>
> **Resource leverage,** and the company's agenda for resource development and resource appropriation.

These are important factors in the equation for creating strategic and economic value. We will address these in more detail in Chapter 07, in an expanded discussion on value creation. At this point, we need to emphasize that natural goals and leverage are the reason we do strategy...to create strategic and economic value. A surprising number of companies embrace a so-called strategic plan that does not connect with value creation goals. They suggest a direction and execution agenda, but they lack the assessment of natural goals and leverage, or they lack good cause-and-effect premises. Value creation is why we construct and implement strategy.

Building an agenda for growth, performance and change involves a balanced point of view. Choices have to be made in strategy. Choices that impact revenue leverage, and choices which wrestle with resource leverage. The dynamics of business further complicate the picture, and it's in this context that we build our strategic agenda. We discern and evaluate choices in the context of the company's experience and the assessment of challenges and opportunities on the frontier. How people in the organization look at revenue and resource leverage shapes how they approach the company's strategic agenda. Everyday business choices make a big difference.

BUSINESS CONDITIONS AND DYNAMICS

The upper portion of our framework expresses the conditions that shape the environment for strategy management and leadership. These conditions are external and internal by definition. The external conditions of business tend to get a lot of attention in the conventional assessment of threats and opportunities, as well as discussions about strategic competence and business position. We believe it's important to address business conditions and dynamics on a more discerning basis. We want to build a very keen sense of business conditions and dynamics into the strategic and cultural dialogue of the organization. The elements are:

> **Business Environment**
>
> Conditions, Trends and Dynamics

When people are actively discerning and perceptive about the conditions and dynamics of the business, the broader thought processes of the company are at work. The company can sense opportunities and problems with greater acuity. People at every level of the organization can contribute a point of view, or an idea, or an edge of something that could help move the business along its strategic journey. Here's the issue: everyone in the organization knows something about the conditions and dynamics of the business. This is way too important to be left to analysts and strategic planners. This is what front-line and first-level leadership [FL/FL] is all about. Under this kind of leadership thought and behavior, everybody in the company has a role to play in the tracking of business conditions and dynamics. Again, Basement to Boardroom; everybody has a role in the adventure.

We find it useful to look at business conditions in terms of the major technical, social, market and economic forces at work in the company's setting – both internal and external in scope. In Exhibit 02.C the *external conditions* that should be assessed are grouped and defined for ongoing assessment. The *internal conditions* are grouped and defined in Exhibit 02.D.

Most of these conditions are familiar to companies that have embraced conventional strategic planning techniques. What lies beyond in the basic assessment is more emphasis on how the strategies of competing firms impact the environment of the current and emergent business.

Exhibit 02.C

EXTERNAL BUSINESS CONDITIONS AND DYNAMICS

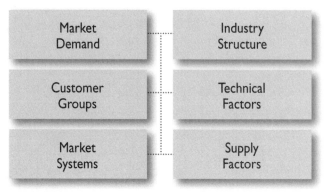

Notes: External conditions make market categories more or less attractive in terms of attainable margins, demand patterns, industry and competitive structure and other factors. Some of these are structural. Some are behavioral. External conditions are dynamic and complex. External conditions may be subject to disruptive forces. They may be stable. They may be subject to glacial momentum or techtonic pressures that could break in dramatic form at some point on the horizon.

The key issues here are the forces that shape demand and supply on the external fronts of the company – their action and energy, and their impact on the company's agenda for growth, performance and change.

Market demand and industry structure usually influence the relative attractiveness of a market category, and the profit prospects for companies that serve the market category. Market systems and supply factors usually influence the competitive conditions of the market category. Customer groups are the arbiters of demand and supply. They have requirements and behaviors that must be addressed. Technical factors such as operational systems or core technologies influence the differentiation of supplier and the segmentation of customers. Companies like Motorola and Monsanto have navigated their respective external environments to become refocused, renewed and redirected in their approach to customer demand and market categories. Companies like Emerson and DuPont have evolved in much the same way. Both have weathered environmental storms over time.

All together, these external business conditions and dynamics are important, but they are not exclusive drivers of growth, performance and change. The real balancing act of strategy analysis combines with a significant range of internal business conditions and dynamics and competitive leverage.

Exhibit 02.D

INTERNAL BUSINESS CONDITIONS AND DYNAMICS

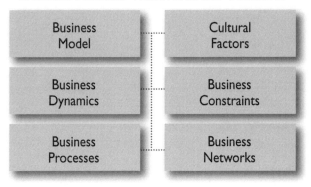

Business Model	Cultural Factors
Business Dynamics	Business Constraints
Business Processes	Business Networks

Notes: Internal conditions define what a company thinks and how it acts, along with its basic competencies, assets and capabilities, relative to goals. Internal conditions surely temper strategic and economic value creation. They shape what a company can, and what it should do. How a company views itself, how it deals with its challenges and choices, and how it moves on its strategic agenda, near-term and long-term, are all part of the internal environment.

The key issues here are the forces that shape a company's thought, behavior and action, business abilities and resources. Strategy goes with structure, and combined, these things make up the capabilities of the business today, and in the future. These are interdependent elements. They interact in the everyday stresses, heat and friction of the company.

Business models and cultural factors go together in many ways to define what a company does, who it works with, who it serves, and how it really gets things done. Business dynamics and constraints indicate what a company faces and how it responds to the realities of the business. Business processes and networks are the individual and collective capabilities of the enterprise. Sometimes these factors are indicative of platforms for competitive edge and differentiation. Sometimes they are merely descriptive elements of what makes the company tick. The emergence of new business models is a concern that every company must explore as a potential threat and a working premise in their strategic agenda. Economic sectors evolve, and we would expect that internal conditions evolve in response. Changes in position are part of the lens through which we gauge internal conditions.

Taken together, these internal conditions and dynamics present the business capabilities and assets of the company. Successful companies have a strong sense of development and evolution with these assets and competencies.

THE PRACTICE OF STRATEGY

The framework for strategy management and leadership is something we can use to guide current and emergent business success. It sets an agenda that works for the *everyday practice of strategy*. It puts things in perspective for people at every level of responsibility, in every corner of the organization. It deals with business reality, and it confronts the real possibilities of the company, along with key risks that are likely to be encountered.

Successful companies tend to have strong cultures and adept, agile structures. Linking sound resources and strategy practice, a company's prospects for growth, performance and change are going to be more positive. The effective practice of strategy reflects the philosophical, mechanistic, intellectual, contextual and evolutionary themes we introduced earlier in this chapter. Practice is one part discipline, one part mindset, one part inspiration and one part foresight. We find these essential parts mixed into the successful practice of strategy in a wide range of company settings.

Managing and Leading the Practice of Strategy

Strategy management and leadership is an organizational asset, and the value of that asset varies widely in companies today. It reflects the people, processes and plans of the business, and it reflects the unique conditions of the company. As we look at managing and leading the practice of strategy, it's clear that organizations need a more complete picture, a more thorough sense of what it means to manage and lead strategy…in every corner of the organization, at every level, with every person, every day. Practice is an appropriate *cultural precept* for leading and managing the company's strategic agenda. Practice drives success in many ways.

ELEMENTS OF STRATEGY MANAGEMENT

For our purposes here, *managing* means setting disciplines in place to guide thought, behavior, action and results. By definition, these disciplines help guide the organization with planning processes, decision support, action programs, stage calendars, target measures and other mechanisms. Managing strategy is a blend of analytics, planning and measures. It provides order, arrangement and rationale, and it puts actions and impact into a kind of sequence, with tempo, rhythm and energy.

ELEMENTS OF STRATEGY LEADERSHIP

Leading strategy involves a great deal of communicating, linking thought, behavior, action and results. It draws energy from interaction as well as discipline. The interaction of people and ideas that inspire the organization is what strategy leadership is all about. The elements of strategy leadership that enable people to function well across the organization include:

> **Competence** about subject matter and conditions that are relevant to the organization's success.

> **Character** in the form of personal standards, values and principles that guide thought and behavior.

> **Connections** that forge effective relationships between ideas, people and plans for success.

These three elements are crucial to the sustenance and evolution of companies. More important, however, is *leadership dispersion* in the organization – at every level and in every corner of the business. When strategic leadership is dispersed, the power of responsibility is dispersed, and the entire organization becomes more focused on business results.

When leadership is dispersed, people take responsibility for their efforts, their actions, and their impact. The days of strategic planning and implementation as an executive circus are dead. The front-line, first-level people of every company have as much to give as they take from the leadership of the strategy agenda. This is FL/FL leadership – good people, fully engaged at every level of the organization, and sometimes beyond the boundaries. Twenty-first century business depends more and more on leadership that crosses over enterprise lines, often with little real authority. This is a critical kind of leadership dispersion.

When leadership is truly and fully dispersed, from the boardroom to the shop floor, from the supply chain through the demand chain, good things are bound to happen. Good people will make good choices. Good plans and efforts will yield good results. Strategy leadership is something that operates in different forms, in different places. The most dynamic companies derive much of their energy from acts of strategic leadership that are closer to the front lines than the boardroom. This is the power of entreship, the creation of new value through everyday leadership at every level.

MANAGEMENT AND LEADERSHIP REDEFINED

In every enterprise, building a sound agenda for strategy requires effective management and leadership. Not one or the other. Not a little of this and a little of that. Both management and leadership. This runs contrary to the populist noise about management and leadership in which academics, writers and consultants have distorted the roles and relevance of both management and leadership. It's disappointing, and it's fraudulent.

Below is a summary point of view that helps redefine what we should expect of strategy management and strategy leadership. We encourage companies to take the time to assess just what these elements mean to their business success formula, and to their everyday thought and behavior. Effective people lead and manage effectively. They do both, with purpose.

Management Redefined for the Strategic Agenda	Leadership Redefined for the Strategic Agenda
Provides discipline	Shapes perspectives
Orders and arranges	Frames values, principles
Disperses resources	Encourages character
Supports sound practice	Engages and inspires
Provides work processes	Forges connections
Gives targets, measures	Encourages relationships
Sets proper boundaries	Provides foresight
Encourages quality	Clarifies direction, focus
Manages risk factors	Encourages thought
Provides information	Shares, exchanges, learns

Source: From internal studies on strategy leadership and management effectiveness, Research 2005, working references and research on Effective Collaboration [Collaboration and Entreship] related to The Future of Enterprise, Dewar Sloan.

As organizations seek to develop management and leadership talent, they should take clear notice of the behaviors, competencies and resources that are essential to the success of their organization. The idea of **benchstrength begins with the development of management and leadership assets**, and their engagement in the company's strategic agenda.

MANAGING AND LEADING STRATEGY

There is an age-old debate on the utility and importance of managing versus leading in business organizations. *In strategy, managing and leading are equally relevant and valuable.* Only those who have not experienced the power and mix of effective managing and leading would argue to the contrary. While it may be popular to fuel this little debate, we subscribe to an approach that develops the leadership and managerial talents of each and every person in the organization. This is the real benchstrength issue.

Good leaders build good leaders, and good managers build good managers. Good managers and leaders propagate good managers and leaders who create value. Companies need both. Some view this as a human capital and talent issue, not just something* for HR. We see this as part of the strategic agenda, and the full engagement of that agenda by people throughout the organization. This is more than some populist debate. Mature strategic thought and behavior is a managerial and leadership asset. Problem-solving and choice-making are everyday priority activities for strategy leaders and managers, and a key zone of strategic thought and behavior.

The depth of leadership and management capabilities in any company is a strategic issue of great importance. When we get beyond all the blather of how people are the most important assets, there are some truly glaring challenges on the line. Benchstrength is as much about **competence** as it is about **character** and **connection.** Badaracco deals with this stream of thought and behavior in *Questions of Character,* 2006.

Benchstrength emerges from putting the right people in the right place to learn and do the right work that drives personal and business results. Benchstrength comes from thoughtful people selection and effective people development. Benchstrength is gained through experience and preserved through sound learning and retention culture. Benchstrength in its finest form is a two-way street; experience is exchanged and enabled across and vertically, throughout the organization. Talent at the individual level is important, but collective, connected talent is what comprises true and sustainable benchstrength.

---

* In an August 2005 Fast Company article, *Why We Hate HR*, the authors tackled some of the mainstream issues behind employer concerns about HR management. Behind everything, it seems, there is a deep-seated issue with credible approaches to benchstrength development and talent management.

THE FOUR DIMENSIONS OF LEADERSHIP

The practice of strategy is supported by leadership thought and behavior in different ways, and in different patterns. We refer to these as the *four dimensions of leadership*, and these dimensions include; *individual self-level leadership, functional group-level leadership, cross-function process leadership* and *cross-boundary network leadership*. These are illustrated further in Exhibit 02.E below.

Exhibit 02.E

THE FOUR DIMENSIONS OF LEADERSHIP

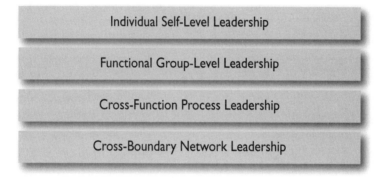

Individual Self-Level Leadership

Functional Group-Level Leadership

Cross-Function Process Leadership

Cross-Boundary Network Leadership

Source: Developing the Four Dimensions of Leadership from research papers in the Dewar Sloan B-202 project and references in leadership development with an emerging open-source project, Collaboration and Entreship, 2005-06.

Leadership inspires and connects people in the ventures and journeys of the organization. Leadership gives purpose and principle to individuals and groups. Leadership provides standards and it sets ground rules. It exchanges ideas and it engages learning. Leadership puts things in perspective and it demands that we think and act with passion. Leadership opens doors to possibility, and it puts individuals and groups in the center of things. Leadership is transformative and emergent. Leadership is adaptive.

When leadership thought and behavior is dispersed across organizations, everyone gains in the exchange. Everyone develops greater awareness, understanding and engagement in the practice of strategy. Everyone has input opportunities and responsibilities. Everyone has a hand in the evolution of the business. Everyone has a role to play, a task to serve. Everyone leads, or they're not engaged in the strategic agenda. Everyone is responsible.

COLLABORATIVE LEADERSHIP

For several years, we've worked on a research initiative that deals with the nature and meaning of collaborative leadership. This is the kind of leadership that connects people within and beyond the boxes of the organization chart and the boundaries of the enterprise. The *cornerstones of collaboration* are part of an emergent way of thinking about strategy leadership, and this is essential for the evolution of conventional and net-centric companies.

Collaboration, as shown in Exhibit 02.F below, shows how people would be prepared and resolved to work effectively with a combination of four concerns in mind. First, the clarity of common goals and principles. Second, the use of practical working structures for collaborating. Third, the assumption of partnership behaviors. And fourth, the use of realistic systems and practices for engagement. More and more, business people have to lead effectively without the benefit of conventional laws of power, authority and control. That is what collaborative leadership in strategy is all about...working outside conventional boundaries. These component themes represent the source of a lot of heartburn in everything from supply chain management to product and service development. They define how value edge is created and maintained.

Exhibit 02.F

THE CORNERSTONES OF COLLABORATION

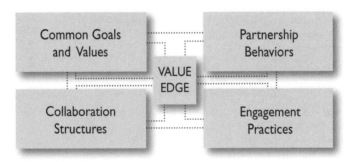

Source: Effective Collaboration, 2005 id Strategy Conference Presentation sponsored by the Institute of Design. See also the open-source project Collaboration and Entreship, referenced at www.dewarsloan.com/research, 2005-06 studies.

PROCESS POINT OF VIEW

Strategy management sometimes looks like a process. It deals with matching a company's situation and business conditions with a collection of plans, decisions and actions that drive success. Strategy management puts into motion certain activities that help connect people and ideas with targets and roles. The process components of strategy management help us make the strategic choices of a company more disciplined. Processes help make execution more orderly and adaptive. They help frame strategy in a way that makes priorities and responsibilities more clear and more tangible.

The disciplines of business process management and process evolution have produced a lot of strategic and economic value for companies with serious commitments to quality, resource management, innovation and leverage. However, when the processes of a company morph into behaviors that blur their original purpose and intent, people can lose track of the strategic agenda for growth, performance and change. Then they can stumble.

Think accountability for actions and results...Strategy leadership often looks like a process. It deals with matching the company's many possibilities and realities with the collective and individual talents of the organization. Strategy leadership provokes and promotes strategic thought and behavior. It shapes business culture and subculture. It sets principles and standards for the organization. Strategy leadership is a process that is powered by communication. *The communication engine is what moves people from awareness, to understanding, to engagement.* Leadership may or may not emanate from the top. Subcultures can be significant in shaping the agenda and they serve to define what is relevant and meaningful to stakeholder groups across the organization.

Think accountability for actions and results... We favor a view of strategy management and leadership that reflects the true work that is needed. That work brings together the agenda for strategic direction, integration and execution. Some people stress over the difference between managers and leaders. We care little for this debate. We need the mindset about strategy that embodies great management and leadership together, a melding of thought, behavior, action and results, at every level and in every reach of the organization, and often, beyond its boundaries.

COMMUNICATION CONSIDERATIONS

In the practice of strategy, new ideas and arguments travel through the organization. These ideas and arguments shape expectations about the business and the plans for the business. Expectations, in turn, shape individual and group behavior, and then, behaviors ultimately drive the performance of the enterprise. The communication systems and pathways of the organization are important to the practice of strategy.

> **Expectations** ┄┄┄▶ **Behavior** ┄┄┄▶ **Performance**
>
> Communication Throughout the Organization and Beyond

Expectations are created and finessed at different levels of the company. Investors cast forth certain expectations for the company's approach to creating strategic and economic value. Customers share their expectations relative to product quality, experience value and service quality. Employees frame their expectations with regard to work process, mission, plans and business goals. In every case, these combined *expectations are part of the company's cultural and strategic setting.* Expectations can be very technical and specific, or quite vague and ambiguous. They can originate from a simple discussion, or they can be part of a more extensive, long-term assessment of data and issues. Expectations are formative and sometimes transformative in their roles vis-à-vis the strategic agenda. Expectations can and do evolve over the course of business life and times.

When we turn to individual and group behaviors in the practice of strategy, another set of communication factors enters the mix. In most organizations, we want people who use their best talents to help the company succeed. But what does that really entail? It means that we want people to use their insights and knowledge to solve problems and venture forward. It means we want them to act in concert with principles and exercise good judgment. It means we want them to collaborate in effective ways with people, subject matter, resources and change. Most companies are interested in effective behavior, plain and simple. However, most would argue that the full talents and knowledge of their people are often untapped. One of the reasons they are untapped is that the communication practices that surround basic strategy are broken, or simply not in place at all. That is a very big issue.

The performance of companies and the relationship of performance issues to the practice of strategy is the third facet of communication. This involves a lot more than reporting quarterly results and standard measures against plan. Performance criteria should be linked to strategic actions, business processes and strategic results. The communication elements that bind these together are part of the framework for strategy management and leadership. While there tends to be a lot of talk in companies about complex performance criteria and measures of performance, it's not always in sync with the broader practice of strategy. We will deal with these issues further in Chapter 07, in the context of specific value criteria.

The conveyance and communication of strategy is a dynamic that is truly unique to every organization. It reflects cultural and subcultural factors as well as the more formal work structures and relationships of people in the business. It pulses in different dimensions and through different channels. Social networks and connections are conduits for strategy communication. Collaborative actions and events are active elements in the strategy communication formula. Each of these factors influences the knowledge and experience of people who are involved in the practice of strategy at every level of the organization.

PERSPECTIVE, KNOWLEDGE AND EXPERIENCE

Companies blessed with good strategy practice tend to have a blend of thought that is comprised of well-developed perspectives, knowledge and experiences in the business. Those perspectives can be common or quite diverse. The knowledge base should be broad, relevant and connected by key ideas. The experience issue is critical. Judgment and business intuition come from experience. Entreship comes from experience. Functional intellect comes from experience. Leadership and managerial capability in strategy come from experience. How do we value perspective, knowledge and experience? Ask that little question of people at different levels of your organization, and consider the answers you get. This could be humbling and surprising. In fact, this may be the most important question that we could ask at the boardroom level. How do we capture and consider the value of perspectives, knowledge and experience in the organization? Judgement comes from experience, and it's a maturity asset of organizations.

TOWARD THE AGENDA FOR BUSINESS SUCCESS

When the framework for strategy management and leadership is established and reinforced with everyday practice, we get an agenda for business success and evolution. This agenda reflects upon the backbone elements of strategy, the natural goals of the company, and the conditions that shape the challenges and prospects of the business going forward. Exhibit 02.G represents the ingredients in terms of strategy direction, integration and execution.

Exhibit 02.G

ELEMENTS OF THE STRATEGIC AGENDA

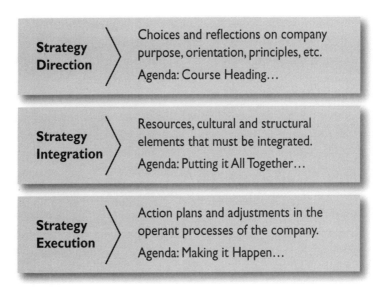

| Strategy Direction | Choices and reflections on company purpose, orientation, principles, etc. Agenda: Course Heading… |

| Strategy Integration | Resources, cultural and structural elements that must be integrated. Agenda: Putting it All Together… |

| Strategy Execution | Action plans and adjustments in the operant processes of the company. Agenda: Making it Happen… |

Notes: Major problems and miscues in strategy occur at each of these junctures of strategy management and leadership, even in so-called Excellent Companies. For more, see www.dewarsloan.com/research and the work of Peters and others in research on *Re-imagine! Business Excellence in a Disruptive Age*, Tom Peters, 2003.

Chapters 04, 05 and 06 of this book examine the details and nuances of strategy direction, integration and execution, along with the theme of leadership and management engagement of the strategy agenda. These are the essential elements of the strategic agenda; they constitute the everyday context for the *who, what, how, when of strategy.* Strategic choices made and strategic resources applied by people shape business results.

NUANCES IN THE STRATEGIC AGENDA

The company's strategic agenda may encounter nuances that temper and season the approach of the organization. We live in a time when *clear and unambiguous plans are a luxury*. There are emergent issues and occasional bumps in the pathways that define a company's journey. It's important to recognize these business nuances for what they are – punctuations and subtle brushstrokes in the agenda for business growth, performance and change. Exhibit 02.H illustrates some of the nuances that we encounter in the strategy management and leadership agenda. Ambiguity is often part of the equation. How knowledge is engaged and applied to plans and choices is a major nuance. How decisions are crafted, finessed and engaged is nuance-rich. How the interfaces of ideas, people, plans and actions work is full of meaning, and the meaning-making schema is nuanced.

Exhibit 02.H

NUANCES IN THE STRATEGY AGENDA

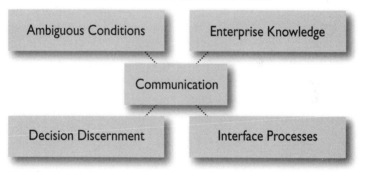

Notes: The common denominator in this complex environment is communication. That means information sharing, engagement, conversations and thoughtful, pragmatic, resourceful debate. How organizations recognize, discuss and explore their strategic issues is a cultural mattter. The way companies communicate is part of their thought and behavior edge, the edge that yields their unique strategic agenda. Military agencies have reset their training cultures to address the inherent volatility, uncertainty, complexity and ambiguity of the conditions under which they serve. This so-called VUCA theme is a useful idea for companies as they tackle their strategic agenda in the context of uncertain and evolutionary business environments.

The days of simple, clear, concise business conditions are over for most companies. The days of five-year plans with modest risk and little change were probably a fantasy of post-war economic times, shaped by steady predictability. Going forward, the strategy agenda of most companies is subject to a greater array of technical, market and economic turbulence. These nuances percolate across and beyond a company's strategy agenda.

Nuances Explored Further

A sound framework for strategy leadership and management is one that considers and contemplates ideas that influence the options a company might entertain. At the same time, we would want our people to act in ways that are decisive, aware, prompt and connected. Government leaders in wartime and peacetime are called upon to recognize and account for the nuances of actions and the absence of actions. Inventors and integrators are called upon to combine their perspectives and their perceptions to conceive new things and new ideas. We look at nuances in the strategy agenda as part of the success equation for companies. To understand these nuances may itself be a source of competitive edge. To contemplate the effects, risks and choices brought about by these nuances may be a special scheme that powers the most innovative companies. Serious questions from the boardroom, and from senior executive discussion might sound something like this:

> What is the real value of the accumulated knowledge of the organization, and who is working to create and sustain the value of knowledge? Who owns this knowledge and its linkages?

> How are simple and complex strategy decisions made in the organization, and by whom, and when? What kind of dispersion of leadership, decision power and authority makes sense? And, how are business decisions engaged by the people of the organization? What engagement risks are in play?

> What is the right formula for crossing and matching the many functional and resource processes of the organization, and who is involved in this work? Who balances the agenda?

While it would be wonderful if the answers to these questions were precise and concise, it's the additional issues that get raised when questions like these power and engage strategic thought and behavior. In their 2005 book, *Freakonomics*, Levitt and Dubner described the importance of looking at the world of nuances through multi-faceted lenses. We look at this as an opportunity to engage the people of the organization in a continuous conversation on strategy. Perspective and thoughtful, pragmatic engagement of people is critical stuff. Looking beyond the current reality of a company requires time for discernment, and in many cases, it requires a greater base of open communication, providing the basis for true strategic foresight.

SUMMARY NOTES AND THOUGHTS

The general framework we advance in *Prepared and Resolved* is relatively basic and widely adaptable to organizations. It has a few simple themes and a concise set of disciplines:

> Strategy management and leadership is really all about the focused connection of strategy direction, integration and execution disciplines.

> Strategy is a responsive and prospective discipline that operates within the context of dynamic and sometimes ambiguous business conditions.

> Strategy management and leadership is a focused and collaborative process for driving the creation of new strategic and economic value.

These themes are part of a puzzle, a puzzle that is complex and dynamic in nature. The work of strategy management and leadership is building an agenda for growth, performance and change. When entire organizations get on the agenda, they will likely be successful. Whether their success is sustainable over time depends on discipline, and sound discipline depends on practice commitment and strategy engagement in the hearts and minds of people at every level and in every corner of the company.

03

CONSEQUENCES OF STRATEGY

Consequences...what happens as a result
of plans and actions; impact intended, and
unintended, near-term and long-term.

The effective management and leadership of strategy helps a company evolve. For most organizations, business evolution is a journey across an ever-changing set of frontiers. As business executives, we hope to cross those frontiers with purpose and readiness.

Successful business evolution is a general consequence of effective strategy direction, integration and execution. As executives, we make strategic choices and set direction. We integrate strategy, resources, structure and culture. We execute plans and we measure impact and consequences:

> **Predicted Consequences –** the planned and programmed
> results of our strategy; targeted goals and objectives met.

> **Emergent Consequences –** challenges and forks in the road
> that emerge en route; surprises, both good and bad.

> **Unintended Consequences –** things that occur as a result of
> our efforts and plans; again, some good and some bad.

Consequences are outcomes, mixed with risk factors. They reflect what we intend to do through business strategy, but they also reflect the fate we experience in the contemporary world of business. People at every level of the organization live with the consequences of effective management and leadership of strategy. One of the most powerful dimensions of strategic thinking in business is our common sense about consequences.

THOUGHT PATTERNS IN STRATEGY

How well have your people thought through their plans? How are the elements of those plans tied to consequences? What about emergent and unintended consequences? These are questions that mix foresight and judgment. They ask for an appreciative look ahead, a discerning sense of impact, and a practical sense of implications. They pose important issues in a clear manner, to be challenged and considered, judged and articulated with a disciplined approach to impact analysis.

Anticipation is part of the process. It's more than looking ahead, and it's more than hope about the future. Anticipation is a basic building block of strategic preparation. What should we anticipate? We should anticipate the content and context of effective strategy, and for most organizations, that exercise should reflect upon the following:

> **The consequences of strategy direction** – making the
> right directional choices, and adapting to changing conditions.

> **The consequences of strategy integration** – getting the
> key resources and structure of the business aligned to succeed, and
> again, adapting as necessary to drive results.

> **The consequences of strategy execution** – making it happen
> with people in sync, action plans, resources, calendars, etc.

Preparing for business success begins with good anticipation and with thought patterns that embrace a disciplined look ahead. Vision and a sense of the future is part of the process, but it's not enough. Too many companies have fallen into naïve traps of over-vision and goals that exceed the company's grasp. This can wreck a culture, and it can seriously constrain disciplined, critical thought on business strategy. Companies need more than platitudes about destiny, no matter how attractive we craft those vision and value statements. More substance is needed. More creativity, more analytics, more foresight and more relevance are what we derive from systems analysis and system thinking, as defined and framed by Jay Forrester in his landmark 1961 book, *Industrial Dynamics*. Business results are system consequences. They become results as a function of cause-and-effect systems. Judgments made on the impact, costs, benefits and consequences of strategy are part of the scheme of successful companies. Thought patterns capture judgment.

BUSINESS ADAPTATION

Better choices and chances go to the prepared. Investors, philosophers and coaches have restated that principle many times. Warfighters, teachers, athletes and engineers know this principle very well. The consequences of preparation begin with anticipation. Better choices go with the deployment of capabilities that are matched to the challenges of the business as it evolves. What does that mean? What is encompassed by adaptive capabilities? The answers are listed in Exhibit 03.A below.

Exhibit 03.A

ADAPTIVE CAPABILITIES AND BUSINESS CONSEQUENCES

Capabilities in Preparation	Consequences of Adaptation
Product-Based Capabilities	Product and service positions that are more or less competitive and more or less profitable...
Market-Focused Capabilities	Customer and channel positions that are more or less sustainable and more or less profitable...
Resource-Based Capabilities	Technical and operating resources that are more or less efficient and more or less differentiated...
Capital-Based Capabilities	Financial and human capital that is more or less sufficient and more or less transferable...
Network-Based Capabilities	Technical and partner networks that are more or less proprietary and more or less appropriable...

The business literature is rich with definitions and restatements of strategic capabilities and competencies. Most of these competencies enable the company to compete effectively on tangible and intangible platforms. These capabilities are dynamic assets, and they are not neccessarily owned or housed in a single enterprise, but rather, across networks and collaborative systems including supply chains, tech clusters and trade groups. Business capabilities are dynamic.

Each of these areas will be addressed in more detail in Chapters 04, 05 and 06 as we deal with the dynamics of strategy direction, integration, and execution. Adaptation, or perhaps the risks of adaptation are incumbent in the broader strategy management and leadership process.

HEALTHY DOSES OF CONCERN

The effective management and leadership of strategy require good judgment about choices and risks. It demands good thinking about possibilities as well as challenges. It takes some patience, and it takes some debate. Good judgment is learned through project experience and substantive leadership. Sometimes it comes from consequences themselves. Some healthy paranoia is part of the mix in some companies. Scenario assessment is part of the rigor in some companies. Futures research is part of the process in some companies. These are thought patterns that organizations use to build a clear stage for looking ahead, planning ahead and moving ahead on critical business frontiers. Perspective is valuable, and it takes work and wisdom.

PRACTICE: GETTING READY FOR CHANCES

Practice may not make perfect, but it helps get a company ready for consequences and it helps get organizations focused on results. Let's take a look at three areas in which practice drives strategic value.

> Companies with steady routines of product and service planning realize better break-even times on development and better category management success in general.

> Companies that manage smaller, more integrative M&A activity realize more strategic and economic value from smaller proportionate changes in their business models.

> Companies with learned processes and planning disciplines in their supply and demand chains are more likely to find incremental and disruptive options for business growth.

Better choices and chances go to the prepared. Better results accrue to those organizations that practice with the disciplines and craft, which anticipate, adapt and respond to the conditions of the business. We develop strategy management and leadership thought in practice. Practice yields new learning. Practice accrues through experience in creating, driving, framing and dealing with consequences – predicted, emergent and unintended consequences that exist in every company. Practice yields strategic experience, knowledge and judgment that can make a huge difference at crunch time.

DYNAMIC RESOLVE

When an organization is resolved to succeed, the people in that organization share a sense of destiny and commitment. They draw strength from the meaning of the strategy and they get energy from the process and the results. Dynamic resolve is a term that reflects how people adapt their efforts to succeed, even when things change. Dynamic resolve is based in strategic principles and in the culture of the organization. When teams of people are resolved to adapt and respond in ways that take them out of their comfort zones, they have dynamic resolve. When they're asked to sacrifice, they're asked to engage in hearty commitments for a cause. That is dynamic resolve. It sustains the heart of the organization, and it feeds ambition.

The consequences of a company's strategic journey are shaped in many ways by this notion of dynamic resolve. When things get tough, can people respond with their best efforts? When conditions are such that we need leaps of faith, can people cross the borders of risk and change? Can we depend on the dynamic resolve of people in every corner of the organization to provide their best thought, behavior, action and impact to the cause? The issues encompass risk factors, focusing on results, and consequences. How do people rise to the occasion?

Neurobiologists suggest that our sense of consequences is a brain function that we learn over time, and through experience. Parents know this story pattern very well. Teachers live with this promise, and philosophers ponder the prospects for thinking about, living with and acting around consequences. Scientists develop experiments to know more about consequences. Improv actors, musicians and comics thrive on consequences, and Pavlov's dogs are conditioned by them. Dynamic resolve is a way of thinking, and a mindset about consequences. It becomes part of strategic thought and behavior.

In an organization with dynamic resolve and a true sense of business consequences, people will find ways to lead at every level, from every corner. They will anticipate and they will adapt, and they will contribute to a cultural base from which decisions and action plans have *consequence checks.* Strategic and economic value is created in the wake of this ever-present sense of consequences, especially when everyone is engaged in the strategic journey of the company. Dynamic resolve is in the soul of companies that are truly ready, fully engaged. They expect to be challenged, and they spawn efforts that get things done in the face of adversity.

ESSENTIAL QUESTIONS THAT FRAME STRATEGY

Getting prepared and resolved for business success requires the posting of several questions. These are questions about intent, focus, purpose, process, people, action, control, order and risk. Moreover, they are questions about the consequences of plans to be framed and decisions to be made. They are questions about the consequences of policies, ideology, beliefs and systems. They are questions about the consequences of structure, leadership and management discipline. Essential questions such as these help frame the experience and the prospects of a company. They are reflective as well as prospective. They help capture the empirical bent of our corporate Aristotle and the pragmatic quest of our more contemporary partner, Wilbur Beall. Here are five queries that we believe should be part of the agenda at the management and governance level, for every company. They are questions that deserve the weight and energy of conversations that get to the very core of the company's strategic agenda.

01. What is your business definition or model, and how is it adapting to the environment in which you operate, or intend to operate? What are your core concerns and challenges?

…the evolution of your products and services?

…the evolution of your markets and customers?

…the evolution of your systems and resources?

02. What is your organization's level of awareness, understanding and engagement in your strategy? What does your stated strategy really mean to your people, across the organization?

…do your people appreciate the intentions?

…do they understand their roles and tasks?

…do they embrace and engage in the plan?

03. What is your agenda for dealing with the three greatest issues that stand before the company, and what do your company's stakeholders think of this agenda? What is the level of commitment?

…the three greatest issues; what are they?

…the meaning and impact of these concerns?

…the plans and priorities to address them?

04. What are your prospects for success, for attaining results against your business agenda, if you adhere to and realize the agenda as it has been framed? What if the conditions change?

...the likely impact on financial performance

...the likely impact on competitive advantage

...the likely impact on customer connections

...the likely impact on corporate stewardship

05. What is your assessment of how well the broader organization is prepared and resolved to deliver business results? How do your people relate to the strategic agenda as an unfolding journey?

...in terms of profitable business growth

...in terms of performance improvement

...in terms of meaningful business change

When we ask these questions of senior managers, we provoke a lot of discussion on plans and intentions, risks and choices. We also stimulate a level of thinking about the perspectives that circulate within organizations, and around the markets they serve. The most important issue here is consequences. Each of these questions raises the specter of consequences to be considered. What about the consequences of the strategy?

Exhibit 03.B suggests that leaders and managers take a hard look at the positive and negative consequences of their work. What shapes the success or degradation of the business model? What counts with regard to internal strategy communication? What about the agenda and focus ideas? What about the specific and natural goals? What about the people? Are we really prepared and resolved to get everyone focused on business results?

The right answers are those which can power the journey, and the creation of strategic and economic value. The wrong answers, or muted answers, or mixed answers, or fuzzy answers can easily drag a company's prospects down, near-term and long-term. Consequences are terminal as well as instrumental. They are part of our focus on results, and they are part of our journey, the process, and the adventure. They reflect cause-and-effect in strategy management and leadership, and they reflect our sense of success, as well as barriers to success. Consequences are the stage gates in business life, and they temper the success of the company as it evolves.

Exhibit 03.B

STRATEGIC QUESTIONS AND CONSEQUENCES

Essential Questions for the Entire Organization	Some Positive Consequences	Some Negative Consequences
Business Definition; Model Evolution	Effective Direction; Thoughtful Evolution	Direction Confusion; Mistaken Evolution
Communication and Engagement of Teams	Full Understanding; Good Engagement	Limited Awareness; Partial Understanding
Focus of the Agenda on Impact Issues	Focused on Results; Targeted Priorities	Undeveloped Focus; Conflicting Priorities
Prospects for Success Against Key Objectives	Clear Natural Goals; Dynamic Resolve	Unclear Intentions; Mixed Commitment
The Preparation and Resolution of People	Fully Prepared Team; Fully Resolved Team	Clearly Unprepared; Clearly Unresolved

Source: Dewar Sloan studies of effective and ineffective strategy in business units and in collaborative ventures, 2001-05.

The difference between espoused strategy and actual business consequences has been addressed in the business literature for many years. One of the most common issues is a declared strategic plan that is poorly connected. Another common issue is the lack of *discerning, focused conversation about the difference between positive and negative consequences.* This is a huge concern, and a great, great need for leaders and managers at every level. Professor Eugene Jennings of Michigan State University framed this as part of *reality sense.* Reality is often a judgment call, and it changes.

Surrounding every choice, decision, plan and policy is a "what if" question. What if we move and we're wrong? What if we don't move and we lose out on the chance for growth and change? These and a hundred other consequence questions are part of the everyday thought and behavior of organizations. This is what individuals, groups, teams and partnerships do on the strategic trek. They manage and lead for consequences. Somehow, in some manner, those consequences add up to the relative success of the business, some measure of impact, some outcome and some business result. We live with these consequences; they are the result of a strategic agenda.

74

STRATEGIC MEASURES AND INDICATORS

Successful companies give a great deal of thought to measuring performance. In fact, the discipline of business measurement has been escalating with the business planning and control sciences that came into vogue more than a century ago with the industrial revolution. Earlier ideas in efficiency have been complemented by advancing ideas about quality, along with some fundamental ideas in microeconomics. These provide companies with a vast business measurement menu. Maybe too vast a menu for some tastes.

We tend to look at business measures as planning and consequence gauges. These gauges help companies lead and manage, but more to the point, they help people define how to think and behave in their roles, and in the tasks they serve. What gets counted gets attended to, or so the logic goes. In more basic terms, measures help us drive activity that, in turn, drives results.

Most organizations can discover and develop a few measures that define most of what really counts in mapping business success. While mountains of indicators may be interesting, a few practical measures are really more relevant and meaningful guides to organizational behavior. We suggest that companies develop practical measures in three areas:

> **Strategic measures** help gauge the tracking and progress the company is making on its growth, performance and change plans. These are critical, higher-order metrics.

> **Operating measures** help define the effectiveness and efficiencies of the company's ongoing business systems, platforms, operations, capital resources and throughput.

> **Process measures** help gauge the methods, disciplines and systems for doing things. These reflect corporate functions and capabilities, pathways and networks.

Practical measures are communication signals and mechanisms for the organization. They help the people of the organization understand and engage in the agenda for growth, performance and change. They provide meaning and the context for people to conduct themselves, at every level, and in every corner of the organization. They help the organization relate its strategic agenda to an ever-changing business environment, and to the people who engage in the everyday work of making things happen.

MANIC MEASUREMENT

Today, we have the capability to measure everything from the quality of materials and the capacity of a machine, to the compliance with processes and the attitudes of employees. We can measure product system contributions, overhead valuations, capital efficiency and resource appropriation. We can measure cycle times, group culture, innovation, constraints, risks and people. We can benchmark almost anything. We can gauge "green" product and process impact. We can track customer trends. We can measure technology patterns and economic growth. From the vast reservoirs of data that companies possess, we can measure sales efficiency and maintenance costs, knowledge assets, supplier value and channel conflict, customer loyalty, demand chain traction and service recovery. We can measure the work of measurement itself, and some companies are doing just that.

At the end of the day, what really counts is what we do with all these measures that helps create strategic and economic value. Are we measuring the right stuff, and how do we know? What is the validity and reliability of these measures for the people who work in the organization? Do we measure things that are not relevant? To what end should we go to capture and convey all these measures? What kind of measurement is enough?

What do these measures mean in the cause-and-effect realm of the company? Do they help us sense consequences? Do they confuse or enhance our strategy, and our structure? Do they help us frame and act upon the agenda for growth, performance and change? Do they keep us focused on results? Do they enable people to manage, collaborate, lead, integrate, serve and perform to the best of their abilities and character? Do they confuse and distract people? Do they engage the best thoughts and actions of people?

Measurement-manic organizations get caught up in the adventures and nuances of measures. Some of these companies get so distracted with the science and analysis of measures that they take away from the cultural and behavioral nuances that made them successful in the first place. This is a serious problem. We need to take measures seriously. But we need to use common sense as well. Measure the stuff that really counts, and get on with managing the business of business. We like measures, but we work the stuff that measures gauge. Perspective is everything, so for the measurement of everything, focus on the systemic cause-and-effect elements.

NEAR-TERM AND LONG-TERM OBJECTIVES

Understanding the relationship between near-term and long-term objectives is part of the discussion on consequences. If we take the work of business evolution seriously, we need to consider the nature of both near-term and long-term business objectives. The strategic agenda must reflect near-term and long-term themes and challenges in the appropriate context.

For most companies, near-term means the horizon out to about three years hence. The near-term horizon is relatively predictable in terms of technical, market and economic forces. Most companies have a good sense of what lies ahead in this near-term frame. In the near-term, the strategic agenda must focus on these main areas of concern:

> Generating strategic and economic value in return for the investments that have been made, and the efforts that are being engaged and expanded in the business agenda.

> Getting the company prepared and resolved for growth, performance and change in the future, as conditions, risks and opportunities emerge in its environment.

Strategy management and leadership are for today and tomorrow, and our near-term strategy agenda should address the realities of today, the realities that lie ahead, and the consequences faced in planning and decision-making. The platform for future business success is based on what a company does in the near-term, to a large extent. Today counts, especially for organizations that are struggling to survive near-term threats.

The long-term frame asks for something in addition to what we think and do in the near-term. The long-term ideas for strategy management and leadership open up bigger questions about the categories of the company, the nature of the enterprise, and the company's evolution as a technical, social and economic entity. We normally press for a ten-year horizon when we look at long-term strategy with a company. Then, we work back to the present, in two- or three-year increments. This forces a sense of sequence, time and resource into long-term thinking. Being prepared and resolved serves both time frames. Both views must come together in practice. Both near-term and long-term perspectives are relevant and meaningful to the stakeholders of the enterprise.

OPEN PERSPECTIVES AND ADAPTIVE MINDSET

When companies approach strategy with open perspectives, they are considerate of ideas and thoughtful about issues that can impact the success of their business. Keeping open perspectives also supports a dynamic and discerning sense of business consequences – the connections between strategic initiatives, ideas, actions, behaviors and business implications that may or may not materialize. Perspectives are learned in practice.

In business, *open minds are very hard to beat.* They are naturally prepared and resolved to succeed. They are valuable assets and they are the vessels of ideas that drive growth, performance and change. Open perspectives are mindful of consequences, and consequences, in the end, reflect why we manage and lead. When a company has the perspective to understand its realities, the organization is simply more able to:

> Contribute to customer and category development with relationship building and innovative products.

> Drive productivity at important impact points, with collaborative efforts and new technology resources.

> Balance resources, capabilities and operational processes with practical innovation and business system leverage.

> Develop the organization and its business ethos with learning pathways, systems thinking and cultural leadership.

> Contribute to the positive evolution of any barriers with ideas that help forge new value and options for change.

Effective stategy management and leadership depends on disciplined, open perspectives. Perspective is a key ingredient in business learning and attitude. It provides filtration for thought and behavior. It helps us keep a sense of awareness, priority, order, risk, creativity, balance and persistence. There can be little in the way of strategic collaboration without wide open and shared perspectives; this all takes a lot of practice. As a consequence of sound strategic management and leadership, the open and dynamic minds of people in a company are the sparks that drive every measure of success. How well do people think in your organization? How well do they think with their peers and leaders? *How is open entreship behavior engaged?*

CREATING NEW VALUE AS A CONSEQUENCE

Most companies would say that among their business goals is the creation of new economic and strategic value. Making a reasonable return on invested capital is a necessary and obvious piece of the puzzle. Some would also say that the creation of new strategic value is important, and perhaps every bit as relevant to the business as economic value. The mix of value themes deserves open dialogue, and open and energetic conversation.

Both economic value and strategic value are created in the stream of consequences that flow from business plans and decisions. In this context, we need to look at strategic value creation as a consequence of effective management and leadership in these areas:

Growth Management Question:
Are we prepared and resolved to drive revenue growth that is profitable, capital efficient, and to some degree, catalytic to business evolution? Is growth management part of the strategic mindset of the company?

Performance Management Question:
Are we prepared and resolved to drive performance efforts that shape efficiency and innovation while sustaining a healthy forward-focused organization? Is performance management part of the strategic mindset of the company?

Change Management Question:
Are we prepared and resolved to drive the learning and behavior of a truly dynamic organization that exploits change as part of its competitive edge? Is change management part of the strategic mindset of the company?

When we assess the strength and value of a company, a lot of what we look at is the economic status of the business. Operating statements and balance sheets express a great deal of information about economic value. But they don't tell us much about growth, performance or change. The elements of strategic value demand a more discerning look at the linkages of strategy, resources, structure and culture. In Chapter 07, we will explore these consequences of sustained value creation in greater depth.

STRATEGIC THREATS AND OPPORTUNITIES

A casual survey of the business literature gives business observers some important lessons on the consequences of failures in strategy. These are not unique patterns, and they are easily recognized by anyone who has been through a major project or two – in any business enterprise. They most often reflect a blend of missed opportunities and transformative threats.

Missed Opportunities

Companies miss opportunities when they fail to recognize them at the right time or in the right form. Entering or exiting a market category, investing in technology, scaling operations, balancing capital, open collaboration and a host of other themes are common in this area. Among the consequences of missed opportunities are investment errors, strategic distraction and disconnect, resource displacement and performance degradation. Missed opportunities occur in every area of business, from product development and customer development to resource management and operations management. Missed opportunities can have huge, lasting consequences.

Transformative Threats

Companies and entire societies have been assaulted by different kinds of transformative threats. These threats can undermine the bases for profitability of a business sector or trade group. They can force the rearrangement of supply and demand chains. They drive obsolescence of product groups and market categories, and they can destroy brands and market equity. Transformative threats change the rules of the game, the standards of business practice, and models of business. They alter the economic and strategic logic of companies and the markets they serve. Transformative threats come in technical forms. They also come in the form of product and service innovation and marketing innovation. They appear as new competition, or new channel structures. They come as evolving market category standards. At this juncture, our intent is to simply define these as consequences. Nobody wants to miss opportunities. Nobody wants to be blind-sided by transformative threats. But these shape the realities of business, and they should temper a company's sense of strategy consequences. Reality sense comes into play, and it forces a dynamic view.

SUMMARY NOTES AND THOUGHTS

This chapter expounds upon the consequences of effective strategy and the effective management and leadership of strategy. When we look at the very nature of consequences, we need to ask questions about a company's sense of itself and its realities. Are people aware of the consequences of their thought on behavior? Are they prepared and resolved to do what needs to be done in order to move forward with the company's agenda? Do they have perspective? Can they adapt? Are they truly discerning? How do they learn about consequences? How does any of this shape their behavior?

We believe that the success of an organization depends a great deal on the sense of consequences people bring to their work. Nowhere is this more important than in strategy. How people think about strategy direction, integration and execution is a significant value factor in business success. Consequences reflect themselves directly in business results, organizational behavior, and in the future success frontiers of the business.

The business environment for most companies today is growing more complex and dynamic. The consequences of missed opportunities and transformative threats are clearly important in every organization. How companies look ahead, plan ahead and move ahead should be conditioned by the *organization's view of consequences*, in the broadest perspective. The energy people invest in managing their world of consequences is part of the basic strategic agenda for business growth, performance and change. Now, let's get focused on business results.

STRATEGY DIRECTION, INTEGRATION AND EXECUTION

Based on the premises of strategy management and leadership we outlined in Part One, there appear to be some missing links in common practice. Throughout Part Two, our task is to define and develop the disciplines of strategy direction, integration and execution as the framework for business growth, performance and change. This is the heart of the agenda.

Throughout Chapters 04, 05 and 06, strategy direction, integration and execution are explored in depth, with references to the kind of thought and behavior that must be engaged in successful companies. This is our general framework for dealing with the purpose and challenges of strategy, and it serves large companies as well as small companies and new business ventures. The same framework serves the public sector.

04

ISSUES IN STRATEGY DIRECTION

Direction...guidance of intent and endeavors,
based on the realities and conditions of
the business and the company over time.

The paths a company travels and the choices it makes say a great deal. These paths and choices define what a company stands for and where it's headed. In the most basic terms, this is what strategy direction is all about. Business principles, intentions, definition and evolution are essential parts of strategy direction. They are the building blocks that shape our corporate paths and choices. Strategy direction frames a company's possibilities.

Earlier, in Chapter 02, we suggested that as many as 30% to 40% of operating companies were moving forward with plans based on strategy directions that were flawed or wrong. One could ask, how can that be? Are half the companies charging down the wrong path? Are they making erroneous strategic choices and taking bad risks? Are they aiming at the wrong target, with the wrong agenda? To a large degree, our answer would be yes, that is, if their ultimate objective is to create new strategic and economic value.

This chapter opens the discussion on the management and leadership of strategy direction, its meaning and its relevance. Our approach to strategy is powered by the common sense development of strategic thought and behavior which links the work of strategy direction, integration and execution. Depth in these areas drives better company results. The bonds between these areas are the cement that keeps us focused on business results.

CONVENTIONAL WISDOM

The most common approach in strategy practice today commences with exercises that deal with assessments of business conditions. These exercises migrate to thoughts about what the company could or should do to advance growth, performance and change. Then, most companies cast forth a program of themes, goals and ideas that frame its agenda for the so-called planning horizon. Much of this happens in a formal strategic planning cycle, during which people scurry through data and presentations to discover and rationalize how to plot the forward plan. Meetings are held and declarations are made. Research data is shared and conclusions are drawn. Occasional debates are encouraged. Visionary ideas are floated and courted. Operational issues and glitches are presented. Creative and analytic energy is dispersed, and people are brought into the discussion to exchange perspectives, experiences, biases and personal and professional concerns.

Most of this happens with senior managers, staff analysts, business advisors, planners, function leaders, project people, and others who are in the know. Sprinkled with some politics and seasoned with dramatic words and images, the conventional approach to strategic planning moves from a seemingly exhaustive review of the organization's situation to a more forceful sense of direction and a better sense of priorities. Often, it sounds something like this, "*we're getting a strategy on the table that has substance, a meaningful plan and agenda.*" To this agenda, companies attach some measurable, actionable goals, some relevant targets that seem like they go with the plan. "*Ready, set and back to the work of running the company. Hopefully, the strategy makes sense. Hopefully, we can keep the business on track as things unfold, and as business conditions evolve.*" This is very common, and it reflects the rhythm of orthodox planning and control methods that most companies use.

This is roughly the pattern of strategic planning in most companies today. With the best intentions, we gather to set and clarify direction based on analytics and planning. We work through the issues, toward some kind of consensus on challenges and priorities, and then we nail a few key goals on the wall. Next, we agree to work hard on those goals. And, then we go to work. And, then we wait for results. There are serious disconnects in this conventional linear approach, however, and these disconnects are both pervasive and costly. They undermine a company's prospects in many way.

THERE MUST BE MORE

In an age where it's clear that more and more companies struggle with strategy and performance, something must be askew. Intentions and results are disconnected. Our research and a growing body of knowledge in strategy theory and practice suggest a number of problems in the conventional approach to strategic planning. Following are some of those problems, and the implications they impose throughout the organization. We define these under the terms: *reality sense, impact sense and factor sense*.

Reality Sense

In practice, it can be very difficult to capture, understand and address the changing business conditions that shape a company's potential for success. The assumptions we make about the most fundamental issues in our business environment are critical to the strategic paths and choices we select and manage. These assumptions reflect background and experience, and the knowledge base of the entire organization, from basement to boardroom.

As a matter of course, we attempt to evaluate the nature of technical, market, social and economic trends that impact the business. We seek to comprehend the current and emergent issues that shape our fortunes. However, there is plenty of evidence that we are slow to deal with these realities. Sometimes we fail in foresight, but more often we fail in reality sense.

Also, as a matter of course, companies go through the exercise of stating their so-called core capabilities and strategic edge resources. This takes some introspection and integrity, and it's often hard to be properly critical when programs, personal concerns and processes are on the table for debate. Reality sense often takes a blow in these areas. There isn't enough thoughtful reflection here. Companies make assumptions that don't make sense. Discernment and perspective are casualties along the way.

When business models and plans are built on shaky ground, there will be problems in strategy. Reality sense is what managers and leaders have to build into the process of strategy, particularly in the work on strategy direction. Emergent realities in the marketplace and the everyday realities of the organization surely deserve better consideration, discernment and contemplation. There is not enough thought or discussion in practice.

Impact Sense

In practice, it can be very difficult to envision the direct and indirect impact of a company's plans, forged in the work of strategy direction. We can look at impact in the context of natural goals. Are we really creating new strategic and economic value for the company in the context of the four natural goals of business? How do we expect business impact to unfold? How does business impact evolve? How will business results emerge in the cause-and-effect streams of the business plan? Consider the relevance of the company's natural goals as impact is gauged.

Financial Performance
Competitive Advantage
Customer Connection
Corporate Stewardship

Natural Goals of Business

In our earlier discussion on consequences, we also asked about the mix of intended and unintended outcomes of strategy. As a matter of course, do we really think about the full consequences of our strategic direction? Do we understand the best case and worst case outcomes? Are we prepared to manage these issues? Are we equipped to lead the organization around obstacles and constraints? Does the culture of this company sense impact and the implications of strategy impact in a manner that is truly prepared and resolved for success? Or, do we simply hope for the best?

Impact sense, in our view, is a significant piece of the puzzle for strategy direction, and a thought mode that is often missing in action during the conventional strategic planning process. This is more than connecting the dots of cause-and-effect; it involves more than alignment of strategy and resources. Impact sense is part of how we engage true strategic thought and behavior in the entire organization. Impact work goes all the way down to the implications of strategy direction for each stakeholder – the customers, employees, investors, suppliers, partners, etc. What is the full impact of the company's strategy direction on these stakeholders, and their perspectives? And how is impact secured and understood? Who needs to be engaged in order for strategy direction to have meaning and results? To whom is this relevant? What matters and who cares? Impact is a big idea here, and in most companies, business impact gets short-changed in the discussion.

Factor Sense

Another consideration in strategy direction is the definition of key factors that influence or drive growth, performance and change. These are usually defined in terms of corporate capabilities and resources, or some advantage in the marketplace. There are a few factors that our economist friends would suggest are key elements that need consideration. These include capital factors, margin capture and market factors. Maybe those economists have something useful and relevant to say about strategy after all.

Capital factors can be defined in terms of hard assets like plants, technology, systems and cash. They can also be defined as less tangible asset forms like the operating processes or brand positions enjoyed by the business. Understanding the capital factors of a company gets surprisingly thin attention by the conventional strategic planning exercises of most companies today. We will address the broader portfolio of capital and resources in more detail in Chapter 05, Strategy Integration.

When we turn to **margin capture,** there is growing attention to value streams, and the distribution of margin creation activity and traction in businesses. For some companies, the toughest margin capture issues lie in market structure and channel systems. For others, the issues rest in problems with excess capacity or radical shifts in production resources and networks. When companies join together in collaborative ventures and value streams, margin capture schemes change. In any case, the true nature and dynamics of margin capture is one of those issues that needs more rigorous assessment in the work on strategy direction. How does the company make its money? And, what are the levers to pull for value creation? What are the trends that shape margin capture, near-term and long-term?

Finally, we have a group of **market factors**. These include everything from market demand and customer action to competitive edge and differentiation. New technology, distribution transitions, category competition, customer segmentation, market sector fragmentation, product and service category blurring…these all contribute to the challenge of understanding the market factors which are germane to strategy direction. Even the accountants get these factors, and they are increasingly important subjects in governance oversight. Markets change, and that reshapes much of what we deal with in the formation of strategic choices and direction.

COMMON SENSE AND STRATEGY DIRECTION

If business success goes to the prepared and resolved, how can we build more common sense into the strategy direction work of organizations? How can we engage better reality sense, impact sense and factor sense into the strategy management and leadership process? How do these get infused into the strategic thought and behavior of the organization, at every level, and in every corner? When does this become part of corporate culture? Where does it take shape in organizational structure? Who takes this on as a mission-critical theme? Where is the common sense meter on strategy?

Those are questions that belong in the dialogue and language of companies as they approach strategy direction. The realities, impact points and factors discussed in the last few pages are dynamic. They are part of the dynamic formula of strategy, and they temper and influence options and risks in strategy direction. These realities, impact points and factors shape what a company could do, as well as what it should do. They set the boundaries of business opportunity. They frame the conditions for creating new strategic and economic value. They embody the challenges that test the resolve of organizations. They set the table for strategy direction.

We believe these issues belong in the collective responsibility and mindset of groups and individuals throughout the organization. Discerning service technicians and sales operatives know about customers. Production people and distribution teams know about quality in context. Cost accountants and design engineers know a lot about issues that belong in development capital discussions. People who study the origins and flow of knowledge in companies suggest that the way we acquire, manage and apply the know-how and issue sense in most companies is a great resource, and a potential base for building competitive edge. This is a kind of knowledge and idea management that lies at the heart of successful business development.

Building the knowledge to master all of this is part of the agenda for strategy management and leadership. How does a company get smart? We believe there is a basic discipline for driving knowledge up and down the organization, a *practice of common sense and conversation* that serves analytic and creative exchange at the most basic collaborative levels. The engines of common sense are learning and intuition and practice.

In her 1998 book, *The Wellsprings of Knowledge,* Dorothy Leonard suggested that knowledge management, or KM, is underutilized in the analysis of strategy and strategy direction. In our view, that is a reality for human kind. In a July 2004 *Special Report* in *The Economist,* commenting on the intelligence used to plan and prosecute the Iraq War, the authors outlined the difficulties with managing strategic data and planning. They defined intelligence data as often "fragmentary, accretive and inconclusive" in nature. The same is true for a lot of the business information used in strategy direction. *Deeper Smarts,* [2005] by Leonard and Swap, takes these ideas about knowledge management and discernment to yet another level. Our sense of strategy direction practice derives from conversations between and among thoughtful people at every level of the organization.

There are two very important insights here. First, the common sense and knowledge that is available for use in strategy direction may be dispersed in the minds of people across the organization. That is true in larger and smaller organizations alike. Second, putting the know-how and smartsets we have to better use in strategy direction is often harder than it looks. Good companies often make bad decisions because they misfire with inadequate information and knowledge. They don't use what they actually know.

In the formation of strategy direction, we need to encourage a more inclusive process of assessment and issue management. This means accessing the radar and knack of people across the organization and people who have relationships with the company. This is a continuous process, not some annual ritual with trappings of official foresight and wisdom. Smart organizations get that way by tapping into their senses and knowledge bases. They understand and engage in these issues as part of their everyday discourse. Teams act as subcultural nodes of the organization, sensing the realities, impact points and factors that will drive business success at the front lines and rear deck.

From GE to the smallest private company, executives say they want their people to think and act more strategically. This means different things in different companies. But the common ground is this: we must capture the combined knowledge and insights of our people as they engage in strategy direction, and the paths and choices shaped for our companies. We seek to develop this in the ***everyday strategic thought and behavior*** of organizations. Asking the tough questions. Holding fierce conversations.

ALWAYS BEGIN WITH THE END IN MIND

Strategy direction is important in many ways. The direction of the company gives us a working view of principles, intentions, definitions and evolution. It provides a certain relevance and meaning to the business, and it frames our strategic paths and choices. It sets a reasonable course, and it provides some room to maneuver as business conditions evolve.

The starting point for every company must revolve around the end results, the end game and goals of the business. Surely, it's important to look at strategic direction in terms of competitive stance and operating excellence. However, those are means, not end results. The creation of new strategic and economic value is what we need to recognize as the essential, ultimate goal, the end result that counts in every company. In our earlier discussion on strategic cause-and-effect, we examined the measures of effect as the relevant indictors of value creation. These themes are usually expressed in financial, operational, strategic and process metrics, as one kind of detail or another. Those functional metrics may or may not be well-settled.

The key end in mind is value creation. For some companies, this will be interpreted as a matter of **business growth.** In other companies, the key issues will evolve around **performance enhancement.** In other companies, new value will hinge on **business change.** Creating new strategic and economic value in a company may require substantial re-engineering, market development, or some other fairly radical step in business focus and definition. No company gets an easy ticket. The paths and choices cast in the name of strategy direction have short lives with respect to value creation; even shorter half-lives for plan relevance. The formula for value creation is always evolving because business conditions evolve.

SPECIAL CONSIDERATIONS

An organization might suggest that its roles and responsibilities in corporate stewardship should over-arch its value creation goals. As admirable as that sounds, business owners need to take a look at their natural goals in balance. Over the long-term, it would be tough to be a great corporate steward unless your company creates real strategic and economic value. In fact, capitalism serves human society through its capacity to create new strategic and economic value. Value must be created before it's shared.

ELEMENTS OF STRATEGY DIRECTION

There are four prime elements of strategy direction. These elements deal with business ***principles, intentions, definition and evolution.*** Each of these reflects what the company stands for, and where it's headed.

Strategy and Principles

Business principles include certain disciplines, values and standards that guide the company. Principles give the organization its rules and boundaries, its ideology and its purpose. In a business world rich with complexity and ambiguity, we need people in our companies with a clear sense of business principles in order to succeed in the journey. Principles frame what counts. They provide background and rationale for plans and actions. They define right and wrong. They give clear meaning to the direction of the business, and they define a company's commitments in several areas:

Product and service quality
Technical product innovation
Customer and channel equity
Operational and systems edge
Process and resource leverage
Category dominance or edge
Business network positions
Specific growth alternatives
Specific economic patterns
Benchstrength management

Commitments are made in the strategies and cultures of companies. In his 2003 book, *Survival of the Fittest*, Donald Sull defines several different types of strategic commitment, including those which are transformative in nature. Other business leaders emphasize commitment, but the heart of commitment is manifested in behavior, not visions and platitudes.

When these principles are manifested in company culture, people have clear guidelines for thought and behavior. In fact, their thought and behavior becomes infused with ideas and precepts that reinforce company principles in a cultural and technical sense. These principles provide a source of energy and an inventory of valuable ideas for the formation of strategy direction.

Putting Principles In Perspective

What are the business principles that give meaning and purpose to your organization? How are these relevant to the stakeholders of the business? Would your employees, customers, investors and suppliers agree that these are reflected in the culture of your company? What meaning do they provide, and what purpose do they serve? Are these principles well-engaged by the organization, or do people miss the mark and get confused about purpose, standards and principles? Here are a couple of test statements that help gauge the depth and relevance of business principles in the organization.

> There are active, ongoing conversations about the direction, challenges and purposes of the company at every level of the organization. People have a clear sense of what the business really stands for and where it's headed. They collaborate to adapt and guide decisions, and to evolve. A sense of principles bonds people together in the agenda for business success. Everyone has a chance to speak up. Mostly true or not?

> There are people at every level of the organziation who are actively seeking the ways and means to drive growth, performance and change. This entreship and foresight serves to channel energy to opportunities and problems that must be solved in order to drive value creation. This energy is continuous, and it draws other people into the discussion on strategy management and leadership. Mostly true or not?

In business, we have evolutionary conditions that require people to think and act more independently in the organization. Part of what enables them under these conditions is their sense of business principles. This is more than organizational culture, and more than casual belief systems. Business principles are an essential element in the prepared and resolved company. They frame expectations, and to a greater degree, they convey to the organization how things are done, and how responsibility is dispersed to people. These are anchor points, guideposts and moral codes. They are value system ideas that guide thought, behavior, action and results. Unless these are welded onto the strategy direction, that direction can get seriously out of sync. People need to connect with these principles, or they are not likely to engage in the company's strategy at a personal level.

Business Intentions

Another element of strategy direction is often referred to as the company's business intentions. These address the course heading of the company, or perhaps where it would like to be headed. They also address the company's expectations of what it would like to become as it crosses over the frontiers of its strategic journey. Intentions provide greater meaning and purpose to the standard strategy direction statement, and they contribute some sense of adventure to the strategic agenda discussion.

Business intentions often relate to the plans a company espouses in terms of its broader strategic management and leadership agenda. These reflect upon the organization's agenda for business growth, performance and change. They can also reflect upon its agenda for resource leverage or investment in new areas. Business intentions are important as a kind of course heading. They say something about the who-what-how-when of strategy. They give the organization a sense of its frontiers along with the strategic journey that has been plotted or assumed for the business. Lewis and Clark had serious intentions, even though their early maps may have been imprecise.

Business intentions say something about the unique personality of a company, how it presents itself and how it approaches issues. Some companies have business intentions that are modest, well-crafted and focused. Others have business intentions that are hugely visionary and optimistic about everything on the agenda. We know companies whose business intentions reflect their faith in spiritual as well as secular grounding that guides their strategic paths and business choices. Companies including S2Yachts, J&J, Melroe and Sauder have serious deep-seated, creed-based business intentions. These intentions give meaning to the stakeholders of the company.

In their 1996 book, *Competing for the Future,* Professors Hamel and Prahalad suggested that strategic intent was cast in the form of business direction, discovery and destiny. We believe that business intentions have a certain level of anticipation built into the mix. Business intentions are, by their fundamental nature, future-oriented. Organizations need a sense of where they're headed and for what purpose. Thoughtful discussion about business intention is thus an important element of strategy direction. A key question is that which forces everyone to reflect more; what do we intend to become? And further, how will our strategic intent evolve over time?

Business Definition

Business definition is another critical element of strategy direction. It frames the company's model for creating strategic and economic value. It defines the boundaries for growth, performance and change. It sets the structural agenda for operating the company. Business definition provides a way of approaching near-term and long-term strategy direction in a manner that ensures focus and exploration. Exhibit 04.A below is a summary framework for business definition. This reflects upon ideas from thirty-plus years of professional dialogue on competitive advantage and business model analysis. Every company and business unit can be assessed in this manner.

Exhibit 04.A

BUSINESS DEFINITION AND MODEL CONSTRUCTS

Business Constructs	Scope and Focus	Competitive Edge
Products and Services		
Markets and Customers		
Systems and Resources		

Inspired by Abell's 1980 book, *Defining the Business,* and contemporary work on business models expressed by several observers in the e-business arena including Amazon and eBay, etc. Current research in value propositions also drives the analytics of business definition. Current research on category development strategy is also part of the creative puzzle.

Companies need to address several key issues and questions in this framework. Which products and services could we or should we provide? Serving which markets and customers? With what systems and resources? How do these scope and focus parameters shape the competitive advantage of the business model as defined? How is that likely to be tested as business conditions change? How do these elements and constructs blend?

For each of these business constructs, what should be our scope and focus? And, what could be or should be our basis for constructing competitive advantage? These are simple and critical questions. They are questions that often get side-tracked by strategic fantasy and hype, along with miscues in business premises. Business definition deserves serious and rigorous debate, with an eye on consequences and a sense of business dynamics. Business conditions evolve. What are the implications for your business definition?

Product and Service Themes

Product and service considerations define the scope and focus of most companies. These considerations help frame the answer that responds to the simple and fundamental question, *what business are you in?* Even those so-called "solution companies" whose products and services are formulated to meet very specific customer requirements face this powerful question. Business definition depends very heavily on the product and service themes baked into the company's scope and focus.

The company could answer that *business definition question* in a number of ways. Here are some common responses we hear in reviews:

> We're in the business of providing unique solutions to customers…very specific to customer requirements.

> We provide complete experiences for the customer, and that means we shape the overall customer experience process.

> We're in the business of creating value for our customers, and their customers…in sequence and with partnership.

> We match product and service options to customer requirements, on a systematic and integrated basis.

> We're partners in business with our customer segments; we're dedicated to addressing their natural goals of business.

Beneath all this customer-centric language is the reality that those customers want something in the form of products and services. And, to be considered a relevant source of supply, a company must have products and services that are competent and credible. While there is a lot of discussion about how companies compete in a market category, the product and service base, its quality and its relative cost, value and risk positions are more important. Without some kind of edge in products and services, it's tough to stake-out relevant and profitable ground in a market category. These are fundamental issues in competitive advantage. Customers engage products, data and services to address a variety of needs and conditions. Technical, social and economic criteria are framed and served in the ongoing exchange between suppliers and customers. These elements evolve naturally over time. The solutions and experiences that are framed and delivered in a company's value proposition cement these ideas in the strategic agenda.

Product and service themes are essential and defining constructs in the formation of business strategy direction. They help frame the scope and focus of a company. And they help set the foundations for competitive advantage. From commodity goods in agribusiness to proprietary tech components, the product and service elements of a company define the business and set its course for competing in the marketplace. Product and service elements are the essential building blocks for business growth, performance and change.

Market And Customer Themes

Market and customer considerations are clearly part of the framework for defining a business. The fundamental question in this area is often posed as, what or who are your target markets? And do the customers know this? How do those customers define their attachment to their sources and suppliers? Are they engaged? Are they connected in a valuable relationship? Do they care? Are they conflicted or are they advocates?

There are different answers to the basic questions, of course, and they depend on the company's points of view on what constitutes a customer, and what is meant by a market. Stated differently, good companies can debate market and customer definitions and relevance. Here are a few elements that are necessary parts of that discussion:

> The characteristics of markets, market categories, market segments, market channels and market niches. Market spaces, viewed in different ways. Core and collateral markets.

> The characteristics of vertical market structure and the stakeholders that populate the marketplace. Networks of suppliers and customers are emerging and evolving over one another. Value streams and intermediaries.

> The characteristics of customers themselves and the different types of customers served in the category. Segments and dynamic sub-segments of the market. Situational customers.

Most companies are sorely tested by their knowledge of and connection with market sectors and customers. Yet it is a fundamental piece of the business definition equation, and the equation is always evolving.

With all of this, a company might assume that their customer is the ultimate user of the product or service provided to the market. They might view their customer base as a collection of technical, operating and economic stakeholders whose disparate needs and concerns must be addressed. They might recognize their customer as a collaborative group.

Perhaps their customer is a value-added intermediary whose functions are to arrange and disperse product supply. These and other perspectives are key themes for the formation of strategic direction. They focus on results through the creation of strategic and economic value at all junctures.

Market and customer themes define a company's focus within the context of market categories and segments. These are dynamic considerations. Market categories migrate in response to technical, customer and economic focus. Customer segments change in response to everything from geopolitics to fashion, and technology to retail structure. Markets have their own natural cycles of transformation, and these are matched by cycles of technical and economic change. Think about personal computing since 1980. Think about retail market and brand structure in the home improvement trade. Think about the auto business, or the health sector, or department stores.

Customer-Centric Strategy is a general concept that is tossed around without a lot of discipline. Getting close to customers, hearing their voices, seeking to know their needs, gauging their desires, scoping options for their experiences, scoping new and better solutions, and getting beyond the experience context…these are all expressions of customer-centric strategy and the market-wise focus of organizations. The bottom line is a special blend of respectful attention, disciplined knowledge of customer experiences, and a purposeful, sound framework for attracting, managing and sustaining profitable customer relationships. This can be a complex frontier, and it's a big frontier with regard to strategy direction.

For nearly a century, business researchers have argued what it means to be customer- and market-oriented. The early tenets of marketing held that companies needed to get closer to real customer interests and requirements. Today, it's popular to get into the needs and behaviors of customers to understand how to address them better, smarter, cheaper, faster, etc. All of this is good, provided the agenda is legitimate, disciplined and applicable.

Systems and Resource Themes

Systems and business resources often define what a business can do and how it does what it does. The key questions in this area are, *what competencies really drive your business results? How do these really work?* Systems and resource themes are the third ingredient in business definition.

There are many ways to approach the systems and resource elements of an organization. While one would naturally expect that strong competitors have unique systems and resource competencies, there is typically more to the question. Consider these issues:

> Capital systems and resources may represent the structural elements that provide a company its bases for sustainable competitive advantage, and its evolution.

> Capital systems and resources may represent the structural elements that enable a company to move its business model forward in the market, across development frontiers.

> Capital systems and resources may represent critical boundaries for the ways people in the company think and take responsibility for results, how they work in collaboration.

We define capital systems and resources as the collection of tangible and intangible assets. These can include production assets, infotech systems, processes, technology bases, network relationships, operating assets, human capital, brand and channel assets, etc. For some companies, organization culture is a valuable resource. Supply chain and demand chain systems are valuable resources or critical barriers to growth, performance and change. The collaborative value edge built in chains can be powerful.

These scope and focus elements set the ground for what a business does, and how it does its thing. Systems and resources distinguish competing companies as they joust for customer favor and market advantage. They also explain why companies fail, strategically and operationally. Companies with great products and weak channels are destined to struggle. Companies with weak quality systems and coarse information systems are destined to struggle. And so it goes with these assets. Much of the discussions we hear on core competencies are suspect and shaky, as competencies are unclear.

Business Evolution

World economic history is rich with examples of business evolution. Commerce itself has evolved with shifts in technology, global trade, societal development, culture and human relationships. In the process of business evolution, suppliers, intermediaries, employers and customers are impacted. These evolutionary forces in the business environment reshape the processes of value creation. And that, in a nutshell, is the relevance of business evolution to strategy direction.

Let's examine business evolution in more detail. What are the structural factors in business evolution, and how do they impact strategy? Further, how can we infuse the ideas of business evolution into our strategic thought and behavior, particularly as we examine the formation of strategy direction for the company? Here are some ideas that should stimulate some interesting discussion. These should pose debate points, not empty chatter.

> In general, the attractiveness of a market category tends to evolve with known technical, social and economic forces in the commercial environment. Those forces are readily trackable. What forces are reshaping the category and how?

> When a market category is examined as a commercial system or network, the relationships among and between technical, social and economic forces will become more clear. Who are the principals in that system or network? What is their agenda?

> The participants in a market category exist collectively in a manner that creates, arranges and deploys value; this value collaboration model is inherently dynamic in nature. If there is value in network collaboration, what is it? Who has power?

These ideas have percolated for centuries. Business evolution is shaped by macro forces like technological changes, renaissance movements, economic transformations, geopolitical confrontations and a host of other important issues. Business evolution is also powered by the more specific nuances of a singular market category. One competitor, with a shift in a business model can alter the evolutionary course of an industry. Think FedEx, Microsoft, big steel, Toyota, Dell, big media, Wal-Mart, Enron, big pharma, etc. These and other examples reflect the evolutionary nature of business.

EVOLUTIONARY MINDSET

The prepared and resolved company looks at business evolution in pragmatic and disciplined ways. One aspect of evolutionary planning is the knowledge management and experience base of the business…

> How does the organization view its own evolution in the context of the evolution of its business categories?
>
> How does the organization view its own evolution as a commercial entity? Is the company destined to:
> - Perish from evolution?
> - Cope with evolutionary forces?
> - Adapt with the evolutionary pattern?
> - Force the evolutionary pattern for advantage?
> - Make category evolution its imperative?
> - Manage its own perpetuation?
>
> How does the organization view its own evolution in the context of everyday thought and behavior?

The evolutionary mindset is part of a company's anthropology and its capability. Very few organizations are revolutionary. Most companies are evolutionary. Their approach to business evolution depends on leadership and management discipline, and it all starts with *getting prepared.* It sustains itself by *staying resolved* in the sometimes uncertain and ambiguous trek of business evolution. Evolution is an unsure adventure, and strategy direction is a dynamic thought and behavior practice for guiding the adventure.

ENTRESHIP REDEFINED FOR BUSINESS EVOLUTION

Our Danish friends at KaosPilots *[www.kaospilots.dk]* have advanced the definition of entreship as a pattern of business thought and behavior that responds to evolution. These precepts are relatively simple and broadly applicable. The KaosPilots educational program in Denmark blends project design, business design and process design into the behavioral practices and disciplines of individuals and groups. Collaboration, personal responsibility, communication, integration, knowledge management and leadership are infused at every level of this program. This works for strategy direction.

EVOLUTIONARY AGENDA

The prepared and resolved company looks at an evolutionary agenda as part of its strategy leadership and management routine. This agenda has several analytic themes, reflecting internal and external conditions. Exhibit 04.B presents some of the analytic elements that should be part of the process for discerning, pioneering, scoping, debating and considering the company's evolutionary agenda. This is part of strategy analytics.

Exhibit 04.B

ANALYTIC GUIDE FOR THE EVOLUTIONARY AGENDA

Evolution of External Business Conditions and Dynamics

Market Demand
Customer Groups
Market Systems
Industry Structure
Technical Factors
Supply Factors

How are these external forces and facets of the business evolving, and what are the implications for company growth, performance and change? Near- and long-term?

Evolution of Internal Business Conditions and Dynamics

Business Model
Business Dynamics
Business Processes
Cultural Factors
Business Constructs
Business Networks

How are these interal forces and facets of the business evolving, and what are the implications for company growth, performance and change? Near- and long-term?

Notes: Gauging external and internal business environments is a basic piece of the foundation for strategy management and leadership. The expanded constructs for this framework are company- and industry-specific. Strategy audits must address these factors, and the practice should be continuous, ongoing, robust and well-dispersed throughout the company.

Think about these questions and ask your team about them on a regular basis. Get beyond the basic questions and answers. Search for risk and opportunity. Search for the emergent and the discontinuous. Provide the setting and the context for constructive conflict and open, fierce, robust conversations on topics that need to be reviewed and debated. Enable the arguments that challenge every aspect of the business model.

EVOLUTION AND BOUNDARY SENSE

Our research on *category boundary strategy* provides an interesting look into the impact of business evolution position and profitability. Companies with category-changing strategies tend to actively nudge the boundaries or edges of their market spaces in ways that:

Capture new customers with new solutions.

Upset the order of competition in the base category.

Alter the creation, arrangement and capture of value.

Reframe the power and orientation of the base category.

Shape the demand curve in adjacent market spaces.

Capture margins from differentiated offerings.

Revalue the economic base of the category.

CATEGORY BOUNDARY STRATEGY

From more than 20 years of study, our research and planning team has developed a framework for *category development and management.* This reflects upon the everyday challenges of marketing, product and service planning, brand, channel system and operations management for consumers, industrial and technical solutions. Categories change at the boundaries.

Examples abound, and very few market categories are lacking in boundary strategy evolution. Think about the acquisition of recorded music circa 1960 versus today. Think about home improvement products and services, and the evolution of Home Depot, lumberyards, Sears and trade contractors. Think about the 50-year evolution path of Toyota. Think about the current transformation of the global steel business, or the transformation of the infotech megatrade. Or the grocery trade, or health diagnostics.

From agribusiness to healthcare, and aerospace to entertainment, companies have engaged in category boundary strategy as a means to their competitive ends. This is about business evolution. And as the old adage goes…there will be companies that *make things happen,* and companies that *watch things happen,* and sadly, a great number of companies that *wonder what happened* as their business evolved. Focus on those boundaries where new gates open and competing business models often emerge.

THERE IS MORE TO STRATEGY DIRECTION

There is more to strategy direction than first meets the eye. We've examined four important aspects of strategy direction in the last few pages. These considerations include:

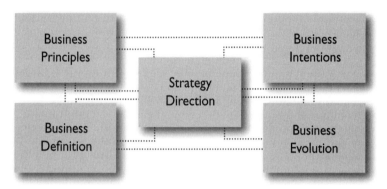

Strategy direction entails the essential choices a company makes relative to *growth, performance and change.* The assumptions used and the perspectives shared are influences that shape these choices. Therefore, an organization must ask itself the following questions:

> Given our **business principles** and the realities of the business environment, **what choices can we consider?**
>
> Given our **business definition** and the realities of the business environment, **what choices can we consider?**
>
> Given our **business intentions** and the realities of the business environment, **what choices can we consider?**
>
> Given our **business evolution** and the realities of the business environment, **what choices can we consider?**

In too many companies, these questions do not get the depth and range of debate they deserve. Strategy is difficult work. It requires discernment and analytic deliberation. It requires perspective and evaluative integrity. We see the formation of strategy direction as an ongoing task, a process that flows like a river, a story that changes in process. Strategy direction is a dynamic argument, a conversation in time. It takes some contemplation, some patience and some judgment. Put energy and intelligence into those conversations and the benefits will be transformative and powerful.

COMPETITIVE ADVANTAGE AND CONFUSION

Strategy direction always takes place in the context of competition. Since the dawn of commerce, companies have played off each other's positions in the battle for market favor, power, edge and value. Economists and business owners might argue over language, but at the end of the day, most would agree that competitive edge is gained with advantages in:

Products and Services

Markets and Customers

Systems and Resources

Edge and advantage may derive from industry structure or specific position, or some combination of operational assets as suggested by Kahn and Greenwald in *Competition Demystified*. Business models reshaped by web assets are also in play here. Business models are built upon advantages in one or more of these areas that contribute to the basic definitions of most companies. The question then becomes more directive. What do we do to compete? Further, how do we keep our competitive edge relevant and focused? Since the competitive conditions and category characteristics of most business sectors are in a constant state of evolution, this is key. Some companies talk of reinvention. When they do, they are called to reset the business agenda with something better in products and services, markets and customers, systems and resources. These are the core business definition elements. They explain how competitive structure and advantage play out in the creation of new strategic and economic value.

Popular discussions that liken business with warfare have some metaphorical value in this discussion. And while various stories from this army campaign or that navy campaign are often loaded with blather, we can draw together some useful terms for the formation of strategy direction. Deterrence, preemption, frontal and flanking maneuvers, avoidance, prevention, retreat and overwhelming force are common language. So too, we have the notion that in our modern networked business environment, we have competitors who may also serve as our collaborative partners. That is a growing reality in market categories whose supply chains and demand chains interconnect in critical ways. Thus, the very notion of competitive advantage is evolving, and many of our economist friends are struggling to fit these new realities into their theories and constructs. The boundaries are dynamic.

VALUE PROPOSITION MODEL

Strategy direction should reflect a value proposition, or an exchange between the company and its customers. This exchange speaks to the content and context of experiences companies share with their customers. It also brings together the processes through which strategic and economic value is created and managed over time, and as conditions change.

The value proposition model we find most practical is one that spans the strategy management and leadership horizon. This model has three elements, and they align with our system of strategy. Exhibit 04.C illustrates the basic elements and relationships in this value proposition model.

Exhibit 04.C

VALUE PROPOSITION MODEL

The Promise of Customer Experiences	The Promise of Delivering the Experience	The Promise of Business Consequences
Positioning in the Category	Operational Capabilities	The Results of the Experience

The nature and relevance of value proposition models in strategy management and leadership have been evolving for many years. Contemporary thought in this area is supported by work in marketing, operations and finance. Inspired by ideas from the 1998 book, *Delivering Profitable Value* by Michael J. Lanning, and the 2004 Value Prop Research Program at Dewar Sloan dealing with advanced solution strategy and customer experience strategy.

The promise of customer experiences is essentially what companies do when they position products and services to targeted customers. The delivery processes include everything from production and logistics to customer relationship management to aftermarket services. This involves critical development work. Finally, the measure of business consequences is an exercise in gauging the impact of value propositions on the customer, the company, and the stakeholders that influence and support the business. In a company's work on its value proposition, what counts is more than the promise of an experience. That part can be too easy. The alignment of delivery processes and impact management makes for business results. That can be very hard. Companies often short-change this development work.

LEADING AND MANAGING STRATEGY DIRECTION

Earlier in this book, we framed a contemporary set of leadership and management constructs. Our intent throughout is to redefine how companies must lead and manage strategy in dynamic ways.

The kind of leadership and management thought needed in strategy direction is an interesting blend of preparation and resolve. This blend appears to be different from that thought and behavior we need in strategy integration. And its different from the thought and behavior we need in strategy execution.

In this chapter, our subject is the formation of strategy direction. In Chapters 05 and 06, we will cover the related challenges for strategy integration and execution. And in each area, we will tackle the common concerns of strategy leadership and management practice.

The elements of leadership and management we defined in Chapter 02 are reframed in Exhibit 04.D below. This is a general construct we will use to assess the leadership and management imperatives for strategy direction, integration and execution. Results come to the prepared and resolved, and the leadership and management disciplines required are diverse.

Exhibit 04.D

STRATEGY LEADERSHIP AND MANAGEMENT ELEMENTS

Strategy Leadership Elements		Strategy Management Elements	
Perspectives	Inspiration	Arrangement	Information
Engagement	Relationships	Measurement	Procedures
Communication and Accountability			

Notes: Refer to the expanded Leadership and Management definitions presented in Part One of *Prepared and Resolved*. Companies need higher-order management and leadership disciplines in their strategic agenda, regardless of organization scope, structure and scale. See page 58. These apply at every level of the enterprise, and across company/network boundaries.

LEADERSHIP ELEMENTS REASSESSED

Our definition of strategy leadership is based on three elements that weave their way into the processes and cultural foundations of successful companies. These include competence, character and connection. Naturally, we need to explore these important leadership themes in the context of a company's situation and challenges. The leadership issues in strategy direction must reflect on the company's *principles, intentions, definition and evolution.* These considerations will reflect on the company's specific challenges with regard to business growth, performance and change.

The relevance of competence, character and connection have been examined earlier, in Chapter 02. Those leadership elements are, quite simply, the engines of effective strategy thought and behavior. They are usually signaled from the top of the organization. However, they are also active at other levels. Leadership in strategy direction reflects upon learning systems and process. People at every level and in every corner of the organization have a stake in strategy direction. That is how they become more prepared and resolved for success. How do we engage people at different levels in strategy direction? Here are some thought-starters:

> Open the awareness – understanding – engagement process.
>
> Pose assumptions and questions that people can respond to.
>
> Open the gates for disciplined exchange and hearty debates.
>
> Give competence, character and connection room to grow.
>
> Recognize the ideas that lurk in the culture, sub-cultures.
>
> Provide protective cover for wild hares, crazies and rebels.

In the formation of strategy direction, we want effective ideas and open dialogue from everyone in the organization. Knowledge and perspectives of an organization can sometimes be buried in the caverns of experience. Senior management may be smart, but they cannot lead the agenda without the technical and informal knowledge of the broader organization. The leadership elements of strategy direction must expose ideas and inspire people to saddle-up for the journey. People at the front lines of the business have a lot to contribute to the work of strategy direction. How are those ideas collected? How are they brought into the strategy conversation?

MANAGEMENT ELEMENTS REASSESSED

The management elements we've considered thus far include analytic, decision and activity processes that shape strategy direction. Strategy has certain intellectual and mechanical attributes, and these relate to the processing of plans, activities and ideas. There are two cautionary notes we can post at this point. First, effective strategy management requires a certain level of **order and arrangement**. Second, order and arrangement can constrain the flow of plans, activities and ideas. This is a simple paradox that wrecks strategic management and leadership in many companies. The process czars need to be cautious here. They are the people who issue all the charts, templates and schemes for others to address. No matter how well intentioned, the process czars can derail the thought and behavior of key individuals and groups as they attempt to contribute to the formation of strategy direction. There must be some flex and latitude in the process.

Let's examine the basic strategy management elements that apply specifically to the formation of strategy direction. Consider the following issues:

> **Analytic Processes –** who is responsible for bringing the strategy analysis together, and what is encompassed? What level and type of information should be included, shared, derived and reframed for strategy analysis?

> **Decision Processes –** who is responsible for crafting the primary strategy choices of the organization, the ideas that cast direction and intentions, and the considerations and assumptions that impact the evolution of the company?

> **Activity Processes –** who is responsible for plotting the journey, activities and priorities of the organization? How does this combination of agenda factors come into phase so the organization is clearly focused on business results?

These are the basic management elements that shape the effectiveness of strategic thought and behavior. Together with strategy leadership elements, they make for more effective strategy direction work and impact. Make way for these processes, but protect the organization. Beware of the tyranny that process overkill can impose upon the organization.

ENGAGEMENT OF LEADERSHIP AND MANAGEMENT

The term engagement comes from the ancient principle of coming together in common purpose and trusted thought. When we look at the contemporary business applications of engagement, there are two similar principles at work in strategy direction...

> We want the organization to engage in common purpose in crafting and shaping the direction of the company...

> We want the organization to engage in trusted thought between and amongst individuals and working groups...

Leadership inspires people to engage in the formative work of strategy direction. Management provides certain processes that support and encourage practical engagement. This is a social and technical crucible for strategic thought and behavior. We get people engaged so the company can be *prepared and resolved.* The most successful companies have worked hard to generate the culture in which individuals and groups across the organization are:

> Knowledgeable about the formation of strategy direction.

> Motivated and competent to tackle strategy direction.

> Experienced in bringing together ideas, perspectives, facts.

How important is strategy leadership and management at different levels of the organization? Opinions vary, but our view is that people grow in their strategic thought and behavior through engagement. And, the more exposure and engagement, the better. The technical and operating subcultures of companies have a great deal to offer in the formation of strategy direction. These people and their combined experience are truly hidden assets of the organization. Successful companies find ways to tap into that walking-around knowledge, and they find ways to engage people in the leadership and management elements of strategy direction. Earlier in the book, we suggested that 30% to 40% of companies are working on errant strategy direction premises. Most of the time, we can trace those errant premises to the failure to engage more people in the formation of strategy direction. The challenge is complicated when tough choices are in play.

EVERYDAY CONCERNS IN STRATEGY DIRECTION

Strategy direction for most companies is a ritual exercise that takes into account key issues and challenges. The traditional mindset for the formation of strategy direction presumes that senior executives and managers have the prerogative to do this important work. Among the considerations that find their way onto the agenda for strategy analysis and direction are the following common elements...

> Challenges related to competitive advantage or the impact of evolving competitive conditions...
>
> Issues related to market attractiveness and evolving market opportunities for profitable growth...
>
> Concerns related to changes in several market categories and their impact on the business, it's boundaries, etc...
>
> Transitions in supply chain and demand chain structure that could impact the business...
>
> Issues related to the capital and cost structure of the business, and the impact on profitability and perpetuation...
>
> Concerns related to market category demand and the risks of revenue and margin degradation...
>
> Challenges related to technical and operational shifts in the network of suppliers, intermediaries and customers...
>
> Issues in the evolution of the technical, social and economic environment of the business...

Each of these elements is relevant in forging strategy direction and each presents implications for growth, profitability and change. The realities that frame each of these elements are constantly evolving. In the context of that constant evolution are problems and prospects. Effective strategy management and leadership face these elements with a combination of foresight, analytics, perspective and patience. These are everyday issues, and they're part of the work of everyday teams. Strategy happens every day in the unfolding ideas and debates that people share at every level, and in every corner of the organization.

DIRECTION FOR VALUE CREATION

The strategic agenda for successful companies reflects on value creation. We look at the formation of strategy direction as a foundation for value creation via growth, performance improvement and change.

Companies create new strategic and economic value in a number of ways. New business value may accrue to the company's investors, suppliers, employees, customers, partners and other stakeholders. Companies may approach value creation from different angles, and with different perspectives. A customer-centric perspective might encourage value creation through product and service innovation or bundled product and service solutions. An approach that is more operations-focused might address quality, systems efficiency and resource initiatives as part of its scheme for generating new strategic and economic value. In a more technical setting, a company might invest in specific technology management resources in order to capture new and differentiated value. Being open to different strokes and different intentions is part of the task of setting and guiding strategic direction. Openness to new and sometimes opposing points of view is essential.

CATEGORY CHANGE AND DISCOVERY

When a company pushes back the boundaries of established market categories, it opens the potential for important changes in the order and profit potential of the business. Market categories are shaped and influenced by a variety of technical, customer and economic forces. In almost every business sector, there are examples of category-changing strategies that enhance the stakes of some companies at the expense of their competitors. Technology substitution in medical procedures provides a good example of category change; these alternative methods, including pharma and intervention therapies, take on established surgical and medical approaches. Economic alternatives for capital equipment usage and finance have emerged in the project contracting and rental sectors, reshaping categories. Customers seek different ways to access recreational experiences and transportation, and in the process, categories are impacted. These and other examples should alert companies to the risks and prospects for category change and discovery. These can alter the value network of entire business sectors. Discovery of these opportunities can reflect both planned and haphazard experiences.

APPROACH AND IMPACT

A company's approach to the formation of strategy creation says a lot about its **knowledge of the business** and its **temperament for success**. While knowledge and temperament are key ingredients in approach, we see the true effectiveness in strategy direction in terms of how people manage their thoughts and behavior about their future. Are they optimistic or paranoid? Contemplative or reactive? Risk sensitive or adventurous? Truly confident or openly concerned? Defensive or adventurous? Aggressive or passive? Collaborative or independent? Rigid or improvisational? These and other themes represent important signs for the company's formation of strategy direction. Regardless of temperament, this is the part of strategy management and leadership that sets the course heading.

How prepared is the company for growth, performance and change? This fundamental question is one that most companies cannot easily address. It may be a result of challenges of foresight, as executives find it difficult to see around the next bend in the river of the business. It may reflect the lack of strategic engagement at key levels of the organization. It may be a function of readiness at different levels and in different corners of the company.

Being prepared is a state of thought and behavior. In the context of strategy direction, being prepared is about choices and commitments made in the journey of growth, performance and change. Companies make strategic choices and set priorities based on assumptions about the business environment, the company environment and the chances for success deemed worth the efforts and risks expended. Being prepared is part mindset and part energy. Being prepared is a valuable strategic asset.

Being resolved is a state of thought and behavior. In the context of strategy direction, being resolved is about courage and intention cast in the dynamic arena of business evolution. Companies make strategic choices based on working premises and assumed truths. They set a strategic agenda based on the desire to generate new value. They enter into the fray of demand and supply with the awareness that something technical, social or economic is bound to change, for better or for worse as their strategic direction unfolds. Being resolved mixes with confidence, perseverance and adjustment. The act of being resolved connects the mind and the heart.

SUMMARY NOTES AND THOUGHTS

The formation of strategy direction gets a lot of attention in most companies. However, much of what passes for direction is not very effective. Errant premises, readiness problems and shallow analytics are part of the dilemma. In addition, companies routinely fail to access and leverage their own knowledge bases. Despite the stated customer focus of companies today, most do not present a consistent value proposition to their customer. Most cannot express the linkages between their principles, intentions, priorities and challenges. How can direction become more clear, meaningful and relevant to the rest of the organization? This is a classic dilemma in strategy direction, a dilemma that can paralyze an organization.

Seasoned business leaders and managers have taken a page or two out of the modern doctrines of warfare. The new realities of business are pre-formed with *volatility, uncertainty, complexity and ambiguity.* Normally, these issues would be in opposition with effective strategy direction. However, when strategy direction is predicated on these presumptions, the company whose strategy direction is most prepared and resolved to succeed is quite likely to have the disposition for competitive success. Chance and destiny favor the prepared. The resolved are those who capture their chances and convert them to business results. Everything starts with sound strategy direction. Without this strategy direction platform, things can be difficult.

05

ISSUES IN STRATEGY INTEGRATION

Integration...bringing together the essential
resources, processes, networks and elements
that contribute to business results.

In this chapter, we address the second key element of the discipline, strategy integration. This is where the essential how and who of strategy management and leadership come together. Strategy direction gives a company a sense of what it stands for and where it's headed. Strategy integration gives a company the ways and means to press forward with the agenda for making strategy happen. Companies face many issues on the journey of strategy management and leadership. Many issues emerge and evolve in ways that shape strategy integration. And they pose uncertain and ambiguous signals for the company. Integration is dynamic and emergent work.

How does a company deliver on its promises? Who has to work together and in what manner of process and structure to get things done? How are resources acquired, managed and leveraged? Who balances vision and reality en route to the goal? These and other questions form the heart of the challenge in strategy integration, the work of getting it together.

This chapter begins with a discussion on the meaning and relevance of strategy integration for people serving at different levels of the organization. Our general approach is one that recognizes strategy management and leadership as an ongoing and continuous process of thought, behavior and results. The work of strategy integration is different than the work of strategy direction and strategy execution. It's a critical bridge between them.

CONVENTIONAL WISDOM AND EFFORTS

The most common practices in strategic planning allow for the separation of strategic and operational plans. Once strategic direction is cemented, the task becomes focused on deployment. People are charged with activities, and resources are aligned and arranged. Priority programs and so-called imperatives are structured, and the arduous trek commences. On the surface, this usually looks good. Matching people, goals, plans and metrics makes sense. It's logical, and it's linear. It works nicely with flow charts and punch lists. Frankly, it's the way most companies go about planning.

However, the conditions for making strategy happen are not that simple. Realities of the business are not fixed or uncomplicated. Strategy integration takes place in a volatile and uncertain realm in most organizations. Technical, market and economic realities are complex and ambiguous. Supply chains are dynamic entities. Demand chains evolve with customer needsets and market behavior. Category forces change and entire industries are remapped in response to everything from consolidation efforts to competitive storms.

Inside the organization, there are a few issues as well. People come into the strategy integration process with different talents, ideas and experience. Resources may or may not be plentiful. Systems and processes may or may not be effective. Culture is a consideration. Management assets and leadership assets may be well engaged, or not. All of this is to suggest that most organizations have something less than the proverbial clear runway from which to take off. The setting for strategy integration is more commonly unclear, more unaligned and complex and more ambiguous than people choose to admit. That is the backdrop of integration, and it's ruddy.

Despite those realities, companies entertain phenomena that historians and philosophers define as folly. In her 1984 book, *The March of Folly,* Barbara Tuchman suggests that when we recognize our realities and act in ways that are somehow contrary to our best interests in the face of these realities, we're on the road to folly. This is especially relevant to the challenging work of strategy integration. Many companies have declared strategic directions and intentions that are simply not matched with the realities of the environment or the organization. They build intentions without viable foundations and they expose plans that are out of sync with mindset.

PREPARED TO INTEGRATE

When successful companies get ready to move on with their agenda for strategy integration, they prepare in many ways. There are several issues reflecting the nature of the agenda itself. What can we take from strategy direction that frames the agenda in the most appropriate manner? What really counts here? Another concern is the system of people, resources, processes and culture through which we need to navigate toward our goals. What can we expect of the organization? Who is engaged in the responsibilities and thickets of making strategy happen? Here are some common integration strategy issues we hear from people in large and small companies alike:

> "Senior management has a wonderful vision for growth, but nobody bothered to check out whether we have the capacity to make our way out of the wilderness...it would have been nice if they checked with the front line..."

> "Surely, we all believe in customer focus and quality; however, our systems and processes don't allow us to do even half of what we need to do to succeed in this plan..."

> "The people who talk about the core competencies of this company are not really the ones who are closest to the core competencies. The truth is skewed and that is a very big disconnect in the plans of this company..."

These comments translate in every company. They are the reality of strategy integration. The work of strategy integration starts with preparation, and preparation is a critical part of management and leadership thought. Getting prepared takes foresight, perspective and probing conversation. Being prepared is one part anticipation, one part readiness and one part engagement. When people in an organization are prepared for strategy integration, they've thought through the who-what-how-when elements of plans. They've considered and discerned the realities of their business environment as conditions for successful integration. They've considered and discerned the realities of their own organization, and their supply chain and demand chain partners. Seriously, prepared is prepared. Integration is collaborative work, and it requires strategic thought and behavior.

THE MECHANICS OF INTEGRATION

Strategy integration involves the coordination of resources, people, systems, processes, ideas, culture and risk factors. The integration effort is mechanical in the sense that pieces and parts have to come together effectively.

The dilemma many companies face is that coordination tends to be inherently messy, political, tough, risky and creative work. Mixing the talents and assets of a company takes adaptive leadership and management, the kind we see in a kind of stagehouse where different performers, technical resources and conductors are engaged in creating and delivering special experiences to their audiences. This is the *stagehouse effect of strategy integration*, managing and leading in real-time, with a plan powered by a vision with rehearsed talent and the passion to perform even as conditions are changing. More on this in good order, as we tackle the ordinary issues of integration.

STRATEGIC ASSETS AND INTEGRATION

Companies enjoy different levels of competence and advantage based on a combination of strategic assets and circumstance. The typical list of strategic assets includes factors defined here in Exhibit 05.A.

Exhibit 05.A
COMMON STRATEGIC ASSETS

Technology Advantages…technical edge and energy

Channels and Partners…market equity and networks

Information and Resources…knowledge and communication

Know-How and Resources…processes, systems, methods

Organizational Depth…talent, benchstrength, culture

Network Competencies…capacities and operations

Notes: Strategic assets may be reflected on the balance sheet, but more often, their value is experienced in the integration of strategy. These strategic assets are the basis for competitive edge. They may be organic or external, network-based.

As we explore the challenges of strategy integration, we often come back to this list. Are these things real? Are they part of the scheme and sequence for strategy integration? Alone and by themselves, they are critical.

STAGEHOUSE EFFECT

In the stagehouse of every company are people who perform tasks, and provide key resources that shape the setting and the performance. There are people, ideas and tasks that are behind the scenes. When everything goes right, customers are satisfied, business operations are productive, profits are generated, and competitors are edged and blocked. When things go wrong, and they do, outcomes are degraded. The stagehouse metaphor is useful at two levels - for conductors and performers alike. Strategic thought and behavior in the stagehouse is everyone's task and role. From the concert master to the property crew, everyone is a manager. Everyone is a leader. In the stagehouse of strategy integration, there is an assumption about preparation, collaboration and adaptation. In the stagehouse, the mechanics of integration distinguish strong performances from those which never realize their potential. The stagehouse features live performances, and every day is a new day for strategy integration; the work is always in progress.

The stagehouse metaphor is very clear for those who have worked "behind the scenes" to enable a concert or play or any form of artistic presentation. Stagehouses are very technical in nature. They enable dramatic effects, acoustics, scene changes and the control of time itself. Stagehouse managers and roadies do a great deal of complex integration work, shaping the flow of performances, serving audiences and performers. Stage crews are critical, they lead and manage. What lies behind the scenes is critical.

The stagehouse is where the real management and leadership of strategic assets takes place. It's where the experience, knack and knowledge of the organization come together. It's where the judgment, wisdom, foresight and courage of people combine to put ideas together. It's where decisions are made with an *acute sense of what works*. The blend of contemplation and speed reflects in the stagehouse. The *improvisation experience* of working with constraints reflects in the stagehouse. Performers screw up their roles and conductors send mixed signals. Technicians create and accommodate. Producers plan and scheme. The rehearsal blends into performance, and performance blends into experience. The stagehouse of strategy integration is shaped by technical, market and economic conditions and dynamics. Nothing is forever; the audience has access to alternatives. Realities unfold in unique and complex ways and in business, that's strategy integration.

THE FOUR TYPES OF INTEGRATION

As we look across the business settings of the 21st century, most companies must deal with four different types of strategy integration. In Exhibit 05.B, each of these integration types are framed for more detailed discussion.

Exhibit 05.B

DIFFERENT TYPES OF STRATEGY INTEGRATION

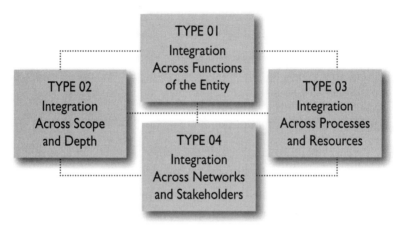

Notes: These four types of strategy integration bear out in the research on effective strategy, organization, development and resource management. These also turn out to be among the key leadership and management frontiers for companies.

Integration across functions is a common requirement and concern. Getting marketing, finance, resources technology and operations on the same page is sometimes an adventure. Strategy integration across functions is shaped by various management and leadership elements, structure, culture and conditions. Clearly, this is harder than it looks. It takes more than crossing the functional silos and fiefdoms of the organization, and more than linking project teams together. This takes patience and knack.

Integration in scope and depth is an organizational issue that relates to business investments, communication efforts, entreship efforts and operating leverage. How a company organizes for development is a depth and scope issue. How executives determine resource mix and timing plans are depth and scope issues. Integration in depth and scope is part of the challenge of working with alliances, and to a greater degree, depth and scope issues shape the framework for M&A decisions and new business development.

Integration of processes and resources is a common type of business challenge. Matching technology investments and capacity utilization is the focus of this kind of integration. Connecting the company's planning processes with those of its demand chain and channel partners is essential in almost every business sector. The disciplines of collaborative planning, forecasting and response management are geared, in part, to enhance strategy integration in trading relationships. In collaborative technology management, resource control and process integration are critical to product innovation. In collaborative supply source development, resource and process integration are the reasons for being, the essential purpose of the enterprise. Supply chains and R&D networks are integration vehicles.

As process management and resource management practices have become more sophisticated, their relevance in strategy integration has been elevated. In everything from warfare management, to sports management to arts management and business management, how processes and resources are developed and leveraged is relevant to the creation of new strategic and economic value for the enterprise. Resource management is critical.

Network and stakeholder integration is a major strategic challenge. This fourth type of plan integration involves the kind of stakeholder resource and network development that a growing number of companies must accept and master to survive. This is network and stakeholder integration in the sense of suppliers working with customers, regulators, specifiers, authorities, partners, investors and channels to deliver on the strategy agenda. Pharma and biotech companies develop products in this manner. Construction firms build projects through stakeholder and network integration, fused together with project management. Small companies work with their peer networks to generate value from best practices and asset sharing. Large companies collaborate to form industry standards and trade platforms. Producers work with inventors, agents, resellers and influencers. These are common strategy integration challenges, and they often spawn new business models.

Given the nature of these four types of strategy integration, it should be clear that business success is very much dependent on getting the *right ideas, people and plans* on the same thought and behavior page as the *right tasks, effort and work*. This is the meaning of strategy integration in a nutshell – it's essentially the *scheme for making strategy happen*.

EXCHANGE AND ENGAGEMENT

Strategy integration happens through an *exchange environment* where ideas, people and plans are blended in thought and action. Through the exchange of various elements of business knowledge and intention, companies are enabled to get things done. This exchange practice covers a variety of things, most of which relate to the understanding of:

> Market and customer requirements
>
> Quality and productivity elements
>
> Business operations and resources
>
> Economic patterns of the business
>
> Technical platforms of the business
>
> Source and supply chain elements
>
> Political conditions of the business

Much of what is possible in strategy integration is based on the deeper knowledge and intentions of the organization. Exchange depends on shared understanding of these areas. Understanding combined with higher levels of engagement provide the competencies needed to integrate ideas, people and plans. Engagement takes place when the knowledge of the organization is embedded with passion, credibility and resolve. *Engagement is part capability and part commitment.* People need to engage in learning and sharing important ideas that will shape the company's bases for success. Effective strategy integration depends on engagement.

Exchange and engagement efforts occur in all four types of strategy integration as they're defined in Exhibit 05.B. Organizations learn the art and discipline of exchange and engagement through experience and practice. Some corporate cultures have great foundations for exchange and engagement. These cultures tend to be more open and ready for collaboration. They have communication patterns and processes that support the management of ideas. They have effective radar for new points of view and new angles on old ideas. People working in these positive exchange and engagement cultures possess many advantages based on the *positive value of working together.* Effective cultures drive positive exchange and engagement cultures. The same is true for the subcultures and network cultures of the business, and it's true as companies operate with partners.

GETTING PREPARED FOR IMPACT

Strategy integration deals with matching resources to objectives in the context of business conditions and realities. In this preparatory process, we make key choices about priorities and sequences. The emergence of more sophisticated project management methods has served to help prepare companies for these choices. The preparatory process also depends on knowledge management practices for its value. Through their strategy integration efforts, companies exchange and engage knowledge in decision-making, resource appropriation and contingency planning.

Much of the impact earned in the Allied battles for continental Europe during World War II was based on strategy integration practices that unfolded through practice and preparation. Political, economic, technical, resource, weather, operating and calendar factors all played fundamental roles in the success of this campaign. There was preparation, framed by the huge stakes. The plans conceived and directed by the Allies for the war were built upon a vast platform for strategy integration that reflected resources, structure, culture, political and strategy options, as well as great and terrible risk. Much the same is true with regard to the broader Pacific Theater campaign of World War II, although this was fought with a very different set of resource and practice integration challenges.

The success of emerging business ventures force preparatory challenges that compare in many ways to world-changing military actions. Consider the strategy to integrate business operations after M&A transactions. Preparing people to connect disparate resources and cultures in the quest for synergy and strategic leverage is not a small issue. Consider the prospects for joint ventures that depend on technical, marketing and economic collaboration from competing entities where getting prepared takes special effort.

COMMUNITIES OF PRACTICE AND PREPARATION

Across every business discipline there are communities of practice or groups defined by special business and management interest. These communities share and compare ideas. They benchmark methods, processes and systems. They compare and contrast new concepts. They share knowledge and practices in knowledge management. They help each other learn and prepare for strategy integration. Exhibit 05.C explores communities.

As people get together to prepare for strategy integration, we need to keep in mind what is really happening. They are exchanging and engaging. Getting prepared for impact is more effective when the value of what is being exchanged and how people are being engaged is focused. How people exchange ideas and engage each other shapes the competence of the company in the work of strategy integration. Research and common sense tell us that exchange and engagement is powerful where open participation, accountability, smart procedures and learning temperament are positive elements in the cultural base. The preparation effort is continuous.

Exhibit 05.C

COMMUNITIES OF PRACTICE AND PREPARATION

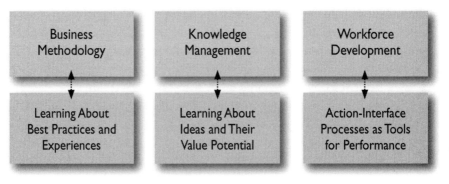

Notes: Organizations learn how to integrate strategy through preparation, practice, experience and assumptions about business reality. Working together in teams and groups provides the laboratory for management and leadership learning.

DISCERNMENT AND STRATEGY INTEGRATION

The strategy integration efforts of successful companies tend to work with a high degree of discernment. In other words, people make the effort to think deeply about the cause-and-effect connections of their strategy direction, integration and execution work. This is a cultural commitment to discuss and debate everything they know about their customers and market categories. It reverberates in companies that make great investments in the right areas, with the right goals, at the right time. Discernment helps connect key ideas, people and plans. Discernment embeds contemplative learning and preparation at key levels of the organization. Discernment is learning and understanding. Without these relatively high levels of shared and active discernment, strategy integration can be a tough and bumpy road.

ANTICIPATION

Forward-looking plans and actions are based on anticipation, and to some extent, entreship behavior. In the work of strategy integration, anticipation involves some additional elements and some nuances. One of these is *curiosity*. We need people to think about what could be and what could happen in the course of integration. Another issue is *creativity*. We need people to consider new ways to make things happen and new ways to see the business itself. One major mistake companies make in strategy integration is to block out creative practices with hard-sided processes and practices that constrain the flow of ideas and perspectives. More on process management later. The point here is simple – don't block creativity.

Yet another kind of behavior for anticipation is basic *foresight*. Some companies have very sophisticated disciplines in place for scenario and environmental analysis. Foresight tends to focus on basic technical, market, social and economic trends. However, the details of foresight often spawn ideas for modest enhancements in products, services, methods, resources and standards. Forward-looking is forearmed and forewarned of challenges as well as opportunities. Foresight is critical to strategy integration.

Understanding trends and futures is not all that difficult as it turns out. Large and small companies alike can appreciate the relevance of trends in everything from globalism to competition at the category level. Shifts in demographics, technology, economic order, industry structure and customer requirements are open to study, and open to effective anticipation. These efforts apply in strategy integration as they help organizations prepare for the evolutionary shifts in business. When companies have the active sense to anticipate, they have the foundations in place to exchange and engage ideas that will help them succeed. Further, when anticipation is baked into a company's culture, the practice of strategy integration will become more prepared and resolved to make adjustments in priorities and plan sequences.

Anticipation is part of how companies get agile. It provides sensors for *readiness and improvisational energy*. Again, some companies watch things happen, some make things happen, some wonder what happened. Integration is the strategic bridge. Anticipation is practice for possibility, risk, challenge, avoidance and change, and it serves all stakeholders. The occasional hint of strategic paranoia should be welcome.

IMPROVISATIONAL ENERGY

Back to the stagehouse for a moment. In the business world, we are confronted with new problems, issues and concerns on a regular basis. Operating problems. Technical glitches. Market disruptions. Category cleaving. Political wrinkles. Competitive moves. In each of these areas, managers and leaders have opportunities to adjust on the move. They improvise. And when they improvise, they practice the best kind of ready communication an organization can ever achieve. Improvisation requires the reception of signals, the discernment of ideas, the conveyance of responses, and the sequential learning of everyone in the act. *Companies learn to improvise and adapt through practice, and this is fundamental.*

Improvisation in the stagehouse of business is part art and part discipline. Improvisation yields a form of communication and deeper thought process. Mental acuity and verbal agility are components of this process. But there is more to the equation for people involved in strategy integration. Improvisation engages the risks and speed of action. It may run counter to analytic methods and practices. It takes a certain kind of intuition and a certain kind of perspective. Improv skillsets come from practice and learning in creative, constructive settings. As people exchange and engage in strategy integration, improv is what enables them to sense what to do, how and when. It prepares them and resolves them to do things where plans and policies provide no good path. Strategy integration is shaped by thoughtful people who improvise using their combined experience and judgment.

Educating intuition and improvisation in the company is an artform in itself and much too often, it's relegated as an occasional task of staff training. In his 2001 book, *Educating Intuition*, psychologist Robin Hogarth explores the relevance of disciplined intuition in decision-making and planning. Organizations with a cultural bias for active conversations and experience sharing are fundamentally smarter than those with no vehicle for exchange and engagement. Intuition is a function of collective experiences and learning. Improvisation is a knack factor built from conversational smartsets. These things take practice, and practice requires attendance from the people who lead and manage the organization, at every level, in every corner. Creative tension and courage are improvisational assets. The bias for improv is part of agile cultures, and it can be a key engine for strategy integration. This represents a key organizational asset that must be learned.

LEADERSHIP AND STRATEGY INTEGRATION

Credible leadership is essential to strategy integration. The projection of energy, trust and effort is much of what leadership means in the strategy integration process. We can break these factors down further.

> Energy in strategy integration means intensity, edge, urgency, power, force and the ongoing resolve to generate impact. One can readily sense the difference between a high-energy culture and a culture that lacks resolute energy. This is most relevant in settings where integration faces complex, dynamic and unfolding business conditions.

> Trust is important at the personal and team level, and it represents a catalytic ingredient in the formula for successful strategy integration. Trust really counts. It brings together shared intentions, predictability, integrity and judgment.

> Effort is directed force and specific knowledge, applied to situations for the purpose of moving ideas, people and plans toward some point of impact or outcome. Integration requires that we apply effort in the right manner and context, with the right people, power and plans, in the right sequence. Effort stems from focus and force.

Most companies have leadership development avenues at the very heart of strategy integration. This is where people learn how to lead people and programs through the dynamics of projects and processes. They learn about their own individual competence, character and connections. They learn about the business environment and the realities of uncertain and ambiguous conditions that shape their adventures in business. Learning happens with people working together in the strategy integration stagehouse.

MATURITY AND READINESS

Strategy integration requires a certain level of cognitive and emotional maturity to succeed in making strategy happen. More than anything else, leadership in strategy integration requires an attitude toward working hard to solve puzzles and move the agenda forward. Emotional intelligence and self-leadership are foundations for this kind of readiness.

COMMUNICATION ELEMENTS

Integration happens through relationships across and between parties of the organization. Most of these relationships are forged not by formal authority, but with personal knowledge and influence. The communication issues are thus very important. Exhibit 05.D suggests the structure of the communication tasks in strategy integration work. Note the sequential and integrative nature of these tasks. People learn how to grasp the agenda and take responsibility for results in the flow of knowledge and influence. People become competent performers through the communication experiences of strategy integration. They become engaged in the practice of strategy leadership and management on this conversation platform.

Exhibit 05.D

COMMUNICATION AND THE STRATEGY AGENDA

Source: Dewar Sloan research on strategic and operational communication in conventional and collaborative organizations; 2004-2005 Collaboration and Entreship Project and the Front-Line/First-Level [FL/FL] Leadership Program.

These communication elements provide vessels for carrying the company's agenda in strategy leadership and management. They help connect the critical actions and methods that drive strategy integration and impact.

Communication reflects the social and cultural systems of a company. The capabilities and behaviors of organizations function informally and formally, and the nuances of communication hold them together. Strategy integration is dependent on the communication processes that weave through the many sub-cultural systems of the organization. The difference between collaborative success and failure is often found at the juncture of these sub-cultural discussions. People learn how to lead in these volatile and often ambiguous settings. Business success is shaped in these complex settings with communication, and through cultural practices of communication.

DIMENSIONS OF LEADERSHIP

In Chapter 02, we introduced the framework for strategy leadership that defines both the elements and dimensions of effective leadership. The principal issues in strategy integration size up very well with this framework. There are three elements of leadership, and four dimensions of leadership. These variables are summarized in Exhibit 05.E below.

Exhibit 05.E

ELEMENTS AND DIMENSIONS OF LEADERSHIP

	DIMENSIONS OF LEADERSHIP FOR STRATEGY INTEGRATION			
Elements of Leadership for Strategy Integration	Self-Level Individual Leadership	Group and Functional Leadership	Cross-Functional Leadership	Cross-Boundary Leadership
Competence Themes				
Character Themes				
Connections Themes				

Notes: Effective leadership is integrative leadership and it takes form at different levels, with different human assets. This framework is part of a collaborative model for leadership and management development in organizations.

Strategy integration requires different levels of leadership capability. How leaders become more or less effective in strategy integration depends upon their competence, character and connection smartsets. The setting, the nature and risks of the integration challenge and the people involved will shape the *balance of leadership* for effective strategy integration.

People with strong technical competence but weak interpersonal skillsets may crash and burn in their integration leadership due to miscues in making the right connections with stakeholders. People with great social skillsets but limited operational exposure may have difficulty in getting people aligned with critical tasks and processes. *Strategy integration is a great crucible for developing leaders and managers*; it forces judgment in the context of uncertain, complex, dynamic, ambiguous conditions. It forces choice, and it forces ideas into the sometimes challenging conversations among principals. People learn important lessons of leadership through integration.

RESOURCE MANAGEMENT ELEMENTS

Strategy integration is everyday work for every corner and level of the organization. The agenda for making strategy happen is the heart and soul of integration. The everyday work is alive with ideas, people and plans. The practice of strategy integration is dynamic. It pulses with conditions and constraints that make the process of moving forward more or less workable. Everybody is touched by strategy integration, directly or indirectly. The flow, rhythm, pace and tempo of the organization are set and reset by the scheme of strategy integration.

The issues that find their way onto the stage of strategy integration involve resources. We can group these resources in different ways. For the purposes of scoping the tasks of strategy management and leadership, a company's *resource edge and advantage* accrues in several areas:

Capital... operational, financial and procedural

Systems and Processes...methods, mechanisms

Information...systems and knowledge management

Know-How...technical, relational, operational

Position...within demand chains and supply chains

Relationships...people connected to other people

As we explore the relevance and impact of these resource groupings, it becomes clear that companies can distinguish their business development and performance successes based on resource edge. Think about everything that relates to resource integration...action sense, speed, agility, control, innovation, leverage, risk management, decision value, profit margins, capital churn, spending edge, quality, customer value, service, cash flow. Everything is in play here, and everyday advantage is gained or lost in the integration of these resources at different levels of the enterprise. Culture and subculture are framed by these resource interactions.

Almost everything that represents a role in the cause-and-effect stream of strategy management and leadership emerges through the resource integration scheme of the organization. Exhibit 05.F provides an audit of the most common resource management elements, a series of the most critical resource and network management concerns faced by companies.

Exhibit 05.F

RESOURCE MANAGEMENT ELEMENTS

Capital Resources

Modern business enterprise requires different forms of capital resources in order to function. Our punchlist of common capital resource management themes includes:

Economic Capital Access-Debt and Equity
Cost of Financial Capital to the Company
Working Capital and Cash Flow Dynamics
Economic Capital and Scope/Scale Issues
Major Operational and Procedural Assets
Intangible Factors and Capital Valuation

Systems and Processes

The basic and proprietary know-how and methods of a company represent resources that enable it to operate with relative productivity and leverage. These include:

Production and Operations Planning Methods
Logistical and Supply Chain Management
Marketing Systems and Distribution Networks
Product Planning and Development Systems
Talent and Leadership Development Systems
Administrative Planning and Control Systems

Information Assets

Clearly today, it's difficult to overstate the relevance of information resources in business management. Some of the most important aspects of information management are:

Customer Data, Intelligence and Knowledge
Operating Data, Standards, Controls, Metrics
Technical Data, Intelligence, KM Systems
Administrative Data, Standards, Applications
Analytical Methods and Information Conversion
Connectivity, Integration, System Automation

Competence Sets

Competence is capability that provides advantage, and it's easier to talk about than it is to create. Some of the most common enterprise competence areas include:

Technical Product and Service Competence
Operating Capacity; Operational Capabilities
Intellectual Assets; Creative Asset Management
Talent and Leadership Assets; Human Capital
Marketing and Demand Chain Organization
Customer Relationships and Connectivity

Market Position

The term market position, is broadly interpreted as a combined stake and base of power in a market category. Some of the most common resource considerations related to business position are:

Position within Supply/Demand Chain Structure
Relative Competitive Share; Brand Reputation
Position within Market Channels and Networks
Perception by Customers; Stakeholder Equity
Internal Strength of Culture and Organization
Strength Relative to Evolving Market Conditions

Key Relationships

The idea that relationships are essential in the practice of strategy integration is increasingly relevant in the networked economy where serious collaboration drives:

Supply Chain Effectiveness and Innovation
Product and Service Development Programs
Market Channels and Demand Chains
Shared Hard Capital and Capacity to Grow
Shared Soft Capital and Capacity to Change
Resource Access and Asset Leverage

Notes: Internal Dewar Sloan research [2002-2004]and research on extended and adaptive enterprises. These resource management elements are critical audit subjects that bear heavily in strategy integration and the strategy agenda.

RESOURCE CHALLENGES

The integration of strategic and tactical resources is a practice of selection, coordination, connection and commitment to results. In a sense, this sounds like the principles of Management 101, and to some, resource integration is that simple. For most of us, however, the practice is more involved, and perhaps less intuitive. Effective resource integration depends on managing and leading a number of things:

> Understanding of Critical Resources
>
> Discernment of Strategic Priorities
>
> Ground Rules for Collaboration
>
> Sense and Measure of Accountability
>
> Preparedness of Key Stakeholders
>
> Capability to Adapt and Respond
>
> Understanding of Business Realities
>
> Receptivity to Ideas, People and Plans
>
> Perspective on System Connections
>
> Courage to Connect Untested Ideas

In all of this, resource integration depends on strategy management and leadership at the level of operability – making strategy happen. Economists use the term *appropriability* to describe the leverage potentials and priority decisions that surround resource integration. In his 1994 book, *Why Companies Succeed*, scholar John Kay explains appropriability as a critical strategy element that is found in most successful companies. To be more or less appropriable, resources must have relevance and realistic areas of leverage. James Womack and Daniel Jones discuss this in terms of resource value to customers in their 2005 book, *Lean Solutions*. For most companies, all the resources defined in Exhibit 05.F are *appropriable* in theory, but in practice, many are not as readily connected. The emergence of e-business systems and web-centric enterprise moves the whole discourse on resource management to a new realm, enabled by technical assets and enterprise behavior. Resources shape the mindset of a company, and collaborative activity beyond the normal boundaries may have great implications.

EXCELLENCE IN INTEGRATION

Strategy integration means different things in different settings. For people managing and leading a relatively mature business unit, the predominant strategy integration issues often reflect improvements in operational and resource efficiency. For companies dealing with new product and new market development issues, the challenges will reflect several buckets of technical, social and economic concerns. For companies dealing with the integration of alliance or business venture partners or acquisitions, aligning resources, culture and structure will likely be a significant strategy challenge. Operational excellence is general "code" for effective strategy integration. Operational excellence is part of strategy, but it is not the essence of strategy itself. Too much operational excellence blather can degrade integration.

What contributes to integration excellence? Are there natural born managers and leaders that are suited for integration work? Is this kind of excellence learned from business experience or built from technical processes and disciplines? Does integration excellence have a natural lifecycle, or is it sustainable for generations? Can we assume that integration excellence follows from focused, clear and concise strategy direction, and great knack for strategy execution? Are there some common twists and best practices in integration? We have a few answers for these questions. But at the end of the day, integration excellence is a reflection of four things – strategy discipline, business culture, company structure and resource platforms.

DYNAMIC AGENDA

Strategy integration is dynamic work. Customer markets and technical conditions change. Capacity use and access factors change. The flows of specific information and measures change. People change. Budgets and spending calendars change. This cacophony of change makes for interesting work in strategy integration. *When we're prepared for this kind of challenge with a dynamic strategy agenda, and when we're resolved to produce results, we're suited up for integration.* Consider the checklist of integration consequences in Exhibit 05.G. These factors are rarely fixed. They are dynamic, and that is the evolving nature of strategy integration. The evolution and improvisation that supports and sustains these integration factors is a significant part of the strategic agenda.

Exhibit 05.G

A PORTFOLIO OF INTEGRATION CONSEQUENCES

Operational Efficiency	··········▶	Productivity Advantage
Capacity Productivity	··········▶	Leverage and Utilization
Operational Foresight	··········▶	Readiness for Challenges
Speed and Agility Edge	··········▶	Performance Leverage
Cost/Asset Containment	··········▶	Margin and Capital Edge
Innovation Capability	··········▶	Product and Process Edge
Knowledge Advantage	··········▶	Intellectual Advantage
Integration Leadership	··········▶	Resource Adaptation
Supply and Demand Sense	··········▶	Capacity Leverage
Continuous Improvement	··········▶	Quality Value Leverage

Notes: These are often expressed as business improvement objectives, but there is clearly much more in the mix. Many of these consequences have predicted, emergent and unintended versions that shape both results and efforts in process.

OTHER CHALLENGES

Strategy integration can be messy. When integration plans appear in the form of wonderful project charts and spreadsheets, beware, as things may not be as they appear. In the midnight confessions of most companies, the integration puzzle is often resolved by sweat, hard labor and sheer resolve. The real work reflected in all those pretty presentations looks more like coal mining than white glove cribbage. This is important, because legendary methods for strategy integration at all the so-called excellent companies are usually one-part serious discipline and two-parts inspired resolve to get things done, with or without the systemic tools and assets that are critical. Bringing these factors together takes courage, knack and good fortune.

PROCESS CHALLENGES

Process concerns are increasingly relevant in strategy integration, due in part to the advance of process management discipline. Processes and systems are forms of operating assets; they enable certain kinds of integration work to be completed with less hassle and more results. Process assets that encourage lean efficiency and better quality are valuable bases of competitive advantage. For the most part, we regard process development, process management and process improvement as essential ingredients in strategy integration.

However, there are instances where processes constrain and restrict business growth, performance and change. Here are three classic process challenges that can corrupt a company's integration efforts, based on our experience:

01. Product Development and Management Processes

70% to 75% of product planning processes in place don't deliver the growth or change results expected by management.

02. Customers and Channel Management Processes

80% to 85% of customer and channel relationship processes do not deliver on their stated business development objectives.

03. Resource Development and Management Processes

65% to 70% of resource development processes do not meet their targets for investment, leverage or performance impact.

Examples of basic roadblocks in each of these areas are part of the landscape in most companies. Processes can block product innovation, and very often, they inhibit new product success. Processes can get between a company and its customers, undermining key relationships. Processes can confound talent, system and method plans at every level of the business, and in every corner of the organization. Processes gone astray can blow up the best intentions of those responsible for strategy integration.

Process development must address these common realities. Otherwise, processes can run afoul of reality and turn into liabilities, not assets. Instead of creating strategic and economic value, they can degrade value. This is not a broadside indictment of process development and management, but it is a warning that turning process-driven efforts into business results may be harder than it looks, especially in the context of everyday strategy integration.

APPROACH AND EVOLUTION

A company's approach to strategy integration is a significant signal for people throughout the organization. Making strategy happen is what most people do at work. Very few of us actually direct strategy. But a great number of us have management and leadership roles in strategy integration. Companies *prepare* for growth, performance and change through integration. They *resolve* to get strategic things done, deliver results, adapt and respond…all in the work of strategy integration. Individuals do the daily work of strategy integration, at their own levels, in their own course.

Again, being prepared is really a state of thought and behavior. The preparation for ideas, people and plans for strategy integration is absolutely critical to the success of a company. *Further, being truly resolved is a state of thought and behavior.* The resolute courage, commitment and energy that enable people to get the job done is raw organizational power that channels the energy for successful strategy integration.

Prepared is prepared. For opportunities, challenges, problems, risks, changes and chance itself. Preparation drives effective integration. *Resolved is resolved.* Integration can be complex, messy, strange and uncertain work. Perseverance is a key virtue in the evolving realm of strategy integration. Perseverance takes more than guts and more than hope. It's part of the thought and behavior of successful, evolutionary companies.

DEEPER INTEGRATION SMARTS

Professors and consultants have searched for the secrets of conceptual, managerial, technical and emotional smarts for decades. Strategy integration requires a combination of sound judgment, quick learning, analytics, creativity, intuition and systems thinking. Mental acuity, great insight and common sense are part of the success formula for roles in strategy integration. Joseph Badaracco Jr. framed this complex of ideas very well in his 1991 book, *The Knowledge Link*. Exhibit 05.H provides a general screener for the kind of knowledge and behavior that can help lead an organization to its specific version of the Holy Grail of strategy integration success. This list provides a broad and deep roster of integration insights, and it reflets a broad sweep of leadership and management thought inspired by Jennings, Kistner, Badaracco, Leonard, Pfeffer and others.

Exhibit 05.H

GROWTH OF ACTIVE, DEEPER SMARTS AND THE ROAD TO MASTERY

Task Targets for Talent Development and Leverage	Characteristics of Exposure – Level Engagement	Characteristics of Expertise – Level Engagement
01. Specific Subject Matter Knowledge	Learning to Manipulate Subject Matter Expertise	Mastery of Technical and Managerial Subjects; Technical Intelligence
02. Systemic Subject Matter Knowledge	Learning to Integrate Explicit Tacit and Implicit Smarts	Mastery in Connecting the Key KM Nodes and Links Integrated CTEM* Smarts
03. Awareness of Knowledge Gaps	Learning to Comprehend and Cover Knowledge Gaps Fast	Mastery of KM Access and KM Application Integrated CTEM* Smarts
04. Sense of Context and Conditions	Learning to Grasp Contextual Factors that Shape Analysis	Mastery of Context Sense that Support Rapid Insight Integrated CTEM* Smarts
05. Recognition of Issues, Patterns	Learning to Recognize and Understand Business Patterns	Mastery of a Broad Range of Patterns and Challenges; Integrated CTEM* Smarts
06. Foresight for Extrapolation	Learning to Catalog and Manage with Mental Models	Mastery of Organizing Ideas and Experience Bases; Integrated CTEM* Smarts
07. Sense of Measure for Differences	Learning to Differentiate the Key Markers and Nuances	Mastery of Making the Fine Distinctions with Insight; Integrated CTEM* Smarts
08. Decision Process Speed and Focus	Learning to Access and Use Facts - Choose Deliberately	Mastery of Decision-Making with Rapid Fire Assessment; Integrated CTEM* Smarts
09. Navigation of Puzzle Variables	Learning to Comprehend the Key Components of Puzzles	Mastery of Assembly without all the Pieces: Conceptual Intelligence
10. Basic Disciplines, Self-Leadership	Learning to Coordinate Direction, Action, Outcomes	Mastery of Self-Leadership Thought and Behavior Mode; Emotional Intelligence

*There are several kinds of intellectual and behavioral smarts, and this exhibit from our collaboration work connects the nature of business talent with learning constructs, with knowledge assets, with conceptual, technical, emotional and managerial assessments [CTEM Competencies] in the context of subject matter exposure and expertise development.

BUILDING COMPETENCE THROUGH CONVERSATION

People learn about strategy integration in different ways. But there is no question about the value of robust conversation in bringing people together to get at the most challenging issues in strategy integration. Solving resource conflicts, bridging structural barriers and constraints, dealing with capacity problems, avoiding conflict, merging common interests...these are all learned best through experience. And the best teacher in the experience game is strategy integration. People learn to develop and exercise at least six skillsets through the conversations they engage and exchange:

> Technical and Subject-Matter Skillsets
>
> Relational and Collaborative Skillsets
>
> Creative and Constructive Space Skillsets
>
> Critical and Task-Analytic Skillsets
>
> Solution and Problem-Solving Skillsets
>
> Productive and Clockspeed Skillsets

The art of constructive and robust conversation between and among people in the strategy integration arena is a practice field for developing sound strategy management and leadership skillsets. Our collaboration studies are digging into the incentives and constraints of collaboration, and much of the project points to robust conversation and strategy integration issues.

Exhibit 05.1

COLLABORATION AND ENTRESHIP PROJECT

Collaboration as a management and leadership discipline has become a more important part of the business and economic landscape over the last half century. The combined focus of globalization, technology, competitive, evolution, business model innovation and other factors have enjoined stakeholders to reconnect their intentions with structures, processes, behaviors and practices that leverage resource bases and business models.

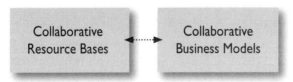

Source: Internal research on collaborative practice education and strategy focused on helping organizations set the cornerstones for effective collaboration. Reference: Collaboration and Entreship, 2006 PDMA conference presentation, Dewar Sloan.

141

SENSE AND SCHEMA

Strategy management and leadership deal with the company's agenda for creating new value. The role and relevance of strategy integration has a lot to do with ideas, people and plans that are part of the schema for making strategy happen. Companies need this sense of method, and they need a pragmatic schema that provides expectations and measures for people.

Based on the realities of the business, strategy integration deals with the bridge between direction and execution. It's quite a bridge. This bridge allows for key parties and stakeholders to work together with available resources, through the dynamics of the marketplace and the organization... to get results. Those results may be gauged in terms of strategic, operational and process measures. Exhibit 05.J below provides an overview of how these factors all come together in the strategic agenda.

Exhibit 05.J

CONNECTION IN STRATEGY INTEGRATION—THE BRIDGE

Notes: The bridge of strategy integration is part resource, part process, part practice, part culture, part structure and a large measure of effective collaboration between and among these strategy elements. The bridge evolves over time.

In the end...strategy integration is the breeder-reactor for much of what is done in the work of making strategy happen. It brings forth the ways and means for growth, performance and change. It bridges the operational gap between strategy direction and execution. It connects everything, and it feeds the adaptation and evolution of the company's strategy in ways that serve near-term and long-term objectives. It provides the essential elements that convert direction to potential results.

SUMMARY NOTES AND THOUGHTS

The conventional approach to making strategy happen involves the so-called implementation of plans. Again, it sounds something like this, *"here is the plan, now go forth and implement, manage the implementation and get results."* Our view is that conventional efforts in implementation do not work very well. They suffer from a number of disconnects, not the least of which is coping ability relative to the dynamics of strategy. Companies need a more capable bridge between strategy direction and strategy execution, a more disciplined agenda for arranging ideas, people and plans. That bridge is strategy integration, and it comes with its own special collection of strategy management and leadership concerns.

Clearly, the most important nuggets in strategy integration include the recognition that there are different types of integration, and these relate to the functions, resources, scope and networks of the enterprise. Everyday ideas, people and plans are engaged and finessed in the company's agenda for making strategy happen; strategy integration enables the cause-and-effect of these efforts. Other nuggets to take away from this chapter are the elements of leadership that engage strategy integration as these are shaped and tempered by energy, trust and effort. The work of strategy integration is, by its very nature, exploratory. This is a great learning space for developing managerial and leadership qualities. Integration success goes to the prepared and resolved – people leading and managing a stagehouse with dynamic, conditions and challenges: prepared and resolved to deliver results.

06

ISSUES IN STRATEGY EXECUTION

Execution...putting into focused action the
plans, ideas and assets that drive business
growth, performance and change.

Execution is part of the language of business plans and strategy. Dialogue on execution tends to focus on tactics, action plans, projects, budgets and targets that help identify what counts and how results will get done. Conventional wisdom holds that breaking down strategy into tactical elements and sequences, with the right metrics and calendar, and the right linkages with other tactics and resources, will deliver results. Sometimes, that works.

While these premises are helpful, there is a lot more to successful execution than meets the traditional point of view of most executives. Our intent in this chapter is to reset the nature and meaning of strategy execution in two ways. The first reset deals with establishing the right *context for execution*. Strategy execution takes place in dynamic settings, not fixed environments where everything is very clear and predictable. That premise forces us toward specific strategic thought and behavior patterns, more prepared and more resolved, as the realm of strategy execution is dynamic.

The second reset deals with *communication factors.* The practices and processes of strategy execution depend on communication effectiveness and the interaction of ideas, people and plans at every level of the business. The way work is coordinated. The way actions are delegated. The way resources are arranged. The way personal accountability is dispersed and absorbed. The way commitments are made. The way problems are addressed. The way change takes place. Communication is what connects execution in everyday thought and behavior, and communication makes or breaks execution.

PRINCIPAL CONCERNS

Good execution is part of what successful companies enjoy if they are on the right track with the right strategy to begin with. While that may seem like restating the obvious, it's a challenge. Faithful execution of flawed strategy haunts many organizations, and it telegraphs in value degradation across entire market sectors. No amount of great work on strategy execution can rescue erroneous strategy direction. However, efforts in strategy execution can improvise for poor direction and integration, and most companies have some experience with this most intriguing truth and paradox of business.

When strategy direction, integration and execution are put together as a connected discipline, companies have a much greater chance of success. When there are gaps or weak connections, the agenda will suffer. In the face of this reality, what is the real problem? Why is execution the troubled child of strategy leadership and management. What causes the disconnect? Who contributes to the problem? Our research suggests a few concerns...

Cultural Factors. The values and behaviors of execution practice are learned in organizations through experience and preparation. How people are developed in companies shapes their execution thought processes and behaviors. Subcultural factors reflecting group interests, values and competence are also in play, and these shape everything from customer service to product innovation. Strong and able execution cultures are prepared and resolved. Execution culture is an organizational asset, weak or strong. Execution capacity and leverage can be a key in competitive differentiation.

Coordination Factors. The basic work of getting things arranged, coordinated and resourced is among the daily challenges of execution. Meetings, memos, and notes are conventional platforms for coordination. But the real work of coordination demands a systemic approach to thought and behavior, one that reflects the conditions of the organization as well as the conditions faced in the business environment. The advance of enterprise systems helps drive and shape coordination, but the crazy human stuff in execution cannot be fully automated through informatics or processes.

Sense of the Target. What really counts, and a vision of the completed agenda are essential contextual stuff for people charged with execution. Some suggest that clear strategy directives and a clear pathway are essential for responsible execution. However, in business, there are many uncertainties that can interfere with clarity and purpose. Ambiguity is part of the strategic agenda in most organizations, and that's a fact of business life that executives recognize. A sense of the target is a sense of intention and purpose, tempered by the resolve to get there under conditions that may not always be favorable, and not always clear and concise.

Responsibility Factors. How is authority taken and then applied in strategy execution? Who has the power to pursue action pathways and gain impact? How is activity tied to results? How are results measured, gauged and considered? What counts? These are essential matters of responsibility, and more and more in business, moving responsibility to the front lines is what companies believe will drive good execution. There is more to this than meets the eye, however. Responsibility takes people who are prepared and resolved to get things done, regardless of conditions. No excuses, just results. That is effective execution, and effective execution is accountable. Responsibility ties back to company culture.

These common concerns exist to one degree or another in every company. Any senior executive who claims these are in perfect order is wrong. The reality in great organizations is built around practice and learning to get better and better at execution. That usually translates in the form of lean and operational efficiency plans, programs for customer-focused performance, supply chain and demand chain leverage, product and service innovation, and a host of other growth, performance and change efforts. But how do these assure execution competence and the capacity to deliver strategy results in the context of everyday business? They're part of the puzzle, but they do not assure successful execution of business strategy. There is more to the strategy execution equation, more than efficiency themes alone. The prospects for discovery and innovation live in the everyday culture and subcultures of strategy execution.

EXECUTION DILEMMA

The adage *practice makes perfect* may apply in circumstances that are consistent and controlled. However, from the first snap of the game, the first note of the song and the first step of the race, the conditions for execution are likely to flex and change. Execution becomes more than pattern tracking and formula work. It becomes improv, mixed with discipline, seasoned with experience and principle. Conditions for execution change constantly.

The execution dilemma is simply the idea that companies must prepare for strategy direction, integration and execution under one set of premises and realities, and then expect that things will change. This is the reality in warfare, artistic performances, sports, poker, transportation, politics, medicine, education, social work, science and business. We face business conditions for execution which are often fuzzy, cluttered and noisy. We need to execute business strategy in these often complex and dynamic settings, and that is where the expectations of strong execution should commence.

The term *press-on regardless,* is an idea that directs us to pursue the goal no matter what. We prepare and resolve to get things done. We prepare the best we can for the conditions we expect. We prepare to adapt and improvise if necessary, and when necessary. We prepare to deliver results no matter what constraints impede the course of action. The resolve we build into our ideas, people and plans is essential. Resolve is the combined smarts and guts and heart to press-on regardless. Resolve is energy in forms that recognize barriers and find ways to complete the mission.

NEVER PERFECT, SELDOM EASY

Preparing for the realities and challenges in strategy execution is more about readiness and agility than flawless plans and actions. That does not bring comfort to people who need great clarity and certainty. But this is the real world of strategy execution. Companies play and compete in market categories with evolving boundaries and complex conditions. Broader technical, social and economic forces drive the mutation of entire industry sectors. If it were as simple as laying down some linear, secure execution plans, business performance data would show better, more sustained results. It's never that simple, and the more we think about what lies beyond the next bend in the river, the better. That is a practical theme in execution.

EXECUTION FRAMEWORK

There are many approaches and methods for linking strategic and operating plans, budgets, calendars, resources, actions and people. Ultimately, these connect with measures of impact and business results. Some companies employ methods that are bonded by project management. Others get things together with initiatives connected by scoreboards. Some companies have very elaborate collaboration and control schemes that connect every person, every action, every result. Our approach here is based on a practical execution framework that has a few very simple mechanical and behavioral elements. This framework helps people engage, learn, contribute and deliver results. It connects focus, action and business impact for everyone.

Exhibit 06.A below represents this general framework for discussion purposes. *The mechanics deal with process considerations and control. The behaviors deal with the people who are charged with leading and managing the execution of business strategy.* This is a simple model, and it reflects the cause-and-effect rhythm of good strategy.

Exhibit 06.A

GENERAL FRAMEWORK FOR STRATEGY EXECUTION

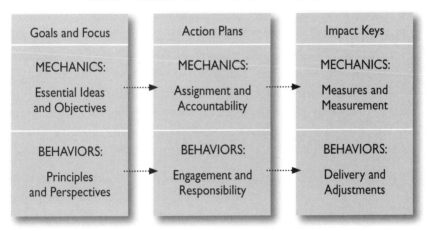

Notes: From Dewar Sloan research and analysis work and ongoing assessments of strategy discipline further related to execution. Keeping this simple is very important; many organizations allow this to get out of control with cascading links and connections that often cripple efforts with redundant checks and endless decision and policy loops. Keep goals forward and plans simple; that allows for rapid adaptation, and purposeful execution shifts in the field.

This framework may seem familiar in tactical terms. However, there is more to the picture. When leadership is dispersed to the far corners and reaches of the organization, we expect a certain kind of thought and behavior for every person engaged in strategy execution. We expect a balance of mechanical and behavioral discipline that assures effective strategy execution regardless of conditions. Expectations of this nature drive broader organizational performance. The mechanical disciplines are *enablers.* The behavioral disciplines are *enablers* as well. All together, these form the competence for successful strategy execution, at every level of the organization.

Goals and Focus

The strategic focus and objectives that shape the execution scheme are obviously very important. Most companies have only a few really critical strategic objectives. These get vectored down into more specific ideas at the execution level. From broader strategic ideas and objectives are born a lot of smaller ideas and objectives. The mechanics of this practice allow us to discern what counts most, what has to happen, what gets what in the scheme of execution, at the right level…the stuff that really counts.

> Focus, Focus, Focus – We have endorsed brief and focused strategy themes, meaning that an organization deserves to present and engage in a strategic agenda that has a handful of core themes. No more than five critical, focused themes, and always geared to results.

Ideas and objectives that network together neatly are attractive and seem to make sense. However, the neat and orderly fabric of these ideas and objectives tends to overshadow the realities of people working together across organizational layers to get things done. If we get going with the end in mind, and if discerning people are aware of the ultimate goal, they're probably on the right track. Focus is a powerful communication engine.

When we look at the behavioral elements of execution goals, the importance of principles and perspectives come into play. The embedded principles of strategy execution help people focus on what counts in everyday action and thought. The perspectives that are shared by people in the flow of strategy execution are reflective of *learned culture*, and *learned methods.* Judgment, knowledge, knack, intuition and execution readiness come from these perspectives. Principle and perspective keep the central themes of strategy execution on the everyday organizational learning checklist.

Clear goals provide meaning and relevance to the organization. When there is personal meaning and relevance in the espoused goals of the company, people are much more likely to become engaged, and much more likely to get focused on results. The communication of essential ideas and objectives must take these issues through the sequential journey of organizational awareness, understanding and engagement.

Awareness is shaped by repeated exposure to messages and symbols that are credible, and more or less attractive to individuals and groups across the organization, and beyond.

Understanding powers a learning and discernment process through which people develop and consider the broader and deeper meaning of the intentions, goals and purpose of the business. Understanding is subject to personal and cultural filters that serve to shape the meaning and relevance of goals. At different levels of the organization, the process of understanding helps set two perceptions in context for individuals and groups:

The Benefits and Advantages of Realized Goals...

The Barriers and Risks of Getting to the Goals...

Behavioral conditions and culture will shape both of these perception sets, and people will exercise their motives and attitudes in this context. For most people, this translates into the *"what's in it for me"* consideration. For people who are really engaged, the greater good prevails.

Engagement is a zone of commitment that people arrive at when they are ready to be part of something that has broader strategic meaning and relevance. People engage in different ways; *a deeper level of purpose, energy and commitment* is key to a meaningful course of strategy execution.

When we introduced these issues earlier as communication factors, we emphasized their importance as part of the mindset of effective organizations. Execution is tough without an organizational embrace of goals and focus. Rarely will every person be engaged, but everyone in the organization must have awareness and understanding of the essential goals of the business.

Action Plans

The mechanics of action plans are often expressed in step-wise forms and formats. Starting with the broader goals and objectives, we move to component tasks that should, under the right conditions, contribute to the main agenda. This arrangement and ordering process helps get assignments and accountability in the right place, with the right people, in the right form, at the right time. Assignment and delegation are part of the process, and execution mechanisms help drive those procedural elements.

The craft of action plans demands sensible work on matching efforts for intended impact. Many leaders and teachers have referred to this craft as the *Do This [Action]...So That [Results]* model, and it puts routine action planning in a pragmatic frame of reference. This model can be made more relevant when we address the critical issues of delegation and responsibility. Action plans become the property of individuals and groups. The caliber of delegation usually dictates the quality of the action plan that is developed. From there, individuals and groups take responsibility for actions and results. The degree to which they are accountable for the stewardship of these actions and results depends on talent and culture. Are they prepared and resolved in ways that secure the intention and delivery of the action plans? Are they prepared and resolved to manage the assigned tasks and roles no matter what happens en route to results? Cause-and-effect thought at the tactical level is something we see in stronger execution cultures.

Action smart is a term found in many successful companies as a descriptor of behaviors that support and enable action plans. Through our research on organizational learning and development, we've isolated several different types of thought that are associated with action smartness. These include subject knowledge, productive edge, creative capacity, problem solving, critical analytics and relational smarts. *Smartsets* addresses this portfolio in more detail. The point here is fairly simple. There are thought processes and practices that reflect *action readiness* as well as *action competence*. This is about more than project charts and process maps. Action smart in practice is being ready for business discovery as well as planning compliance. Leaders would do well to consider this platform of behavioral competence.

We've explored the range of action plan disciplines in practice in a wide variety of companies, and we've debated the virtues of different planning routines with our colleagues. Roger Bean, a development consultant, is an advocate for methods that connect planning and action reviews in a process that completes a continuous learning sequence for action managers. This ties together with evolving military disciplines that utilize a variety of techniques including after-action reviews. The sequential nature of many action plans and management schemes is helpful in the sense that people see the operative connections between actions and intended results. Provided the sequence holds together, action plans can be managed responsively.

What happens when action plans are bumped out of sequence, out of their resource plans, schedules and connective order? What happens when ideas, people and plans are subject to new constraints and barriers? What happens when the stewardship of an action plan is changed and new tactical issues are interjected into the plan? These and other considerations are part of the procedural heartburn that goes with action plans and strategy execution.

People who are engaged in tactical processes sometimes need to shift gears, refocus, align and alter their action plans. In some cases, this requires modest adjustment. In other cases, it may involve major disruptions in action plans, from the people involved to the specific targets of the action plan. The readiness challenge is served by being prepared for change in the execution scheme, and in the broader context of the planning agenda. Things change, and that's the simple reality in most organizations. Change-ready people are focused on results, and they are prepared to hurdle execution obstacles.

The delivery challenge is served by true resolve. In business, sports and warfare, action plans are destined to change in the course of execution. The ability to adjust execution efforts in mid-stream may be a company's most valuable strategic asset. This ability will show up in measures of completed work and delivered results. Companies with this agility are more productive, have higher action capacity, and deliver more results. Peter Drucker would suggest that the winners are simply more productive, a point driven very hard in his 1980 book, *Managing in Turbulent Times*. It's just that way in business life. Things are dynamic in this world, so prepare accordingly.

Impact Keys

Impact measures get a lot of attention in organizations because they help define and communicate how well the business is performing. Common charts and metrics we see in companies address everything from quality management to production factors. In one way or another, most impact keys will tie back to the natural goals of the business. The framework of natural goals is useful in managing what counts. Here are a few examples of impact keys for strategy execution summarized in the framework of the natural goals of business. This is not an exhaustive list, but it should cover the essential subject matter that applies in the goals of most companies.

Financial Performance – Impact and Natural Goals

Revenue Level and Leverage

Margin Level and Leverage

Capital Level and Leverage

Cost and Expense Management

Capital Investment/Return

Capital Access/Management

Competitive Advantage – Impact and Natural Goals

Product and Service Quality

Innovation and Development

Marketing System and Equity

Supply Chain Productivity

Human Asset Management

Business Model and Network

Customer Connection – Impact and Natural Goals

Market Access and Contact

Customer Attraction-Related

Customer Cultivation-Related

Customer Retention-Related

Customer Asset Management

Customer Profitability-Related

Corporate Stewardship – Impact and Natural Goals

Employment Stewardship

Community Stewardship

Investment Stewardship

Supply Model Stewardship

Demand Model Stewardship

Environment Stewardship

The big idea of strategy execution is that impact is gained in ways that contribute to the natural goals of business, directly and indirectly. Strategic and economic value is created or degraded through the strategy management and leadership practice of a company. It gets done through execution, and execution is gauged against impact measures that should mean something in terms of natural goals. Focus on goals that make the most sense.

Getting focused on results is a true learning and engagement process. Some companies have crystal-clear impact keys, and everyone knows them in spades. High-acuity impact keys are about business results, ideas that are germane to business growth, performance and change. In some cases, these are impact keys that define a company's survival. In some cases, they are the basic echo points of business culture. For auto producers, these impact keys range from market share to margin status. For pharma companies, they relate to innovation pipeline and category position. For some companies, it's cost structure. For others, it's technology platforms, production capacity, marketing systems, knowledge assets, network leadership or capital leverage. Impact keys reflect on the broader vision and direction of the company as well as the resource and integration cues of strategy.

The behaviors that surround getting focused on results are relatively simple. People need to embrace and engage in things that count. They need to have a thoughtful sense of what matters, and how these impact keys shape the prospects of the organization. Impact behaviors are often sacrificial behaviors. We give up some things to make other things happen. We redouble our efforts and we recharge our teams to get things done under tough and often ambiguous conditions. We adapt as neccessary, and we trust execution as part of the ongoing journey that makes the company's strategy agenda. The linkage of execution mechanics and behaviors is always evolving.

PROCESS CONSIDERATIONS

In the context of strategy execution, companies can observe the very best and worst aspects of business processes. Effective processes help people gauge what is relevant and valuable, and what makes sense in the organization. Effective process management helps people get ideas, assets and plans connected in ways that produce impact and sustenance. Peter Keen raises some important questions about business processes, their salience and their economic worth in his 1998 book, *The Process Edge*. Which processes make sense in the execution of strategy? Do they help create new value? What about leverage and efficiency? Which processes really drive new value creation? Which shackle the agenda? These are practical questions.

When everyday business processes get in the way of strategy execution, the organization suffers. These situations emerge in many areas. Here are two examples that have common manifestations in strategy execution:

> "…we have a major blockage in our product planning and development system. The process is so cumbersome that we strap 500-pound anchors to every good idea that people offer into the process. That dooms projects from the start. It stops our innovation engine and it kills a lot of good ideas…"

> "…our process for capital expenditures analysis is based on a flat earth with fixed calendars. Budget cycles are all fine and good, but our marketplace is dynamic. We miss opportunities. We take a long time to tackle the important problems, missing good deals as a result. It's really about competitive advantage…"

These and other examples are not an indictment of business process per se. Rather, they point out the challenges of organizations as they go through the mechanics and action behaviors of strategy execution. Exhibit 06.B suggests a few process areas that are especially germane to strategy execution. Our premise is that business processes and systems are important productivity levers for companies. They should contribute to the strategy execution program relative to the linkage of goals and focus, action plans and impact keys. They should not be the constraints of the organization, and they must not block progress. They must be strategy execution assets, not anchors, and we should approach them as areas for competitive edge.

Exhibit 06.B

PROCESS ELEMENTS IN STRATEGY EXECUTION

BUSINESS PROCESSES: Subject to Process Audits and Review	RELEVANCE TO EFFECTIVE STRATEGY EXECUTION Audit and Review Notes…for each major business process and sub-process element:
Quality Management Product Development Service Management Financial Management People Development Customer Management Resource Management Compliance Systems Supply Chain Systems Demand Chain Systems Business Improvement Business Development System Development	Does the intent of the process make sense for effective execution? Who are the central process advocates? Does the organization have the preparation to make the process an effective asset of the company or its resource networks? Where is the process edge? Does the process enable better, smarter, faster, leaner action – every day? At every level? Across networks? Does the process lay any traps or blocks for effective execution, or does it clear the way for legitimate business progress? Does it bridge gaps? Does the process stimulate, limit, challenge, block or neutralize new value creation? Where does power reside? How is power dispersed? Does the process have practical platforms and paths for effective collaboration and business communication? At every level of the organization?

Notes: These process elements represent assets and activities that can enhance or constrain strategy execution. The questions posed on relevance tie to broader organizational ideas and imperatives in Collaboration and Entreship, 2005 study, Dewar Sloan.

The good, the bad and the ugly of business processes show up in the everyday work of strategy execution. The challenge is to put together processes that connect strategy direction, integration and execution in effective ways – in the context of messy, complex, noisy business environments. This requires wise strategy leadership and management efforts at every level of the organization. It requires a *well-developed strategy culture, with a sixth sense for effective execution.* Organizations need to be watchful of the *execution friction* caused by their processes, cultures and structures. And, they need to be open to opportunities for process improvement.

BUSINESS CULTURE AND EXECUTION

Some companies are blessed with strong execution cultures. They have the knack and the collective behavior to execute strategy under even the most difficult conditions. The culture of great execution is one in which talented people are prepared and resolved to get things done. Targets and accountability are usually valued in these organizations. *A sense of urgency is a common facet in strong execution cultures.* Execution cultures are learning cultures. They manage experience and knowledge and intuition at every level, up and down the organization, and in group settings.

Strong execution culture means readiness and total responsibility. People are good at making things happen in these cultures and subcultures. They practice what are often referred to as *the five senses of execution smarts,* and these are defined as follows:

> Sense of focus on business cause-and-effect...understanding what really drives the impact of strategy execution...

> Sense of concentration of effort and resources...putting the energy into things that count the most in execution...

> Sense of knowledge, learning and perspective...leveraging what people know and how they put learning to work...

> Sense of foresight, improv and option plays. Readiness for whatever happens, and the resolve to deliver results...

> Sense of accountability for business results...commitment to fight the good fight, to be the engine of performance...

Business culture manifests and evolves in ritual thought and behavior in every corner of an organization. Subcultures and counter-cultures exist in every company, large and small. These serve to temper and season the organization. They can be part of a check-and-balance scheme that prevents certain bureaucratic diseases from crippling the company. They can also stimulate creative work in mission-critical areas that often materialize in the strategy execution arena. Culture is part of the business system and it is largely a sensory thing. It helps shape the effective execution of business strategy. Cultures and subcultures influence the conditions of execution, and in many companies, they set the context for success.

Execution culture is hatched and learned through communication and signals that are issued through strategy leadership and management. Effective communication provides for awareness, understanding and engagement. Again, the idea for strategy leadership and management is to encourage the company-wide engagement of people. Execution culture is one part engagement and one part execution talent. Of the many definitions of talent that have been floated by people over the centuries, we like a variation of the talent scheme framed by the Gallup organization. This formula for talent reflects on three principle ingredients, as defined in Exhibit 06.C below.

Exhibit 06.C

TALENT ASSETS AND STRATEGY EXECUTION CULTURE

Talent Ingredients	Strategy Execution Culture-Strengths
Competencies	Engagement of Deep Competencies
Motivation/Drive	Self-Leadership and Personal Edge
Relationships	Interpersonal Maturity and Respect

Notes: Talent as defined by human resource and human capital professionals tends to build on central ideas in competencies, motivation and relationships. Gallup and Caliper are popular talent scoping resources. Other important references on talent management, benchstrength, human capital and team/group development, and employer/manager/employee of choice themes are addressed in HR/Strategy references at www.dewarsloan.com.

Execution cultures are developed through experience. Companies might ask themselves a few questions about their agenda for building more effective strategy execution cultures through experience. Do we provide the right experiences and execution exposure for developing individuals and groups? How do these experiences impact the cultural energy for individuals and groups? How do these experiences pose threats or counter focus to the existing culture? How do subcultures operate in the context of everyday strategy execution? Can we attract people into our organization with natural execution culture appeals? Can we redirect our talent assets and the structure of individuals and groups for more effective strategy execution? How can we make execution, competence, motivation and relationships part of the growth, performance and change engine of the company? Surely, it takes people who are prepared and resolved to get things done.

EXECUTION BENCHSTRENGTH AND BEHAVIOR

The talents of an organization reflect in many ways. Human capital drives strategy execution in fundamental efforts aimed at outcomes. Despite this reality, and regardless of a thousand clichés about the importance of our people as valuable assets – the benchstrength of most companies is lacking. Executives and boards of directors report privately and sometimes publicly that they do not have the horses to pull the load of their strategy programs. That is clearly a big concern, and it constrains many companies.

Execution benchstrength is essential to effective strategy leadership and management. This is where companies must step up to the truth of their situation with regard to people development. Do we have the right kind of talent, assigned to the right execution posts? Do these people have the personal qualities and talents to get the execution job done? Do we put individuals and groups in appropriate learning situations? These and many other human captial questions are often separated from the strategy execution exercise. This is a problem for two reasons:

> Benchstrength is catalytic to implementation, and in creating
> or degrading the practice of strategy execution.

> Benchstrength is conditioned and committed in the work of
> strategy execution – through experience and learning.

Strategy execution is a crucible for building benchstrength. People learn what needs to be done and what it really takes to succeed in the practice of strategy execution. They learn the markers and nuances of strong execution culture on the playing field of execution. They learn the value of being prepared and resolved when they are called upon to muster up everything they've got to get things done. They learn to work with the best and worst qualities of their co-workers, partners and their company when they do the messy, bloody, crusty, grubby, musty work of strategy execution. The elegant schemes for action planning and project management tend to lose their allure in the trenches where the everyday work of strategy execution happens. Benchstrength is a condition for positive strategy execution and it's built by experience. It emerges from positive experience, learning and exposure as recognized by advocates of "trial by fire" opportunities. This is the crucible for leadership and management development.

Experience is instrumental for building the talent of a company. Over the course of human history, in ancient governments as well as modern organizations, people have grown through experience. People have been tested and challenged through experience. They have been exposed to the fires of strategy execution through real experience. They learned to exert their personal and collective talents through the arena of strategy execution and through practice. ***Practice grows competence and confidence.***

Morgan McCall, Jr. captures many of the developmental issues of learning to lead and manage strategy execution in his 1998 book, *High Flyers.* The experience of groups and individuals provide learning content and context. Knowledge is gained through everyday experience. The proper applications of business knowledge are learned through the cumulative common sense of groups and individuals. Jagdish Parikh, Fred Neubauer and Alden Lank refer to the creation and application of learned know-how and knack for execution in their 1994 book, *Intuition: The New Frontier of Management.* From Socrates to modern day warriors, we get the message that benchstrength is built through experience, practice, and the grind of everyday strategy execution discipline. This may not be glamorous, and the work can be thankless at times, especially for those who are grinding away at the block-and-tackle front line work that often goes unrewarded. But it can be the source of natural rewards to individuals and groups.

EXECUTION BEHAVIORS

The behavioral qualities of a great execution group can be defined in a number of ways. Here are some of the execution behaviors that our strategy studies suggest are most important, along with some "code" words. Each of these manifest at the individual, group and enterprise level.

> **Established Habits and Patterns.** There is a certain pace and rhythm in strong execution groups. Acute focus and energy are part of the pattern. The habits are intense and ready. Execution is practiced. ***Firehouse ready.***

> **Structure and Flexibility.** There is clear structure that shapes execution priorities and deployment. But there is also a degree of latitude that supports new ideas and the occasional diversions for innovation. ***Accommodation.***

Barrier Recognition and Removal. There is an ability to deal with constraints and obstacles. Part of this derives from perspective and experience. Part of it is built from sound tactical problem solving methods. *Adaptation.*

Constructive and Optimistic Attitude. Great execution over time lives or dies on the basis of positive signals. People need positive signals at every level, not only for the motivation, but also for looking ahead. *Perspective.*

Sense of Clockspeed and Pace. Execution creates value through systemic combinations of ideas, people, plans, actions and impact issues. The faster these are combined, iterated and performed, the better. *Speedmaster.*

Personal and Group Commitment. The engagement of people at the individual and interpersonal level to the tasks and goals at hand is essential glue for execution. Part team chemistry and part personal ethics. *Teamwork.*

Meaningful Targets and Measures. Execution behavior is shaped by outcome and process expectations. When these are relevant and clear to the people in the game, better execution behaviors will follow. *Relevance.*

Enriched Communication Practices. Execution depends on regular, meaningful, credible communication across and throughout the organization. This shapes awareness, understanding and engagement. *Involvement.*

Personal and Group Responsibility. There is no room for anything less than complete responsibility practice in the organization. A serious commitment to the cause is powerful stuff in any organization. *Stewardship.*

Compass Check and Principle. Sound execution management and behavior connects with organizational purpose and principle. It engages and discusses intentions and impact; it embodies trust. *Integrity.*

Execution capacity is a learned-action behavior. The research on strategy management and leadership points to preparation and resolve that is learned through experience. If companies want executive benchstrength, they need to provide people with executive decision situations that allow for empirical learning. Source: Dewar Sloan studies on Effective Organizations.

MANAGERIAL CONCERNS

If management is about discipline and method, then the challenges of execution are important to recognize. What specific tools do we need to put in the hands of people in order for them to succeed in strategy execution? What methods and routines need to be in place? What measures will help frame expectations, behaviors and performance? How do we use these disciplines and methods to get everybody on the same page for effective strategy execution? In more advanced terms, how do we build a focused, self-managing execution mode and practice culture that has the energy and appetite for devouring the essential tasks and goals of the company?

In a perfect world, a company would attract talented people with superior execution genetics and behavior. As soon as we develop the diagnostics and targets for that approach, we will shape the method. Until then, a more practical managerial approach must depend on enabling good people to think and act in the best manner with regard to the right tasks and actions, in the context of their conditions. There is little magic here. The common sense realities are really out there for managers to put in place. Exhibit 06.D reflects on the key ingredients of execution management and adaptation.

Exhibit 06.D

EXECUTION MANAGEMENT AND ADAPTATION

Management Criteria	Executive Themes and Concerns
Arrangement	Putting things in good order
Progress Tracking	Sensing the course of progress
Performance	Gauging results and impact

Notes: The managerial mechanics of execution provide the company with a sense of control in the course of the strategic agenda. This allows for making course corrections and adjustments in process encounters. Strategy execution is a dynamic, organic, living practice. Adaptation and improvisation are part of the practice of strategy in any enterprise.

One management ingredient is *arrangement and order,* which entails matching the execution agenda with the conditions for driving results. Arrangement puts ideas, people, plans, tasks and assets together, and it puts calendar and impact measure into play. *Rapid arrangement* is a discipline. High execution acts depend on smart, rapid arrangement. Effective strategy execution really begins with good arrangement.

Another management ingredient is *progress tracking,* and this entails the active engagement of the team in the assessment and interpretation of select indicators. These indicators reflect on the cause-and-effect elements of strategy execution. As tracking considerations, managers learn to guide and finesse their plans. They adapt and adjust tactics and assets in the process. They improvise and shift gears to account for issues that emerge. They manage the energy of the execution program and the balance of resources needed to get things done. The tracking process needs to be visible and relevant to people. Tracking puts execution progress in everyone's view.

Performance is the third ingredient of the management scheme, and this is more than a measure. It reflects on the relevance, meaning and implications of sound execution versus failed execution. The potential risks of failure. The thrill of victory and the agony of defeat. The proverbial last yard and last play of the game. The consequences of deadlines and resource utilization. The quality of performance. The cost of missed performance targets. Each of these factors and more color the managerial concerns of strategy execution. Performance gets defined in terms that make sense for everyone involved in the work of strategy execution, with measures that are relevant.

When self-managing and self-directed teams assume the responsibility for strategy execution, an important act of delegation has taken place. The group accepts the challenge of setting a course to deliver results. They accept the charge of getting things done, in the face of evolving conditions and resource realities. They manage with what they have – methods, habits, schemes, tools, processes, systems, energy, focus, improv, techniques. They arrange, track progress and then perform. They manage expectations and they manage behavior. They manage performance. They adapt as required. They stay the course, and they change course when that is what needs to be done. They maneuver their way through the mechanics and the realities of execution. These are leadership and management endeavors that are often left as the chaff of strategy, relegated to the grunt forces. Such thinking is wasteful because front line people are the assets that make strategy happen. Leadership must be dispersed to the front lines if people are to be held responsible for results in strategy execution. Front-line, first-level leaders are closest to the customer, closest to the operations, closest to the category…closest to everything in strategy execution.

EXECUTION LEADERSHIP

The leadership framework we outlined in the first section of this book prescribed four levels of responsibility for the strategy execution scheme. Exhibit 06.E provides a look at these leadership levels as critical parts of the practical, everyday architecture for strategy execution.

Exhibit 06.E

LEADERSHIP AND STRATEGY EXECUTION

Four Levels of Leadership	Execution Roles
Individual Self-Level Leadership	Personal Level Practice
Functional Group-Level Leadership	Group Level Practice
Cross-Function Process Leadership	Process Level Practice
Cross-Boundary Network Leadership	Network Level Practice

Notes: Leadership engages people and groups at no less than four levels in effective organizations. This general idea is especially relevant to strategy execution because the people who power business results are usually in front line efforts, reaching from the individual to the network level of action. Refer to Part One of Prepared and Resolved for the technical definitions and foundations of the Four Levels of Leadership and leadership dispersion ideas.

The temperament of effective leadership for strategy execution is perceptive, ready, capable, steady and credible. There is a need to inspire the people who are ultimately doing the work of strategy execution. People can be deep in the trenches and may not have a full view of the company's plans and challenges. These people depend on *contextual inspiration*, that which provides meaning and relevance to their work. Leadership temperament is crafted in the work of strategy execution and in strong execution cultures; one can observe the exercise of effective leadership at every level, in every corner of the enterprise. Again strategy execution is a great development ground for building effective leadership and management assets. Nothing happens without leadership, and nothing happens without management. The purposeful and effective work of strategy execution is the perfect training ground for developing leadership and management benchstrength. Front-line, first-level leadership assets are essential in strategy execution.

ARRANGEMENT

There is a great deal of planning that depends on arrangement and order. Terms like alignment, sequencing, getting in sync and process linkage are part of this dialogue. Arrangement is really a matter of bringing together the essential working elements of strategy execution. Arrangement is that part of planning where we get the critical ingredients for execution in the right place, which is a place of readiness. Making order from chaos is part of arrangement, and this goes well beyond the simple alignment of goals and people. Arrangement is an active learning process.

What makes for good arrangement, and who is in charge? Our sense of great arrangement and order reflects a blend of six considerations:

People who are prepared and resolved through learning, practice and courage to focus on critical business results.

Action principles that dictate what counts and how things must take place in order to contribute to natural goals.

Foresight and common sense about the complex and dynamic conditions of the business environment where actions happen.

Respect for the resources and capabilities of the enterprise; tangible and intangible assets, barriers, cultural issues.

Energy to implement action plans under favorable and difficult circumstances; energy leverage and consideration.

Structure that provides control, measure and order in action as well as the flow of ideas and assets to deliver results.

Arrangement is not perfect sequencing or synchronization. It is not perfect alignment. It is not some wondrous orchestration of tactics. The world of strategy execution is way too bumpy and messy for perfection. Arrangement sets into play a place for each asset used for effective execution under uncertain, complex and evolving conditions. Arrangement asks that we are prepared and resolved to deal with the realities of our business world, as they ebb and flow. Arrangement that works in conditions of ambiguity is always good. Arrangement is sometimes smooth and flawless and sometimes more like a goat rodeo, complete with chaotic and strange challenges.

COMMUNICATION PRACTICE

People on the front lines see different things than people at other levels of the organization. People at intermediate levels of a business network see a different view of business realities as well. How these differences are conveyed is essential to good strategy execution. The perspectives of the entire organization are fused, for better or for worse, in a cultural dialogue. If that dialogue is powered up for the effective exchange of insight and knowledge, great. If things are disconnected from any meaningful exchange, expect trouble. Ongoing engagement through communication is key.

Business knowledge that is acquired, managed and exchanged via sound organizational communication puts individuals and groups in the position to act. The communication channels, the nature of messages that are exchanged and the context of communication will shape the execution of strategy. The ways conventional systems approach strategic communication is illustrated in Exhibit 06.F. Note the interference and mediation elements that temper and forge the effectiveness of communication in strategy execution. Also, note the diversity of communication parties on multiple sides of the communication system. These are part of every company's reality.

Exhibit 06.F
COMMUNICATION NETWORKS IN STRATEGY EXECUTION

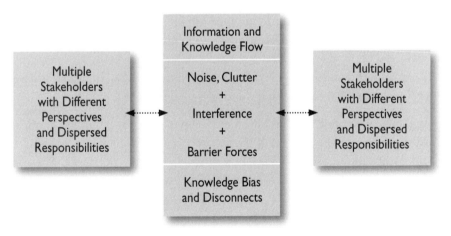

Notes: This involves more than simple communication practices across and between organizations and with stakeholders. Execution lives and/or dies with active conversations and rich communication throughout the network of stakeholders.

EVERYDAY CONCERNS

In every company, there are commonplace concerns that block and hinder strategy communication, particularly in the actions and efforts of strategy execution. These concerns can disable strategy execution in each of the three areas of the framework for strategy execution:

> Goals, Focus…What we're trying to get done
>
> Action Plans…How we're going to get it done
>
> Impact Keys…What we have if we get it done

Furthermore, the disruption of strategy communication practices can poison the execution platform altogether. Toxic communication practices exist in most organizations, to one degree or another. We have experience with large organizations that have serious communication problems that render their strategy all but useless. In one company with extensive process management commitments, the executive team was reduced to its own bureaucratic ashes by the abject lack of communication that would support strategy execution. Senior planning staff people first identified this dilemma as the need for communication processes that would link with their strategic vision. Apparently, this crafty strategic vision was conceived without any communication across or between elements of the organization. There was no communication base to build upon, and there was a cultural bias for disjointed, vertical, unilateral communication. In such an environment, why would people respond to another process scheme as a substitute for respectful leadership and management communication? They wouldn't, which is a big problem in strategy. Boards must deal directly with this even in companies with strong governance-management boundaries. Boards have a role in the oversight of strategy, including execution.

At the business unit level and in smaller companies, we often find another set of concerns. These relate to the linkage between execution prerogatives and the apparent objectives of other stakeholders in the enterprise. There is plenty of room for disconnect here. This is a zone of many mixed messages, and people in the trenches can simply withdraw their energies from strategy execution if communication miscues and random inconsistencies persist. Emergent ventures and transitional companies face these concerns.

EXECUTION RESISTANCE

Many observers of business have commented on the behavioral blocks and barriers to execution. Earlier in this chapter, we discussed some of these constraints. At this point, we need to bring some additional perspective to the issue of communication and strategy execution. Here are a few of the most common points of strategy execution resistance...

> **Lack of Information on Key Ideas –** without the rationale for execution plans and directives, there are serious, legitimate gaps in readiness. This problem is fueled by the lack of credible dialogue that should take place in the exchange between individuals and groups across the organization.

> **Lack of Connection with Other Efforts –** without the sense that operational resources and other people are properly linked in the standard cause-and-effect mechanics of strategy execution, there are likely to be real and perceived blocks to understanding and engagement. These influence preparation and resolve, and they are troublesome.

> **Lack of Performance Impact Measures –** without a good gauge of what really counts in terms of select activities and results, there can emerge many different kinds of resistance. Measures define the real purpose of strategy execution, or they should. In cases where measures confound and confuse, they need to be recast and reclassified for action.

> **Lack of Disciplined Benchstrength –** companies need teams of people with deep competence, high integrity and the disciplines of relationship building at every level of the organization. These factors reduce fear and loathing, and they cut down cultural conflict by getting the right people on board at the start. No benchstrength, tough sledding.

There are other factors that crunch down on execution capacity, but these four points of resistance are like common aches and pains. Our research suggests that the problems infect the governance level of organizations as well as the execution level. These can become big, pervasive problems.

ENERGY, INTEGRITY, ENTHEOS

In those organizations that are blessed with strong execution cultures, there is a certain energy, a sense of urgency, and a sense of enthusiasm that exudes the power to tackle tough goals and deliver results. Coaches and teachers have been charged with developing the energy reserves of young people in academics, sports, the arts and religion. Energy is energy. One can sense the level of energy available in a company by observing how its people interact. Energy is an asset and a derivative fuel of the strongest execution cultures. The presence of energy, or the lack of energy is a key issue in strategy.

Integrity is something related to building execution cultures, and it appears in the bonds of execution standards and principles. The more powerful these standards and principles, the more profound the level and impact of integrity in the organization. With the ethical lapses of every kind of organization in modern times, we have some visible and profound signs of failed integrity. But integrity is really more about commitments to principles and standards than compliance per se. Sarbanes-Oxley and a host of regulatory norms deal with compliance. However, when organizations set down their own mechanical and behavioral stakes and boundaries, we maintain that their levels of integrity will reflect stewardship interests as well as performance targets. It has become popular to restate this observation as a research finding. However, it represents a piece of the free market system puzzle that has brought balance to industries for a long time. Integrity is more than moral guidance and ethical practice. Business integrity is something that enables effective strategy execution. It's obviously more than compliance.

Entheos is a root factor in empathy. Entheos is a structure for wise leadership at the individual and group level. It accounts for an organization's sense of itself and the awesome responsibilities it engages at the individual and group level each and every day. Sending people into tough territory requires a discerning sense of challenges, opportunities and unknowable risk. People working at the execution edge of strategy are front-liners, and they're part of the heat shield for the organization as a whole. They deserve entheos, and they deserve both credit and responsibility for keeping the company stuck to its principles, standards and platforms. Entheos fuels engagement.

SUMMARY NOTES AND THOUGHTS

Strategy execution is obviously an important piece of the puzzle for business growth, performance and change. For a variety of reasons, it often gets separated from the company's strategy direction and integration disciplines. Effective strategy execution is heavily dependent upon communication and engagement across three essential areas of effort…

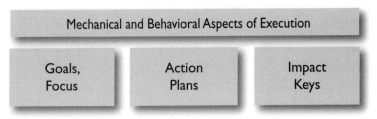

Our research and experience suggest that companies go overboard with the mechanical aspects of strategy execution, attempting to link ideas, people and plans in technical, calendar and economic terms. At the same time, they miss the opportunity to build *effective leadership* practices into these pivotal areas. This is a critical function of the "who-what-how-when" mix in strategy leadership and management. As simple as it seems, important elements of operational context and everyday communication are often left out of the formula for strategy execution. These gaps can severely cripple the efforts of strategy execution, and they can stunt people development.

Strategy execution cannot be an afterthought, staged and plotted once strategy direction and integration are slated. Instead, strategy execution concerns should be part of the thought and behavior of the organization as it goes through the formation of strategy direction and integration. This is critical, and it cements the path of business success.

PART THREE

THE PURPOSE AND PRACTICE OF STRATEGY

Now that we have a framework for strategy in place, our focus can shift to a couple of common concerns. Chapter 07 deals with the subject of value creation and business evolution. Chapter 08 deals with energy, practice and impact themes formed in strategy direction, integration and execution. Chapter 09 explores five common application subjects.

In a sense, Part Three of *Prepared and Resolved* represents the trail back to the beginning of our strategy management and leadership journey. It reflects on the creation of strategic and economic value as the reason for strategy. Further, it points to the personal issues that must find their way into the minds, hearts, guts and souls of responsible employees.

07

CREATING NEW VALUE

Value discovery and exchange is the
basic purpose of business...value for
each stakeholder group.

The goals of business can be viewed in a hierarchy. Among the most basic goals of a business entity is funding for survival, and this is usually addressed by investors and debt providers. At the highest level, the goals of a company relate to sustainable growth and evolution. Beyond these, companies have goals that connect resource management to business development.

The most fundamental and enduring goal of business is the **creation of new strategic and economic value.** What does that really mean? How are these things measured? Is this about near-term or long-term? These and a dozen other questions are addressed in this chapter, through a discussion that connects strategic and economic value issues with each element of our strategy leadership and management framework. In effect, strategic and economic value is shaped in the blending of strategy direction, integration and execution. The failure of companies in their quest to succeed can be attached to problems in their agenda for strategy direction, integration and execution. Failure can be calculated in value creation terms.

The success of companies, near-term and long-term, can be tracked with performance measures. However, all the measures and metric schemes in the business world cannot capture the thought and behavior which percolate in successful, evolutionary, innovative companies. These extras are another kind of success asset. They reflect the way entire organizations look ahead, plan ahead and move ahead. They bond strategic thought and behavior.

ECONOMIC VALUE REDEFINED

The premises of economic value creation are ancient. Companies employ capital to generate goods and services, which have greater market value than the costs and assets needed to produce them. While some companies use more complex models for gauging new value creation, most of what really matters is cash flow. For most companies and in most market categories, true economic value is created when current and projected cash flow exceeds the relative cost of capital invested to operate the business. When an exception emerges, generally there is something wrong. Academics and consultants may argue that there is great complexity to all of this. Any small business can give advice on this most basic of all business realities with simple cash flow patterns which emanate from general revenue, margin and capital metrics. How these relate to cash flow is what really counts.

ECONOMIC VALUE CREATION

While there are many clever approaches to driving business success, companies are most likely to build new value through tried and true efforts that are geared toward one or more of the following ideas:

Revenue Development and Management
Usually involving more value for more customers

Margin Enhancement and Management
Usually involving more value in the solutions provided

Expense Containment and Management
Usually involving cost/quality in context strategy

Capital Development and Management
Usually involving selective capital usage practices

To create new economic value in any business, a combination of the above factors must be part of the agenda. Growth, performance and change will impact economic value creation through the deployment of these ideas. The degradation of economic value happens when revenue, margin, expense and capital forces go in the wrong direction. Extreme value degradation is what drives companies under. Modest value degradation erodes company strength and choices, and it destroys resource options along the way.

ECONOMIC DEGRADATION

On the negative side, many companies have experience in the erosion or degradation of economic value. Every major corporation on our research list, including those with star "cover page" reputations have tested their own version of economic degradation. Some recover. Some suffer through long valley of death marches. Some crash and burn. Some recraft their strategic agenda and become great once again, recasting for new realities. The most common indicators of economic degradation are these:

> **Revenue and Margin Hazards.** Disruptive gross sales revenue patterns, business mix changes and margin erosion. These reflect in demand chain and supply chain problems for the business. Margins are the lifeblood of any business, and when they are in trouble, economic value is jeopardized. What's relevant here is the margin pattern or trend in play, rather than absolute revenue points or margin rates. Look at revenue trends and tempo along with margin shifts and underlying patterns, etc.

> **Expense and Capital Hazards.** Dramatic changes in the cost structure or capital formula of a business entity can threaten economic value creation. Again, it's usually the patterns and trends that count, and few market categories are free from serious expense and capital issues. Global economics, infotech challenges, market category change and other structural factors can alter the pattern. The trend and tempo of spending impact is a principal issue in business growth and change.

Economic degradation is a key force in the marketplace. It operates as a kind of by-product of competition. It can encourage innovation and business investment. It can put a premium on business evolution strategy. Economic degradation, or the risk of economic degradation can be a powerful and empathetic incentive for business change and evolution. Again, the engagement of a little healthy paranoia in these matters can be a great base for guiding strategy and business change. Corporations today are under great pressure from these dynamic forces, and that becomes a survival driver provided the business is prepared and resolved.

STRATEGIC VALUE REDEFINED

The creation of strategic value is an important complement to the creation of economic value. For this discussion, strategic value is created through a variety of efforts that relate to the following:

The company's market equity...with customers, supply and demand chain partners who operate in the category. Market equity may accrue from the reputation of the company for quality or service. It may reflect on the company's knack for product or service innovation. It may echo something as simple as market trust. Regardless of the source, market equity helps ensure revenue and margin leverage for the company and it provides a path for creating value. Market equity is an investment reality faced by companies with and without strong market relationships.

The company's knowledge capital...intelligence and know-how in key areas of the business. Knowledge is a primary soft asset of an organization, and most companies would likely admit to their KM working as an underperforming asset. Creating strategic value from knowledge capital can take many forms. Knowledge assets are often referenced in discussions about:

Customers

Market Categories

Operations

Innovation Models

Business Trends

Networks

Collaboration

Competition

Knowledge capital powers everything from new product flow to lean operations edge. In these and many other areas, effective knowledge management and the crafty conversion of that knowledge into margin and capital leverage is key to near-term and long-term success. This is a key integration asset.

The company's resource platforms and foundations...

can be a powerful edge and a collective source of strategic value creation. Technical, social, cultural, operating, service and resource platforms exist in several areas.

Customer Management Systems and Resources

Product Development and Management Methods

Operations Planning and Management Systems

Supply Chain and Network Management Systems

Social and Operational Business Networks

Organizational Talent Development Systems

Technology Sourcing and Management Systems

Caliber and Engagement of Corporate Boards

In Chapter 05, some of these were examined as factors in resource management and strategy integration. These elements of resource management are ingredients in what makes the company more competent than its competitors. In itself, this is a complex and dynamic notion because the conditions for competitive advantage are dynamic. The value of resource platforms evolve over time, in response to changing conditions.

The company's foresight and natural goals...

can be part of its engine for creating strategic value. Strategy direction may or may not create new value, but it surely influences how the organization thinks and behaves. Strategic value is created through the thought and behavior of employees and business partners, for better or for worse. Foresight bolsters a company with anticipation and it gives essential meaning to reality sense.

Strategic value can be tangible or intangible, realized or denied, recognized or ignored. This is subject matter for serious, humble and discerning review in the most successful companies. Some companies ignore the subject, and in doing so, strategic value can be wasted. We approach strategic value as a business objective that has been below the radar in most companies for a long time. Knowing the nature of the business in its most basic evolutionary context counts large in the enlightened analysis of strategic value.

THE DYNAMICS OF VALUE CREATION

We examine new strategic and economic value in the context of market change and organization dynamics. Exhibit 07.A below introduces the relevance of marketplace and organization issues as value is created in the normal course of strategy direction, integration and execution. We approach these dynamics as ever-present evolutionary forces that shape company success, near-term and long-term.

Exhibit 07.A

THE DYNAMICS OF VALUE CREATION AS CONTEXT FOR STRATEGY

	Marketplace Dynamics	Organization Dynamics
Strategy Direction	What makes the marketplace environment more or less attractive? How will this picture evolve in the near-term? long-term?	What makes the current stance and position of the company sustainable, and is it facing reality? What are the open choices?
Strategy Integration	What demands does the marketplace have on companies serving the customers of the market category? What market norms exist?	What resource leverage does the company need to possess to ensure sustained, profitable growth? Areas of evolution? Areas of stress?
Strategy Execution	What are the requirements for successful category power; and are these changing with the trends? What about risks and rewards?	What operational edge enables the business to stand out clearly from the competition? Are the bases for competition changing?

Notes: Strategic and economic value are not created in a zero-sum world. They are influenced by the character of the environment in which a company operates. It becomes more and more critical that companies gauge the environment in which they play, as it exists, and where it's headed. No business ecosystem is static. There are no zero-sum conditions.

Executives must assume that the answers to the questions posed in Exhibit 07.A are constantly shifting and evolving in response to the migration of technical, market, social and economic conditions. That is one key reason why strategy management and leadership must be considered a dynamic practice. The ways and means for value creation are dynamic. Producers of everything from small aircraft to small appliances know this to be true from experience. So do construction firms, boat builders, hardware suppliers, pharma companies, material converters and small retail operations.

CHANGE PATTERNS AND TRANSFORMATION

Things do not stand still for business. As economist Jagdish Bhagwati has suggested, *the realities of the modern business world are not flat, but kaleidoscopic.* Forces keep moving – sometimes at a glacial pace and at other times, on a more radical, episodic and rapid basis. In much the same manner, intense forces are moving in response to evolving business methods, resource platforms, talent reserves and spurious opportunities that emerge.

Being prepared and resolved for the dynamics of strategy and value creation is essential to success. Having a strategy direction that is appropriately engaged and matched across the organization is part of the answer. Having a complete and responsive sense of the dynamics of the business environment should open the eyes of the entire company to problems, risks and options.

The mechanics of value creation reflect a company's situation and its capacity to convert ideas and investments into products and services that customers are willing to purchase and consume. Over the course of industrial development, the risks of market categories change, and the ways in which new value is created and retained changes in step. Consider the historical paths and sequences of major business categories as they have evolved over the last half century; the names and places seldom remain the same.

> Big Steel and Metals...Nucor, Mittal, Corus, Nippon
>
> Information Technology...Cisco, IBM, Microsoft, SAS
>
> Automotive Manufacturing...Delphi, Toyota, Magna
>
> Energy Distribution...ExxonMobil, BP, Chevron, Texaco
>
> Agri-Business and Farming...Cargill, Monsanto, Conagra
>
> Big Pharma and Medicine...Pfizer, AstraZeneca, Teva
>
> Telecommunication Services...Nextel, Visual Networks
>
> Chemicals and Plastics...BASF, Degussa-Huls, Dow
>
> Healthcare System...Sutter, Trinity, Baptist, Munson

In these and virtually every other market sector, the dynamics of business have opened some new doors and closed some old doors to strategic and economic value creation. How a company balances strategy direction, integration and execution over these cycles of change drives success.

FORESIGHT, FEAR AND DYNAMICS

Creating new strategic and economic value is usually funded by moves that break into new business models or new market categories. Sometimes, business foresight opens the gates for innovation and business change. Sometimes fear of the pending degradation of a business model is the incentive for evolution. Sometimes, providence and good fortune put a company on the threshold of an emerging market category, with just the right product and service portfolio, resources and conditions for success.

Sustained growth and performance is an assumption that finds its way into the precepts and language of many strategic plans. Indeed, the premise of sustained, profitable growth would be attractive for most executives and business owners. Such a premise would make planning less stressful and decision-making more secure. For the next quarter century, companies serving the diverse needs and wants of an aging population, those in healthcare and recreation, for example, will serve a fairly predictable demographic world. This world, in theory, would support the premises of sustainable market growth and performance, at least for this generation of companies and their customers. Other categories would evolve in other ways.

What about market categories that confront more doubtful conditions for smooth sailing and predictable futures? Transportation, for example, where modal competition and energy economics, technology and demand patterns have implications for the market category. Or take the construction business or the furniture business where new forms of global business competition have displaced large portions of traditional market structure. Changes in supply chains and demand chains have disrupted everything from the toy business to the outdoor power equipment trade. Each of these pose functional examples of markets where new players and old players will compete for the favor of a changing customer and channel base.

Companies with a respectful concern about their own degradation and market obsolescence are perhaps most likely to *survive on the energy of business change itself.* The challenge is to craft that foresight through conscious thought and behavior, so it can actively and suitably fuel the agenda for strategic growth, performance and change. Discretionary efforts focused on adaptive competence are highly valuable. Where orthodoxy and processes block strategic behavior, they have to be addressed with toughness.

STRATEGY AND MEASUREMENT

In many different ways, companies measure their results and progress against goals. While it may be fashionable to speak in the language of business metrics, the work of strategy measurement is often not all that glamorous, or all that complicated. In our empirical research on strategy and measurement, we have found a wide range of performance indicators and measures tied to company efforts to gauge results. We have also found a broad array of problems that block the pragmatic measurement of activity and business results. Surely, some of these serve as disconnects between essential plans, ideas, people and actions. Measurement must be relevant and meaningful.

Some of the most common performance measures follow the outline we've forwarded as the natural goals of business. These are the natural goals that have practical relevance and standing in most companies, regardless of the scope or focus of the business entity...

Financial Performance
Competitive Advantage
Customer Connections
Corporate Stewardship

Natural goals of business translated into credible value management metrics and evolving targets.

For most companies, we see a vast locker of *financial performance* measures. These include the usual revenue, margin, expense and capital data, along with *supporting cause-and-effect indicators* that suggest how well capital is used to generate economic returns. These financial performance measures can focus on the near-term and/or the long-term, and they can help the entire organization better understand its choices and its challenges. Financial performance gets the attention of investors, regulators, government, suppliers and other stakeholders including supplier and customer communities. These are the common subjects of those who perform valuation and development work for the investor community.

Financial performance is influenced by conditions, opportunities and challenges that come along in the course of business. Our sense is that companies tend to overlook their shortcomings and overplay their event-specific opportunities as they plan for financial performance.

Measures of *competitive advantage* are typically gauged in terms of market position or standing, segment relevance, category presence, market reputation, customer preference or some aspect of technical, resource or operating edge over market adversaries. We can also look at competitive advantage in other ways. For example, it's quite popular to define competitive advantage in terms of some kind of competence, some technical, market, operating or relational capability that provides unique value-creating power. With the speed of action in most markets, competitive advantage is tough to measure in critical, accurate and temporal terms. However, there are some questions that can be posed as stakeholders review the company's base of competitive advantage:

> A company believes it has the edge in terms of operational and supply chain systems. The question is this; how does this edge translate into strategic and economic value, today and tomorrow? How real and valuable is the edge?

> A company believes it has the edge in terms of new product and service development. The question that needs to be posed is this; how does this edge make money, and how does it sustain itself over time? What is sustainable?

> A company believes it has the edge in terms of its customer base, brand position and market loyalty. The question is this; how could that foundation erode into a problem that replaces value creation with value degradation?

We ask these questions in greater detail with both large and small companies as part of their strategy leadership and management process. What we find most often is that the more successful companies tend to challenge their own internal beliefs with greater discernment and more deliberate criticism than their lesser peers. Lesser performers tend to believe their own press about the nature of their competitive advantage – an almost always distorted view of reality, and sometimes a tunnel of self-deception. Active discussions and hard-nosed discernment are antidotes to the arrogance and denial that grips companies as their customers abandon them. Conversations that get to the heart of tough issues are part of more successful business cultures, and some level of constructive confrontation is part of the mix.

The measures for *customer connections* are also quite varied and diffused. Common indicators derive from three primary kinds of attachment between companies and their customer populations…

Customer Attitudes – perceptions, experience and preferences that temper the relationship between companies and customers. These attitudes can reference anything from market equity and brand relevance to situation-specific preferences, even love-hate relationships with customers.

There are many reasons why companies misread customer attitudes…and these errors can be very, very costly.

Customer Business Capture and Retention – common measures of customer activity is share of category or share of wallet. How much of the total category or spending relevance does a company enjoy, given the parameters of the customer base? Retention is a broader measure of sustainability.

Companies fail to sustain customers, very often without knowing it…customers are assets; they reflect business value.

Customer Rejection – valuable customers tend to consider certain companies as non-starters for their patronage. Researchers may refer to this as the rejection set; some customers want nothing to do with a particular supplier, for any reason or no reason whatsoever. That's rejection, and it's powerful.

There are reasons why customers disregard, disengage and leave a company…and customer loyalty is a costly commodity.

In the course of business development, aggressive customer management requires focused, effective acquisition, cultivation and retention of new customers. No company keeps its customers as permanent assets, although some come very close. Strategic and economic value is created when *profitable customer relationships* are managed for more than the sake of market share, and more than revenue alone. Without focused attention on customer management practices, companies invest efforts in ways that undermine strategic and economic value. This is a big paradox, and a serious challenge, regardless of the scope of the enterprise.

The most common measures of *corporate stewardship* include business efforts geared to doing good works. While stewardship efforts are often related to reinforced stakeholder relationships, there is broad evidence that these efforts miss their true value creating potential. In our work on the natural goals of business, we've found there are several possible avenues for strategic and economic value creation on the platform of corporate stewardship. These avenues include, but are not limited to the following:

Stakeholder Integrity and Relationships
Working with partners to assure common interests

Community Engagement and Citizenship
Working with communities to secure quality of life

Employer of Choice and Employee of Choice
Working with employees to build a magnet entity

Supply Chain and Demand Chain Integrity
Working to build collaboration as a business asset

Investment in EcoSocial Development
Working to sustain environments and humanity

This list could expand, and in discerning companies, it often does expand beyond the *"goodness and light" prerogatives* that are so common. Our intent here is simple, however. Strategic and economic value is created and sustained through sound, considered efforts in corporate stewardship, because that stewardship is a responsible call to relevant goals of society. Under the most conservative blueprint of true market economics, a company's ultimate responsibility is to generate profits and capital results. From that platform, it can be steward-like in everything it does. That is the essence of capitalism, and great companies balance every aspect of their natural goals to achieve the appropriate ends for all stakeholders. Our friends at Sauder, Welch-Allyn, Gore, S2 Yachts and Marriott know this well as do the people at most forward-looking companies.

Ecomagination at GE and other platforms are evidence of this growing imperative. There is more to corporate stewardship than buzz and blather, and the "big vision" stuff must be clear and credible. Stewardship by way of innovation and invention is another value creation arena.

MEASURES AND STRATEGY

The framework for strategy leadership and management we've discussed over the course of this book contains three main elements. Strategy *direction* involves purpose and business heading. Strategy *integration* involves the match of resources and assets with business priorities. Strategy *execution* involves the engagement of people and action plans. For each of these elements, a company can pose specific indicators and measures. A business analysis and review process that connects the appropriate cause-and-effect measures with each strategy element is bound to be very useful.

Exhibit 07.B suggests a general scheme for charting the most appropriate measures, at the right pace for each element of strategy. This is a starting point only. To suggest a more formal cookbook for tracking and control is clearly beyond our scope here. What is more important, in our view, is a perspective for indicators that are baked into the corporate culture. Don't measure for the sake of a cool dashboard or scorecard buzz. Measure to build the preparedness and resolve of the company. Measure to enable business growth, performance and change in the most meaningful way.

In the assessment of indicator content for strategy measurement, it's helpful to reflect on the *relevance and salience of key measures*. Of the vast array of indicators that could be measured, which of these have the greatest strategic meaning across the organization? Which are useful and germane to people at every level and in every corner of the business? Which of these really show how well the company has performed under dynamic business conditions? Which suggest how well ideas, people and plans have come together to deliver on objectives, in the context of business conditions? Which elements really count? How many things do we need to measure?

For most companies, a relatively small number of strategic, operating and resource measures are useful as *principal indicators*, key targets on the strategic leadership and management agenda. Five or fewer key measures can be framed in strategy and forged into culture. This is where strategy thought and behavior blend into a powerful force, and we caution executives not to go overboard on metrics. Measures are good; too much measurement is like too much process noise. Measure what really makes the most sense in terms of the agenda for business growth, performance and change.

Exhibit 07.B

MEASURES BY STRATEGY ELEMENT

Strategy Elements	Principal Indicators	Measures to Consider and Relevance to Organization
Strategy Direction	Engagement of Organization in: Purpose; Intentions Natural Goals Business Foresight Industry Dynamics	Strategic Purpose... Relevant Measures- Market Attractiveness? Competing in Category? Business Model Options?
Strategy Integration	Engagement of Organization in: Thinking Together Working Together Connecting Assets Forward Behavior	Strategic Linkage... Relevant Measures- Resource Management? Productivity Factors? Collaboration Efforts?
Strategy Execution	Engagement of Organization in: Staging Activities Results on Calendar Accountability, Now Learning Practices	Strategic Actions... Relevant Measures- Execution Conditions? Methods, Checkpoints? Adaptation Signals?

Notes: In a 2001 working paper entitled *What Counts - Key Metrics*, Dewar Sloan notes the relevance of business indicators at three levels of measure – the strategic purpose level, the operating performance level, and the process and behavior levels. These help define business opportunity and responsibility, and they help it all make sense for employees.

Companies need to ask themselves a simple question about business measures. Is this about scorekeeping or intervention? At some point, we need the data to keep score, but the impact of value creation comes from plan interventions, improvement, innovation, problem-solving, adaptation and plan adjustment. Measures alone don't lead or manage; they provide signals and patterns for strategy leadership and management. People interevene to evaluate, develop and deploy specific business action. They intervene with good intent and good knowledge, if they have a reasonable and balanced sense of measures. Through strategy leadership and management, ideas, people and actions are engaged to adopt and respond. Thought and behavior in response to business measures are what drives success. Measures inform and influence the process of strategy leadership and management. Nothing more or less, and nothing that business stakeholders fail to comprehend.

PEOPLE ON NOTICE

Measures help individuals and groups set their sights and frame their actions in sync with the greater intentions of the company. Beyond all the charts and graphs, and aside from bonus schemes that put metrics in dollar terms for people, metrics and measurement help in:

Defining **Expectations** in Terms that are Relevant

Encouraging Productive **Behaviors** for the Organization

Defining **Performance** in Terms that Speak Impact

Measures put language and symbols around a company's purpose and intentions. They pose mandates for results. They help individuals and groups get focused on results. They frame the relevance of results. They connect the *cause-and-effect* focus of strategy leadership and management. Measures serve as ritual markers for business thought and behavior. They help engage the collective mind, heart, pulse, guts and soul at every level, in every corner.

CONFUSION AND COMPLICATIONS

Measures put people on notice of what counts and why, and how matters that count shape the destiny of the company. This seems fair and sensible, but things get confounded and confused for a variety of reasons. Our research suggests that people suffer from mixed signals. They're exposed to conflicting goals and resource bases. They're given measures that can be finessed and managed without delivering real results. They're confronted with measures that are simply out of sync with their capacity to deliver impact. In the face of mixed messages and measures, individuals and groups may act out in opposition to the basic goals of the business. Or, they may apply energy to areas of the business agenda that contribute to *unintended consequences,* which can be problematic or opportunistic. When people are on notice in general, they are prepared to learn.

Companies ask people to "do more with less" in many instances. It's not unusual to have austerity conditions in one area and abundance in another. This sets up an interesting arrangement of incentives and barriers to engagement. Measures should motivate and engage. However, they can have the opposite effect. Measures can present and impose paradoxes.

SIMPLER IS BETTER THAN COMPLEX

Research and experience suggest that strategy measurement methods that tackle networks of interwoven indicators become too complex. When the process of measurement becomes a burden to the people who are charged with building the business and generating results, something has to budge. Here are some warning signals to consider in the assessment of business measures and measurement processes:

> **Problems in Data Management** – difficulties with data integrity, accuracy, relevance and timely measurement.
>
> **Problems with Data Association** – difficulties with the match of cause-and-effect measures and business reality.
>
> **Problems with Data Engagement** – difficulties with the behavioral relationships and consequences of measures.
>
> **Problems with Data Cost and Value** – difficulties with the collection, arrangement and application of measures.

Any company can generate an array of measures that appears useful and sensible. However, there is a complexity monster in strategic, operational and resource measurement. That monster can stifle an organization, drive some really bad decisions, and wreak havoc on individuals and groups.

ACCOUNTABILITY FOR THE PREPARED AND RESOLVED ORGANIZATION

Measures are for measurement, and measurement is for assisting people in directing, integrating and executing sound strategy. Measures must tie back to creating strategic and economic value. Do measures help ensure accountability at the personal and organizational level? Do measures serve to convey and reinforce what counts and why? Do measures help people get prepared and resolved? Do measures make a company better, smarter and faster? Do they help it learn? Do they contribute to effective leadership and management of strategy? These are questions the measurement folks need to ask and answer. Otherwise measurement gets in the way of real and true performance goals, and in some cases, it can derail company values. Basic measures provide meaning and clarify intention.

LEARNING AND VALUE CREATION

Companies are dynamic entities, and much of what powers their capacity for growth, performance and change is organizational learning. The appetite for learning seems to be a catalytic part of the culture of successful companies, and this hunger shapes perceptions and attitudes. Organizations learn through research and experience. They learn through dialogue about every aspect of the business, every problem and challenge. They learn by thinking about the past and the future. They learn through discovery and exploration. They learn by observing other companies and other industries. They learn through examples and metaphors, fantasy and theory, stories, fact, mythology and fiction. Companies learn in many ways, and learning can be retained or lost.

Strategic and economic value are captured through new learning and the everyday study of business conditions and problems. Over the 200-year history of the industrial revolution, people have learned to learn in business. They've learned to recognize and generate strategic value and economic value in many different ways. In the operations of a business, they've learned to reframe productivity, quality, value and adaptability. In customer and channel relationships, they've learned to provide product and service solutions that make sense, shape utility and move demand. In the structure of a business, they've learned to recast capacity, assets, supply chain economics and capital leverage. In the human resource realm, they've learned to reset the meaning and development of human capital and leadership as value-creating assets. Learning to create and deliver business results is tough to measure.

Learning to collaborate is part of the success equation. Collaboration influences the blending of ideas, people and plans. It shapes processes for conceiving new products and processes. It tempers the behaviors of people across business functions, and across the boundaries of the organization. Academics including Senge and Argyrs have argued the importance of organizational learning as a collaborative discipline. In his book, *Learning In Action,* David Garvin posed concerns about the content, barriers and context of learning. Our colleague, Len Kistner has suggested that organizational learning is an empathetic process – a ***simpatico experience*** of the organization. Designers are exploring this domain of experience. Learning is quite clearly a critical facet of strategic preparation and resolve. It's a key value creation engine.

LEARNING TO EVOLVE THE BUSINESS

Value creation happens in the context of business conditions that are often complex and dynamic. If a company is to create strategic and economic value on any kind of sustainable basis, it must learn to evolve the business. In some business situations, this may require more revolution than evolution, but the basic ideas are really quite similar, once we get above the hype.

Business evolution can be seeded on several fronts. Strategic and economic value is created or degraded on these fronts. Exhibit 07.C suggests a few pathways for business evolution. Companies must dig into each of these pathways with rigorous debate. In the depths and ditches of these pathways lie some key business evolution issues, along with the challenges that define what evolution options really exist.

Exhibit 07.C

PATHWAYS FOR COMPANY EVOLUTION

Common Subjects on the Learning Agenda of Successfully Evolving Organizations	Learning Targets and Consideration Triggers
Strategic Forces and Orientation - defensive and growth alternatives	Category Conditions
Sense-and-Respond Mechanisms - discovery and analytic procedures	Pattern Comprehension
Operational Forces and Discipline - capacity blending and innovation	Quality and Efficiency
Cultural and Organizational Edge - talent and social network assets	Evolutionary Behavior
Structural Energy and Dynamics - decision and risk management	Approach to Choices

Notes: Companies are organic entities, and they operate in dynamic business and economic environments. The knowledge engines that are engaged by business owners and executives are either engaged or oblivious to these subjects. When they're engaged, companies adapt and evolve through new learning. When they're oblivious, fateful ignorance takes its course.

VALUE CREATION IS EVOLUTIONARY STUFF

The richness of Exhibit 07.C can be found in the everyday discussions of the company. How are people engaged in dialogue and thought about the future of the business? How does the organization prepare itself to look around the river bend? How are people asked to play in the game of business evolution? How broad and deep are the senses and perspectives of people exchanged across the company? How do these learnings contribute to strategic and economic value? How does an organization distinguish the relevant stuff from the nonsense? Who really cares about value creation?

An organization learns in ways that inform its capabilities and its culture. These enable its evolution, along with its ability to create new strategic and economic value over time. We ask companies to explain how they will evolve to create new value over five-year spans, given the challenges of the market categories they serve. The most common response to this planning question harkens back to business definition – the combination of products and services, markets and customers, resources and systems that frame the business. The more reflective and expository question is this: how does a company get prepared and resolved to manage the evolution process? Almost always, the answer involves *learning to evolve.* Without this learning imperative, the company cannot be prepared or resolved to create any kind of sustainable growth, performance or change. Without learning, there can be little new value creation or delivery. Our research shows that *successful companies have curious and brave learning cultures.* It's acceptable to challenge reality and authority in these cultures. Excuses for failing to learn are just not as acceptable in these cultures.

Business learning takes place in many ways, under the leadership and management of people who sense the meaning of experience and the relevance of methods. Long before there were proprietary schemes for planning and decision-making, Socrates and Confucius asked a few questions of their students. These typically yielded answers and new questions. New learning creates new value. The knowledge that is mined in learning can be tangible and/or reflective. Applied to the planning and decision-making agenda of an organization, knowledge drives the creation and evolution of strategic and economic value. Knowledge is a kind of business currency, and that currency can be well-circulated or stuffed in the proverbial company mattress.

MINDSET AND AGENDA

Getting people at every level to a place where they have a role in building the strategic and economic value of the business is no simple adventure. The strategic agenda, powered by effective leadership and management is a framework for engaging people, ideas and actions to deliver business results. The strategic agenda is fed by mindset, and mindset is an active and dynamic cultural element of most business organizations.

Whether people have the capacity to learn their way into this mindset is a concern for every company. In a perfect world, companies are populated with people whose skillsets, attributes, character, motives and behaviors are strong and focused. People with more *volition, the personal attachment to intention* as Professors Ghoshal and Bruch define things, are positive mindset builders and energetic actors in the strategic agenda. If that kind of volition is engaged, and if it gets applied wisely to the strategic agenda, value creation is virtually assured as an outcome. Further, the positive energy of the company's mindset feeds on leadership at every level.

This mindset thing is more than cultural; it's personal, social and technical at the same time. When groups or teams are dysfunctional, one can be confident that the company's mindset has become polluted with both technical and personal assaults on the strategic agenda. Strategic value and economic value are built and destroyed every day through the collective thought and behavior of organizations. The challenge for most companies is to guide the balance of this mindset thing so the forces of business development and creative destruction are properly set. Mindset builds focus, energy and impact. Mindset is the collective thought and behavior of the company and it takes form in everyday plans and decisions.

The mindset that is crafted into a company's strategic thought and behavior must be principled, objective, prospective and adaptive, all at the same time. People regenerate their individual mindsets from experience, from stories, from foresight and from legacy. Sometimes, mindset has to budge and bend and get reset to function. Some people carry their mindset too far; some carry it not far enough. Imagination and possibility blend with critical thought about risks and constraints. These variables evolve as the ever-changing realities of the business.

SUMMARY NOTES AND THOUGHTS

The fundamental purpose of strategy leadership and management is the creation of new strategic and economic value. There are several ways to approach value creation. Economic value is created through moves that focus on revenue, margin, expense and capital measures. Strategic value is created through movement in market position, knowledge, strategic resources and foresight. In everything a company does and says, there is impact on the creation or degradation of value. Value creation is the fundamental issue in strategy.

While companies toil over everyday strategic and operating issues across the enterprise, we find engagement in meaningful business measures to be off the mark in many organizations. The disciplines of business measurement have escalated through a period of business history that has been reshaped by better information, compliance interests and management systems bonded by connective metrics. With all of this horsepower and heartburn, how do companies miss the target in value creation? Our answer to that question would be that, for most organizations, *this is harder than it looks.*

Value is created and/or degraded in the strategy direction, integration and execution platforms of the organization. Great execution of errant strategy direction cannot create value. Great strategy direction without integration competence and character simply cannot drive new business value. This is a central lesson of strategy leadership and management. Success depends on the everyday thought and behavior of people across the organization, in a march for business evolution, on frontiers with ever-changing conditions.

08

ENERGY, PRACTICE AND IMPACT

The strategic agenda emerges from a mindset
that is focused on results, and engaged in
the work of people in everyday practice.

The effective practice of business strategy creates new value. Practice is a very important concept in strategy. Practice is what we do to prepare the direction, integration and execution of strategy. Practice is prepatory thought and behavior; the mental and social conditioning of a company is built through practice. People prepare to engage themselves as well as others through practice. Practice is learning and practice is thinking about the cause-and-effect nature of business growth, performance and change.

As we examine strategy in practice we see a few common problems. First, inertia provides much of the energy and mindset for conventional strategic planning. Inertia may be a very poor base for strategic thought and behavior, even if the company is an "excellent" enterprise. Second, organizations can miss opportunities to engage people in the thought and behavior practices that are critical to business results. Too many companies use strategic reviews to restate the obvious in the dialogue among senior managers who are far from the trenches. Third, strategy is a way of merging thought and behavior into everyday intentions and deployment. As long as companies approach strategic planning as a ritual event, it will remain a ritual event.

Effective strategy leadership and management practice is that which deals with the right subject matter, the right people and groups, and the right blend of analytic and creative discourse. This chapter brings together what should be called *the greater prospects for strategy practice.*

STRATEGY PRACTICE AND RESOLVE

Using common practice metaphors from sports, the arts, warfare and science, the apparent purpose of practice is to prepare for some ultimate performance. Practice makes for readiness, and to a greater extent, practice makes for excellence. The energy we humans put into practice makes us more or less capable to perform under different circumstances. We practice to deliver impact and results. We practice to experience business success or survival or victory or evolution. We practice to learn and discover.

Resolve is an important precept in successful business cultures. The personal and organizational resolve found in companies gives us some insight into the other dimensions of strategy practice. We can look at resolve in terms of the following set of personal and behavioral considerations: Courage, passion, respect, adaptation, curiosity – key elements of resolve.

Courage – an essential element in strategy leadership and management. From a great 2004 essay in *Fast Company,* courage takes on new meaning:

> To search for and find the truth.
>
> To confront risks and hard choices.
>
> To sacrifice, endure, persevere.
>
> To take the high road, with honor.
>
> To force and enforce business change.

Courage is catalytic in strategy leadership and in every aspect of the leadership and management domain. When we examine common strategy problems and constraints, this dimension of resolve has to be a development target. Courage and resolve go together in the prosecution of strategy.

> In every endeavor, great and small, courage is a facet of doing the hard work of strategy that demands leaps of faith. Those leaps require courage, hedged with insight, trust, guts and for many, deep abiding faith in the possible. Courage fires the soul to make decisions.

Energy and Spark – the element that drives individuals and groups to move and keep moving. The combustible fuel that sustains and engages resolve. Part of the inspiration equation that keeps individuals and groups on task and on target – focused on business results. Energy is built and learned through practice and resolve. Energy is depleted and restored in practice.

Accountability – from personal and moral resolve, to project and business covenants, to group and team charters, to budgetary and standards compliance, we find the practice of *accountabable thought* framed in many ways. The resolve to be accountable, to pursue accountable thought and behavior is part of the commitment puzzle that defines individual and group credibility and purpose. Accountability and responsibility go together.

True Passion – more than buzz and noise about purpose, and more than drama about business ideas. The practice of passion in true form and engagement is based on deeply held convictions and motivation. True passion is resolute. True passion is enduring and tough to quench. True passion in practice is contagious among people who are resolved to pursue similar principles, intentions, standards and purposes. Passion shapes inspiration and courage. Passion seeks interest and trust, and it connects through essential cultural and sub-cultural beliefs. Tom Peters describes the next level of passion as "*Bloody-Mindedness*," or fierce focus on impact.

Leadership research at the individual level suggests that people who show passionate practices in their responsibilities possess personal qualities developed in their self-leadership experience. These people are:

> Focused and disciplined to pursue critical goals.
>
> Organized and oriented around key priorities.
>
> Responsive to private, personal, internal rewards.
>
> Open to technical, social and ecomonic signals.

Sims and Manz address these ideas in their "super-leadership" work. Passion in practice is woven with resolve across the spectrum of everyday thought and behavior. True passion is a connector between people. True passion brings ideas, people and plans together in often extraordinary ways. Passion engages, and engagement is powerful in strategy.

Respect – an essential element that is a basic practice in successful organizations, large and small. Respect is not blind compliance or submission to order and authority. Respect is the practice of learning to discern and engage issues that contribute to success, under challenging conditions. Respect supports resolve. Respect is a part of the human value system, the basis on which we manage organizational relationships. Respect is the fulcrum of exchange and engagement.

Adaptability – essential element in a changing and complex world. The practice of adaptability involves more, however. Knowing what to change for...opportunities and episodic issues. Knowing the right scope and focus of change. Knowing how and when to change. Knowing what to expect with the risks and rewards, barriers and blocks of change. Adaptive capacity and judgment come from practice. The resolve to adapt is a state of thought and behavior that balances choices with known and unknown conditions. The embrace of readiness is a fundamental practice theme.

Curious Work – some individuals and groups are inspired by curiosity, and curious work is what they practice. Doing things out of curiosity expands the realm of options and potential choices. Curious work poses questions without answers and ideas that may or may not deserve action. Curious work challenges existing norms and opens dialogue on uncharted ground. It tests the basic rules of strategy and culture, and in some instances, curious work exposes flaws as well as truths in organizational resolve. Curious work may be highly disciplined or very informal. It can be expressed as:

Scenario analysis and planning is applied curiosity.

Innovation research requires sustainable curiosity.

Business process and system planning takes curiosity.

Developing new customer demands takes curiosity.

Managing collaborative projects requires curiosity.

Reframing business models takes curiosity.

Curious work also reflects on the *positive and opportunistic nature* of individuals and groups across the organization. Positive thought succeeds far more often than scoffing, skeptical, critical, negative signals of individuals and groups. Optimism has value-creating power, and it drives the people who engage in curious work. Positive and opportunistic works in strategy.

Can a company learn resolve through practice? Surely, we believe it can, and we believe that practice makes not perfect, but resolved to succeed under the often complex and dynamic conditions of business. Can a state of resolve explain the differences between competing companies, as a marker of success or failure? Yes, absolutely it can. Resolve builds on itself, and in the process, business cultures are transformed with the practice.

RESOLVE TO SUCCEED

At some point in the analysis, business success is gauged in core measures of growth, performance and change. In some organizations, these measures are shaped by the evolution of market categories, or patterns of technical evolution, or the shift in economic structure that defines how new economic and strategic value is created. Success is caused by many factors – good strategy direction, integration and execution. The resolve to succeed is focused on business results. Impact means something to every company in terms of growth, performance and change.

GROWTH IMPACT AND AGENDA

Resolving to grow a business is a matter of setting the balance and blend of strategy, resources, culture and structure for growth. To succeed in driving growth impact, companies get prepared and resolved to address the issues summarized in Exhibit 08.A below. These are critical issues everywhere.

Exhibit 08.A

DRIVING GROWTH IMPACT

The Challenge...	Resolve Agenda...
Define the Nature of Growth Conditions for the Company... Near-Term Direction Long-Term Direction	Resolve to understand the avenues for growth that make sense for the company. The resolve to explore options.
Define the Growth Practice and Agenda that Make Sense... Competence to Grow Capacity for Growth	Resolve to engage the key assets and orientations that enable the company to grow. The resolve to develop.
Define the Choices for Growth that Best Fit the Plan Agenda... Priority Management Portfolio Development	Resolve to appropriate the company's resources and assets for effective growth. The resolve to engage.

Notes: From internal studies on Business Development Strategy, working papers and protocol. The resolve agenda is a key part of the sequence of organization awareness, understanding and engagement of strategy, across and throughout the organization. Driving growth is an entrepreneurial and opportunistic discipline, and in some cases a key to survival.

AVENUES FOR BUSINESS GROWTH

The resolve to grow any business starts with a reality check on the nature of growth challenges and opportunities. In most market categories, real growth comes from no less than four sources. One of those sources of growth is share conquest. Through *share conquest*, a company takes business from its competitors. Share conquest also relates to movement in margin capture and control in the exchange structures that exist in supply chains and demand chains. In effect, share conquest moves can take place between stakeholders at the producer, channel and customer level. Share conquest can be defined in revenue, margin or capital terms. It can be gauged in value-added and value-capture terms. A company can have margin share conquest even while it relinquishes revenue share or customer share.

Share conquest is tough business in most market categories. It usually requires investments in reseating customer and network relationship. Under the common rules of market engagement, that typically means something in terms of product or service differentiation or operational efficiency advantage or shifts in customer and channel relationships. However, share conquest can be funded and exploited with changes in business models and practices. These changes can be radical or evolutionary. In effect, they reframe the rules of the market game. Exhibit 08.B on the following page provides a few examples of share conquest in the context of resolve for business growth. As a reminder, case examples are perishable.

A company could choose to relinquish share as part of a broader agenda to realign its business forces and portfolio. This is sometimes done to exit market categories that are not well-aligned with the evolving business. Rather than commit resources to a category, the company may effectively divest, reassigning resources to a category with greater prospects for growth, performance and change. A company could also choose to invest in a business category for revenue share purposes, with assumed sacrifice of margin share or share of the profit base of the category. These moves are often made in the name of capacity leverage and fixed cost coverage. However, depending on market and operating conditions, these moves put a company on a slippery slope. Margins are critical, and share wars put margins in the breach of profitable, capital-efficient and sustainable growth. Consider the rules of market structure and competitive systems.

Exhibit 08.B

SHARE CONQUEST GROWTH IDEAS

Parlux is a fragrance producer with a portfolio of youth-oriented brands and global market reach. Targeted co-brand development and powerful channel position have girded the share growth of Parlux. www.parlux.com

Nucor has reset the competition stage with several moves that have yielded technology-based and capacity-based advantages in an often turbulent market. Service and cost advantages enable Nucor's share growth, sustained advantage and strategic leverage. www.nucor.com

Target has evolved as the mass market retail player with success in a field occupied with traditional incumbents like Sears and K-Mart, überstore Wal-Mart, big-and-mid-box stores for everything. Target has harnessed design for the masses to grow share in a competitive sector. www.target.com

Samsung has evolved as one of the most innovative and aggressive electronic and appliance products companies in the world, focusing on digital convergence trends and experience-oriented market needs. Samsung is pushing competitive frontiers in its served markets. www.samsung.com

Adobe defines its business in terms relating to document management, from creation to access, to storage and transport. The foundations of content software enable Adobe to address the changing needsets of context stakeholders in every sector. www.adobe.com

ConAgra is an evolving, multi-brand, multi-category packaged food product company with a focused acquisition and conglomerate strategy agenda. Targeting attractive categories with good margin potential and marketing with leverage potential is key. www.conagra.com

Strayer is a private, commercial, adult education service provider that has tapped into business and technical subject matter and delivery models that now reach more than 20,000 students who are seeking quality, access and convenience. www.strayereducation.com

Notes: These examples are intended to illustrate different avenues for business growth, including situations that involve other business challenges. This is not a benchmark or best company roster, but rather, a contextual look at a few, very different growth agenda examples. Attractive share conquest examples may be perishable.

A second source of business development is *demand-based growth* in a market category. Demand-based growth happens when technical, market, social and economic forces come together in ways that increase the consumption of products and services. This is natural growth in the purest sense. Competitors share in the demand-based evolution of market categories. Customers enjoy greater access to products and services that become better, cheaper, safer, smarter, faster and cooler than previous options. Exhibit 08.C below provides some contemporary examples of demand-based growth.

Exhibit 08.C

DEMAND-BASED GROWTH

Cisco has enjoyed the derived demand growth curves of network-enabled markets and the connectivity economy. The company's brand is synonymous with data network design, management and control...strong foundations with demand-based growth engines. www.cisco.com

Qualcomm, another tech sector company, has a stake in the tech standard that is incorporated into most mobile phones, granting a slice of a growth frontier. As standards evolve, however, Qualcomm will need to cast beyond its current standards-shaping agenda. www.qualcomm.com

Cummins builds engines for big equipment trucks, a market which has experienced ups and downs over the years. The current market is experiencing strong growth, reflecting global business trends and capital patterns in transportation gear markets. www.cummins.com

Stryker serves patients and healthcare providers with products that enable surgical reconstruction of joints and bones. With an aging population interested in quality of life, this is a demand-based growth sector that has strong legs and momentum. www.stryker.com

Eclipse Aviation builds light, compact jet aircraft. Demand growth for inexpensive, small jets is driven by changes in travel needs and the service level options available in private aviation. Demand is expected to triple in the 2007–2017 horizon. www.eclipseaviation.com

Notes: These examples are intended to illustrate different avenues for business growth, including situations that involve other business challenges. This is not a benchmark or best company roster, but rather, a contextual look at a few, very different growth agenda examples. These demand-based examples may be perishable.

Category-edge growth is a third source of growth. When a company extends its product and service reach across existing categories or market spaces, it pushes the edges of its core and peripheral business. The category strategy decisions a company faces have a lot to do with its growth agenda, and its strategy foundations. Category-edges are sometimes hard to discern and define. What may seem like a natural and attractive adjacency that matches company and customer interests can turn into a real problem. Conversely, companies can stumble into lucrative trans-category opportunities and find themselves in a growth mode without the pretense of serious planning. They may get lucky, but remember; success goes to the prepared and resolved. Category-edge opportunities involve business change.

Category-edge growth avenues have been driven by producers seeking to provide more complete and differentiated solutions for customers and market intermediaries. They've also been driven by channel and intermediary entities with motives of category dominance in their demand chain and supply chain positions. Consider the impact of e-business systems on the structure, characteristics and movement of a category.

Category-edge growth is usually triggered by some combination of technical, social, market or economic moves. Technical forces put the value of safety features into automobiles and they are in the process of transforming personal entertainment through digital appliances and sourcing networks. Social and market forces have caused growth and demand shifts in everything from transportation to food service, housing, leisure, healthcare, education, security, information and personal expression. Demographic forces influence the market for household appliances in developing country markets and healthcare delivery in advancing country markets. Economic forces alter the balance of demand and supply in different ways, at different levels. The economics of household goods have been reframed by major changes in the retail network over the last 20 years. The economics of mobility and connection have reduced a remote globe to a smaller community of inter-related market systems.

Category-edge growth takes place in the context of market change and evolution. Exhibit 08.D provides some examples of category-edge growth, reflecting on the simple and complex variations of business evolution. Sustaining and disruptive shifts happen at the category level. This is an emerging, major area of strategy research interest focusing on networked enterprises in a collaborative, highly-connected business world.

Exhibit 08.D

CATEGORY-EDGE GROWTH

Google serves its stakeholders along several market fronts and in the process, it pushes existing and emerging market boundaries with customer experiences that are convenient and efficient by design. The category edges for Google are dynamic. www.google.com

Siemens pulls together diagnostic and information technology with process and program solutions in healthcare delivery to better address patient care quality, provider efficiency and capital integration. The category edges are blurring with growth prospects. www.medical.siemens.com

Coleman provides a wide array of outdoor lifestyle products that reflect on changing leisure-time boundaries. Products for backyard and leisure experiences join products for off-grid comfort and food prep in back-up/emergency categories. www.coleman.com

Autodesk serves a range of needs that stem from strong partnerships and collaboration between and among source companies, supply chain networks, design teams, core producers, service providers and others in the concept-to-support value chain. www.autodesk.com

Notes: These examples are intended to illustrate different avenues for business growth, including situations that involve other business challenges. This is not a benchmark or best company roster, but rather, a contextual look at a few, very different growth agenda examples. Attractive category-edge examples are perishable.

A fourth source of business growth is *diversification* in the scope and focus of the company's existing product, market and economic base. Business diversification is most often marked by shifts in the business model that are intended to tap into new opportunities – beyond the platforms and foundations of the established core business. Technical conditions or market and economic conditions could be the rationale for this growth avenue. These same issues frame the relative risks of growth by diversification moves. Under conditions where the basic business is without growth prospects of any kind, diversification may be the best option. As a mode for creating new strategic and economic value, however, diversification is much like starting a new business, with the attendant strategy leadership and management concerns and risks. Diversification has its pros and cons that merit review.

Diversification makes sense for many slower growth businesses, but it should be examined against a company's options for category-edge growth. Moving on growth options at the edges of the core business provides diversification benefits without some of the attendant risks of diversification. Peripheral and collateral moves for growth can also conserve and leverage key business resources under the banner of diversification.

Examples of diversification for "sensible growth" are provided in Exhibit 08.E below. These examples should be considered in their full historical context, as business diversification can be a significant destiny-changing strategy pathway, altering the company forever.

Exhibit 08.E

DIVERSIFICATION FOR BUSINESS GROWTH

FedEx has evolved with changing technical, market and economic conditions through shifts in its product and service portfolio. Adding package freight capacity and the Kinkos service delivery/access systems give FedEx new kinds of market and customer reach. www.fedex.com

Danaher is an evolving manufacturing and services provider with a series of strategic platforms that bring order and focus to its broad portfolio of solutions. The company espouses a proprietary business systems discipline for planning and control. www.danaher.com

Symantec frames its business in the context of managing digital assets, security and storage solutions. Diversification for Symantec involves new avenues for integrating data management and security, aided by a combination of emergent information technology and user applications across a broader range of commerce. www.symantec.com

Sharp has evolved to become a key player in appliances, business products, entertainment systems, mobile electronics and a variety of related consumer and commercial products armed with some key technology assets. Sharp appears to leverage its anchor positions well. www.sharpusa.com

Notes: These examples are intended to illustrate different avenues for business growth, including situations that involve other business challenges. This is not a benchmark or best company roster, but rather, a contextual look at a few, very different growth agenda examples. Attractive diversification examples are perishable.

New economic and strategic value is created through business growth, and as we have suggested, there are at least four different forms of growth for the business enterprise. Share conquest, demand-based growth, category-edge strategy and diversification provide most companies with a broad palette for moving the business toward new value creation. We view most forms and models for growth in a positive, responsible and progressive context. Sustainability is not a zero-sum game in the business world. Growth is a positive force in social and economic development and it's a positive force in business innovation for stakeholder benefit. The absence of growth is a risk factor, and there are difficult social consequences of a lower growth business and economic system. This connects business and social ecology.

PERFORMANCE IMPACT AND AGENDA

Resolving to enhance the performance of a business is a matter of setting an agenda that targets key areas that can help drive new value creation. In Chapters 04, 05 and 06, we covered a wide range of performance ideas that relate to a company's natural goals…

> Financial Performance
>
> Competitive Advantage
>
> Customer Considerations
>
> Corporate Stewardship

The resolve to perform better is an ongoing journey for any business unit or company. Finding and securing options for performance enhancement is the work of the entire organization, as well as its strategic partners.

The quest for **better, smarter, leaner, faster** is often interpreted through an operational lens, focusing on continuous business process improvement, etc. Sometimes, performance improvement has its genesis in product and service enhancement. Sometimes, its origins are shaped by supply chain networks and systems. Options for going to market and improvements in demand chain relationships can sometimes drive critical enhancements in business performance. The ongoing resolve to discover and exploit quality, cost and resource advantage is the heart of performance enhancement. Exhibit 08.F on the following page suggests the main pathways for generating business performance advantage. Again, the general context for this discussion is the creation of substantially new strategic and economic value.

Exhibit 08.F

DRIVING PERFORMANCE IMPACT

The Challenge...	Resolve Agenda...
Define the Performance Marks Desirable for the Company... Near-Term Direction Long-Term Direction	Resolve to understand the targets of performance that are realistic, reachable. The resolve to explore.
Define the Priority Practices that Must Drive Performance... Performance Ideals Performance Levers	Resolve to engage the key drivers of performance at every level of the enterprise. Exchange and enhance.
Define the Specific Agenda for Performance Enhancement... Priority of Selections Portfolio Management	Resolve to put resources and effort into the right programs, for business results. Mix and improvise.

Notes: From Dewar Sloan studies on Business Development strategy working papers and protocol. The resolve agenda is a key part of the sequence of organization awareness, understanding and engagement of strategy, across the company.

Much of the focus in performance enhancement, as we've approached it separately from corporate growth and change, is about operational issues and efficiencies. For most companies, we can explore five basic areas as the sources of performance enhancement. These are outlined on the following page. However, Exhibit 08.F suggests a strategy leadership and management agenda that provides for *priority selection practices* and the blending of resources and action sequences. While most companies have performance prospects geared to revenue growth and volume leverage, our intent here is to focus on issues in operating performance, independent of business growth and change strategy. Surely, a company can grow itself out of a performance problem. But, performance problems can also destroy the energy base and resources necessary for business growth and change.

Making strategy happen involves an understanding of what the company *could do* relative to performance, and what it really *must do* in order to evolve successfully. Performance impact scores and measures in many ways, reflecting margins, expenses, capital and operating cash flow.

Margin enhancement is a huge performance issue in every company because its impact reflects straight through to the bottom line, given the nature of sound business models and structures. Margins can be enhanced in many ways; performance gains are shaped by:

Quality Advantage. Managing quality at appropriate levels reduces relative costs and increases price leverage. In other words, the right quality platform helps realize gross margins that derive from price and cost mechanics.

Network Advantage. Managing supply chain networks and demand chain networks is part of the margin equation. Companies get to *better, smarter, leaner, faster* status through these network relationships, contributing to greater margins and better margin leverage.

Costing Advantage. Managing direct and indirect costs is surely relevant in every company. Changes in commodity costs can pose headaches and/or windfalls for producers and resellers. Operating costs impact margins directly, and non-operating costs are margin forces as well.

Pricing Advantage. Managing the fundamental spread between realized price and actual cost is absolutely critical to margin enhancement. Balancing variable and fixed cost realities with demand conditions is rarely a simple task.

Program Advantage. Managing the critical development resources and operational programs that are behind product plans, service delivery, customer management, channel relationships, sourcing development are key drivers.

These advantages play out in terms of competitive differentiation, which in turn, materializes in the form of margin enhancement. Part of this stems from basic economics. Part of it evolves from advanced methods and disciplines that focus on quality management, process leverage, pricing models and a range of so-called network effects. The quest for enhanced performance is a continuous journey in the life of a business. Better, faster, leaner, smarter. One caution, however, companies will realize diminishing returns on performance improvement without a growth platform.

EXPENSE MANAGEMENT

Expense management is a general discipline that has three elements. The first element is effective spending, which means spending at the appropriate level, tempo and speed in operations and programs. The second element is austerity and cost-containment where and when appropriate. The third element is spending innovation, a concept that is often born of necessity. Some would call this clever spending or turbo-spend.

Expense norms and inertia are part of every organization, and they usually reflect a combination of functional and process conventions that have served the company in its past. When expense management takes on a more strategic perspective, some important and powerful things can begin to happen. Better expense models can emerge. Different operating, marketing, development, field, system, administrative and program spending models can reshape effectiveness and efficiency. Spending models are discovered and rediscovered in practice and everyday experience.

Expense and capital options can emerge. Different expense and capital alternatives can influence the capabilities of a company in many important ways. These manifest across functions and processes:

> Product Development Cycle and Break-Even Times
>
> Marketing, Selling and Service Delivery Costs
>
> Administrative Costs and Expense Amortization
>
> General Expense Rates with Programs and Projects

Expense rates and spend timing can improve. Different spending schedules and spend appropriability can alter a company's approach to solving problems and matching challenges. Order and timing can make a difference in expense management and appropriation.

Expense management does not mean cost-constraint alone. Expense management means the diligent and disciplined remix of spending in general areas above and below the margin line in ways that create new strategic and economic value. There is a difference between good control and smart spending, and this is an interesting lesson to be learned in the everyday work of people across the contemporary business organization.

CAPITAL MANAGEMENT

Capital management is defined here in terms of both economic and strategic capital. Economic capital is typically addressed as technical property, working capital and operating resources of the business. Strategic capital is that which has tangible and intangible value in the form of knowledge assets, technical competence, category and brand assets, talent and human capital, supply chain and demand chain networks, and other similar assets. Here is the principal question in the business performance discussion... *How well is capital used? And further, how could capital be used even better?*

Capital usage is a performance catalyst and a success driver. As we look out across the contemporary business landscape, there are two questions:

01. To what degree are we tapping the true capital base of the company, or what is our rate of capital utilization? What are the deterrents to enhanced capital utilization? Capital leverage?

    This is a question about capital usage alternatives and capital deployment practices and procedures over time, through networks, and relationships. What about collaboration?

02. To what degree is the usage of strategic and economic capital effective in creating new strategic and economic value? What are the trade-offs? The boundaries? The return on effort?

    This is a question of investment and operational effectiveness of the company's capital base and resource appropriations. What about cash? Flow and working capital?

Most companies make plans with assumptions of resource and capital scarcity rather than abundance. This bias provides order and control, but it can be blind to options and opportunities. With the evolutionary changes in play with e-business and net-centric enterprise, the very nature of capital management as a business discipline continues to mutate. Different ways of dealing with strategic and economic assets will continue to emerge in response to technical, market, social and economic trends. Ideas substitute for economic and network capital in emerging business models and can disrupt the order of industry structure, recasting the company's framework for growth, performance and change. This is a moving, dynamic frontier.

PERFORMANCE AS A MOVING TARGET

We routinely ask executives to look at the performance indicators and prerogatives of companies outside their served industry. Interesting things happen in that discussion. Cement producers see new and applicable ideas in the work of hardware retailers. Transportation firms see new performance themes that originate in healthcare delivery. Widget makers see pathways for innovation in the work of solution developers. Just when a company seems quite set with its performance agenda and measures, something comes along in the form of new ideas and applications that can jeopardize or optimize the margin, expense and capital management model of the business. Business enterprise is dynamic, and *readiness for change* is clearly important.

CHANGE IMPACT AND AGENDA

Resolving to change a business is loaded with hope, chance, need, trust, faith, risk, fear and loathing. It's all of these and more. Change management is a given adventure for companies with intentions for long-term success. For troubled companies, change management is a pathway to survival. For emerging companies, change management is the lifeblood of true entreship. For evolving companies, mature and otherwise, change management with all its attendant issues is a source of new economic and strategic value. Exhibit 08.G outlines the realities of change strategy, similar to those expressed for growth and performance strategy in Exhibits 08.A and 08.F.

Change management is like growth and performance in that it requires a blend of strategic preparation and resolve to set the foundations for impact. In the abundant research on change management, several themes stand as important enablers, drivers and servant elements. Understanding the relevance of change for the organization is a starting point. The need for change and meaning of the change agenda is critical to individuals and groups. Employees need to know the relevance of change.

Understanding the pathways for change helps inform the organization about the ways and means of the change adventure, as well as the conditions that are likely to characterize the change experience. Understanding the intended outcomes and continuous evolution of the change agenda is paramount to generating new value. Change is simply a success route, not an end in and of itself; it's part of an organic business practice.

213

Exhibit 08.G

DRIVING CHANGE IMPACT

The Challenge...	Resolve Agenda...
Define the Nature of Change Desirable for the Company... Near-Term Direction Long-Term Direction	Resolve to understand the reasons for change and the broader purpose of change. The resolve to evolve.
Define the Change Practices and Agenda that Make Sense... Change Competence Capacity for Change	Resolve to engage people and resources in the kind of change engines that work. Exchange and embolden.
Define the Choices for Change that Best Fit the Plan Agenda... Priority of Concerts Portfolio Management	Resolve to match the right change initiatives with the right people and assets. The resolve to reset plans.

Notes: From Dewar Sloan studies on Business Development Strategy working papers and protocol. The resolve premise is a key part of the sequence of organization awareness, understanding and engagement of strategy, across and beyond the company, its supply chain and demand chain networks, etc.

Our general approach to change management has been tempered by experience across a wide range of business sectors and market categories. *The one constant in change management is the power of prepared and resolved.* Companies with prepared and resolved cultures are better suited to create new strategic and economic value through change...change in product and service platforms, change in market categories and customers, and change in business resources and systems. These companies have many advantages in a complex and dynamic business world, with thought and behavior that drive value creation and success. They are *change-ready and change-smart.* They hunger for dialogue on change. They find inspiration in the contemplation of change. Business change itself causes some heartburn and anxiety for the organization. So what? Change is a potential source of energy, and learning takes place through and with change practice. Business thought and behavior are more broadly engaged in the experience of change strategy. Change is baked into the culture, passion and mindset of strong players.

ANTICIPATION AND FOREWARD MINDSET

One of the requisite ideas in change leadership and management is basic business foresight. How do we anticipate the evolution of the business? How is the demand for our products and services changing? How is the customer's landscape changing? How are the boundaries of our market categories changing? How is competition changing? How are the supply chains and networks of the business changing? With all of this, how do we prepare for the evolution of the company and the implications that will be re-shaped with the business? Who anticipates, and who responds?

This kind of anticipation is at the heart of being prepared and resolved to succeed. It takes a kind of energy that is often part of company cultures that have been honed over time by shifting revenue patterns and business model concerns. In these cultures, individuals and groups tend to be more sensitive to changing business conditions and strategic implications. The realities of change and response to change are captured through *the lens of experience, a sense of preparation and everyday resolve.* People with greater business experience tend to be more attuned to the practice of anticipating and responding to change. Experience, once again is the great teacher.

Anticipation helps steady the thought and behavior of people at every level of the organization. It helps people engage in the strategic direction of the company. It enables the organization as it goes about the often gritty, messy work of strategy integration. Anticipation energizes the strategy execution process in general, and it helps drive specific efforts that bring adaptive plans, fresh ideas and engaged people together in practice.

POSITIVE FORCE IN CHANGE

Anticipation opens a company to uncertainty. For a positive culture that tackles uncertainty with an *optimistic edge,* that can mean a positive force for change. Positive thought and behavior is energy that enables productive change. Positive energy trumps negative energy. That is a huge intangible in successful companies that face challenges and constraints, threats and risks, barriers and battlefronts. Positive thought is a catalyst in culture and strategy. It serves the prepared and resolved organization in many ways.

COVENANT OF DETERMINATION

Another important theme in change leadership and management is the determined focus of the organization to evolve as an enterprise. In this context, we look at the term covenant as a strategic and cultural promise to drive business growth, performance and change. Covenants can be very powerful sources of inspiration, energy and principle.

What does such a promise contain, and how does it shape strategic thought and behavior? We find *covenant themes* in many forms, shaping the determination of groups and individuals...

> **Survival motives and covenants –** in new ventures with relatively high risks and rewards, determination is part of the covenant and part of the energy that enables people to crank through great challenges with a positive, powerful approach to the strategic agenda of the company.

> **Innovation motives and covenants –** in development work and resource integration work, finding new and better ways to improve the business or grow revenues is part of the covenant. Great determination to get things done, and to tackle work for meaningful results is energy for the organization.

> **Endurance motives and covenants –** most organizations have periods of endurance when things are difficult and the challenges are intense. Getting through these periods can be a matter of sheer will and determination. The grace and resolve to continue, to press-on regardless.

Determination is a cultural attribute that is central to the strategic agenda of companies that are prepared and resolved to succeed. The covenant to evolve is a strategic and cultural ingredient that is critical to organizational engagement in strategy. People get engaged most completely when the covenant brings the meaning and relevance of strategy to them at a personal level. Skeptics and scoffers might ask, **what's in this for me?** The covenant of the organization is a rational and positive promise which answers that question, making strategy meaningful and relevant to those who must engage in the company's strategic agenda. Determination is always a personal investment, but covenants are born of group purpose.

THE GOAL IN MIND

Resolve in groups and individuals is motivated by a variety of themes and goals. Business survival is a strong motivator. Our friend, Lèon Danco, suggests that enterprise survival is an especially powerful and personal motivator in private companies. Contemporary research on corporate stewardship infers that business survival may be the utmost social responsibility of the company. Interesting premise. Business survival is a matter of evolution, *planned evolution is a social covenant, and the goal is ongoing value creation.* This makes the importance of your strategic agenda even greater.

SUMMARY NOTES AND THOUGHTS

Business success is realized through practice. Practice itself is a matter of preparation and resolve. For growth, development and change strategy, nothing is automatic. Everything takes serious work and a sound agenda. This is the hard work of looking ahead, planning ahead, moving ahead.

Throughout this book, we've explored the basic ideas that shape how companies become prepared and resolved to succeed with their strategies for business growth, performance and change. This chapter highlights *the art of strategic practice* – the everyday thought and behavior of strategy leadership and management, at every level. The resolve to succeed is seeded in different motives. But the strategic and cultural covenant of the organization is what brings thought and behavior together as a base of energy. It connects people together with the resolve to succeed through engagement at the personal level, the group level and the enterprise level.

To put this energy into everyday strategic practice, individuals and groups need a sense of the meaning and relevance of the company's growth, performance and change agenda. This conveys purpose and intention. It also conveys realities and implications for the business. Getting people and their groups prepared and resolved to be part of the strategic agenda is the *practice of business.* We direct, integrate and execute the strategic agenda through everyday business practice. We develop people and processes through everyday business practice. We compete in the marketplace through everyday business practice. Companies innovate, improve and learn through practice. Business success is served by the covenant to evolve, and that is framed by the ways we help our organizations get prepared and resolved.

09

MAJOR APPLICATIONS

The issues and ideas presented in this book are intended to support more effective strategy leadership and management. For most companies, that means a different approach to strategic thought and behavior.

COMMENTS FOR GOVERNANCE

Directors of public and private companies are called upon to take more interest and responsibility on issues of strategic oversight. But, what does that really mean? Surely there are compliance issues that need to be addressed. However, strategic oversight is really another issue. If directors were fully engaged in the company's strategic management and leadership agenda, they would already be focused on the specific elements of the agenda...

Strategy direction – governance concerns would include the credibility of business development and improvement investments along with the company's value creation goals.

Strategy integration – governance concerns would include the nature and impact of resource and priority management that supports dynamic capacity and implementation.

Strategy execution – governance concerns would include the connection of people, ideas, assets, options and plans that cause things to happen...and drive business results.

Some might argue that boards should not meddle in the details of strategy integration and execution, as that is the domain of executives. Not true. The agenda for strategy leadership and management is a collective agenda. Boards need to understand the elements that are bonded together in ideas that contribute to and detract from the work of making strategy happen.

Directors in public and private companies are held to greater levels of scrutiny today in the wake of corporate misbehavior and economic transitions fueled by technology and geopolitical trends. There is renewed focus on compliance, and companies are adjusting to new standards and reporting disciplines. Attention to strategy issues often lags however. This is where we need to call upon governance and management to refocus as well. The framework we've provided is very appropriate for governance oversight. It supports strategic awareness, understanding and engagement at the director level, and it enables a functional role for governance that is properly scoped and focused for practical strategic oversight.

Directors are called to serve in governance with their experience, knowledge, judgment and connections. Good directors on boards are active contributors to strategic and economic value, as several authors and observers have noted. Research on governance and strategy suggests that directors must bring perspective, conversation, evaluation and creative alternatives to the table when matters of strategy, direction, integration and execution are engaged. Outside directors, in particular, carry the burden of gauging the realities of the company's strategic agenda and the consequences of guiding the agenda. Research for the monograph *Boards and Strategy* suggests that directors and management are not fully connected on the broader framework for strategy direction, integration and execution. There are political and cultural reasons for the disconnect. More to the point, however, there is very little experience in crossing this agenda with any real depth of conversation.

Strategy leadership and management can benefit greatly from the insights and oversight of directors who engage at the governance level. Here is a short list of the scope and focus of governance concerns and themes that apply to oversight of the strategic agenda...

Strategy Direction – Issues for Directors

What business forces shape the company?

What is the sustenance of our business model?

What is our capacity for growth and change?

What is our basis of intention and principle?

What resources shape our strategy options?

What kind of business evolution makes sense?

Strategy Integration – Issues for Directors

What business processes shape integration?

What resource platforms shape integration?

What kind of benchstrength do we have in place?

What constraints pose blocks to integration?

What are the potential hazards on the horizon?

What could help leverage our integration work?

What elements comprise our networks?

Strategy Execution – Issues for Directors

What are the links between cause and effect?

What are the plans that hold execution together?

What are the plans that need improvisation?

What measures count and what measures guide?

What shapes our capacity for great execution?

What blocks our capacity for great execution?

These are broad questions that belong in the governance discussion about strategy. The discussion between governance and management is an attractive melting pot of perspectives, experience, provocation and constructive arguments. It puts strategic oversight into a format that supports strategic leadership and behavior. This kind of oversight is good for all company stakeholders – investors, employees, customers and suppliers. It helps create new strategic and economic value, and it helps engage people in sound, creative thought about strategy direction, integration and execution.

Our current research on *Boards and Strategy* focuses on the nature of targeted, dynamic conversations that help raise critical strategic issues at the governance level. These conversations are part of the strategic thought and behavior assets of the company, and they are a significant resource of value. Boards must support these conversations with active engagement. When they do, the foundations for trust and energy grow between governance and management. These are important building blocks in the strategic agenda for growth, performance and change. They help drive the creation of new strategic and economic value, and they frame company perpetuation. *Boardroom Insider* chief Ralph Ward advances this view.

COMMENTS FOR SENIOR EXECUTIVES

Conventional wisdom holds the CEO ultimately responsible for strategy. Supported by senior management and staff, the CEO is supposed to craft the vision and agenda for strategy, and so it goes. Our framework takes a different avenue. While the CEO is clearly the lead player in strategy, the collective energy and knowledge of the organization is necessary for effective strategy direction, integration and execution. The role of the CEO under this premise is much deeper than calling the program for the company's annual strategic planning exercise, or calling in the consultants to put some new, hyped aura on the strategy. Consider these roles:

> The CEO provides a working framework that connects the interests of governance with the conditions of the business. This framework must address the creation and sustenance of strategic and economic value...the main thesis of the agenda.

> The CEO builds energy into this framework in ways that drive strategic awareness, understanding and engagement at every level of the organization. The CEO sets exchanges that address company principles, intentions, culture and challenges. These provide the basic leadership and management footings that connect strategy direction, integration and execution.

> The CEO sets a structure in place that encourages groups and individuals to take responsible roles in the agenda for business growth, performance and change. This is more critical than delegation and compliance work. It's where and how leadership and management are dispersed across the enterprise.

What are the essential ingredients here? First, we need to establish strategic *expectations* from the governance level, down through the organization. Second, we need to *engage people, plans and action* that match the strategic agenda, meaning we need an agenda that makes sense to everybody. Third, we need *leadership that inspires and management that connects people, goals and action.* Without these ingredients, the CEO is headed down a very bumpy road, with a very insecure load. Senior executives carry the burden of leadership in their everyday roles as teachers and players. They must set the tone and pace of the strategic agenda.

222

EXECUTIVE READINESS

Companies groom their senior executives to take on ever-greater levels of managerial and leadership responsibility. They invest in the development of technical, managerial and conceptual skills of these executives. They invest in all kinds of support to guide and counsel executives in the journey of strategy leadership and management. Are we ever ready? Or, is this really a continuous journey in learning? Readiness is relative, of course.

Younger managers are made ready through experience and learning. They gather proper knowledge, judgment, competence, character intuition and inspiration from sound experience and learning. More seasoned senior managers are made ready in the same manner. More experience, and more learning. Executives are works in progress, shaped by learning circumstances. The readiness of senior managers and executives can be gauged in many ways, and these reflect a host of leadership and managerial habits that are typical in highly successful organizations. These habits are learned and incorporated through experience, circumstances, barriers and conditions. Executive readiness is reflected in two questions:

> Are the key executives prepared to lead and manage
> the strategic agenda throughout the entire organization?
> Are they resolved to do what is necessary to deliver on the
> growth, performance and change themes of the strategic agenda?

Built into these two fundamental questions is the idea that senior managers must move the entire organization, with its given resources and its given market challenges. With its cultures and subcultures, its problems and its wants. With its structure and its relationships, and its capacities. This is where things can get really tough, because senior executives are the ultimate coaches of the strategic agenda. They convey what it really means to be prepared and resolved. They provide the context for strategy direction, integration and execution. They match the expectations, behaviors and performance of the organization with a much deeper view of the natural goals of business. Emotional maturity, technical competence, personal character and other factors contribute to executive readiness. The strategic thought and behavior we've outlined is an executive development imperative. It's part of the agenda for sustainable business success and part of the engine for growth, performance and change. Senior executives engage the practice.

COMMENTS FOR MANAGEMENT

Management at the program, function and process levels of a business is where the strategic agenda comes together. In these areas, the translation of strategic direction, integration and execution takes place in everyday thought and behavior. How well that translation takes place depends on many factors, not the least of which is the preparation and resolve of leadership and management at every level, particularly the mid-organization levels where the minding and grinding of the strategy agenda takes place.

The interworkings of people, action plans and impact are pivotal to the company's engagement of its strategic agenda. Managers are in the formula in many critical ways. They're the owners of many roles and tasks that spell the difference between success and defeat. Here in brief form are some of these managerial roles and tasks:

> **Engagement** with senior management and governance in the strategic agenda of the company scopes the rationale, the natural goals and challenges of enterprise, and plans for creating new strategic and economic value in key projects.

> **Collaboration** across the many program, functional, business processes and resource boundaries. Collaboration is more than simple contact and control. Collaboration requires a strategic and cultural sense of the following:

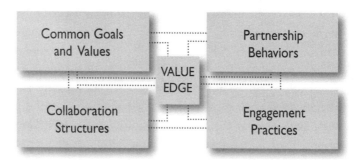

> **Leadership** at all levels, and in all corners of the business is faced with the demands of becoming better, smarter, leaner and faster. Engagement in the strategic agenda and effective collaboration are critical ingredients in the strategy work of managers across the entire organization, and often beyond.

Engagement that connects individuals and project teams across and beyond the organization is key. The challenges of engagement and collaboration are many, and this is where managers craft their knowledge and where they disperse their leadership. Consider the following tasks and facets that managers and leaders must address every day, across the reaches of the organization; how is management effectiveness framed in each of the following areas?

Business Processes

Resource Relationships

Improvised Efforts

Conflict Resolution

Talent, Benchstrength

Innovation Efforts

Change Imperatives

Group Relationships

Revenue Platforms

Capital Resources

External Networks

Specific Competencies

Each of these areas and many more make up the routine work of managers forging the direction, integration and execution of the company's broader strategic agenda. Engagement means a great deal more than awareness and understanding. It means much more than delegation and empowerment, more than dispersion of leadership and management power. It transcends conventional wisdom about delegation and shared responsibility. This is an era of business leadership that will demand a lot more from managers as they impart greater responsibilities and expectations to an emergent generation of self-leaders. Putting the accountability and inspiration gears into motion at the individual level and for group preparedness and resolve is a key part of the recipe for business success and sustenance. The effective organization is all of this, reflecting strategic preparation, readiness and commitment. The effective organization is engaged in thought and behavior. Project teams and groups fail when they break down in the thought and behavior patterns that enable effective strategy management and leadership.

STRATEGY AS LEARNING

There is value in strategy as a learning framework. As people are exposed and engaged in the company's strategy agenda, they are challenged to be agents of that agenda. To become prepared and resolved in the direction, integration and execution of strategy. To contribute to the analytic and creative energy of strategy in business practice. To a broad extent, strategy is engaged and measured in learning terms. It establishes the exchange of ideas in the company, and these provide individuals with everyday gauges to guide their responsibilities and actions. People learn the realities of the business, the pathways of success, and the meaning and purpose of business results through the work of the strategy agenda.

The strategic cause-and-effect sequences that help determine business success are infused with organizational learning. People learn the principles and intentions of the company through the strategic agenda. They learn of culture and subculture through their engagement with the strategic agenda. Groups and project teams learn how to succeed in making strategy happen as they become engaged in the company's strategic agenda. They learn to be effective, responsive and supportive through their roles and tasks pinned to the strategic agenda. Strategy itself is a cultural foundation, shaping beliefs and behaviors. Strategy is part of the experience people exchange in the organization, and that experience is a powerful asset for the company.

DEVELOPING TALENT IN THE ENTERPRISE

How people think and behave toward the strategic agenda is part of the formula for business success. Talent, as suggested elsewhere in this book, is a matter of how people think and behave in their roles, in the context of the strategic agenda. Putting individuals and groups on track with their strategy leadership and management roles is a talent development option, which educates. It exposes people to the work of leadership and management, and it makes the work relevant by way of the strategic agenda. To every degree possible, we believe that people need to be engaged in strategy at every level, in every corner of the organization. Everybody on the team needs and deserves playing time. Otherwise, the capacity to develop talent can be diminished. White House advisor, Karen Hughes, would suggest that strategic clarity, example and optimism are the context in which this happens.

COMMENTS FOR STAFF AND TROOPS

In the best, most successful companies, the strategic agenda touches every person in the organization through processes of exchange. Every technician and sales operative, every customer service agent, every production worker, every support staffer. Every person, in every corner of the organization, has the right and charge to be engaged in the company's strategic agenda. This course of engagement *enables and inspires people*. It puts responsibility and accountability in their court. This course of engagement aligns, inspires and serves the cause of preparation and resolve. It *gives meaning and context* to the work of individuals, frames purpose and provides the light of relevance to goals, tasks and roles. Finally, the strategic agenda helps engage the minds, hearts and souls of the organization as it faces the future.

The communication of the strategic agenda is essential work, and perhaps too often, we leave this work unattended. The conveyance of strategy direction, integration and execution issues is a dynamic and complex undertaking. The general staff and troops of the organization have multi-lateral interests in the strategic agenda. Consider the following touch points of the agenda:

People in the far reaches of the company deserve to know the elements of the strategic agenda that will impact their roles and focus. Only then can they operate with clarity and focus, at full capacity, and with their personal talents and professional gifts in gear, fully engaged. They have a right to know, as they are central stakeholders in every aspect of strategy – direction, integration and execution.

People at every level of the organization have the opportunity to contribute knowledge, ideas, concerns and questions to the strategy leadership and management process. People close to the marketplace and close to technology have especially critical responsibilities to convey their insights and perspectives around, up and across the reaches of the organization. This effort is fundamental to a company's preparation and resolve. This is where the most inspired, responsive, talented people push their organizations and lead from the edges and reaches of the business. They must be engaged however, or these opportunities for growth and change do not emerge as responsibilities. Habits of success are engaged, and habits are part of the mindset and culture of successful organizations.

People outside the organization have a lot to say about the business in general and how the relationships of a company and its communities operate to create strategic and economic value. External stakeholders have views and concerns that have a lot of bearing on company success. Considering the positions of each stakeholder, even if they raise barriers to the progress and performance of the company.

Customers often have a lot to say about a business, and more importantly, they may have a few thoughts about a company that are not easy to harvest from normal correspondence. Companies are discovering more and more from their customers through high-discernment research and co-discovery work.

Suppliers usually have a lot to say, and again, a lot they might not say that would otherwise contribute to the company's strategic agenda. So-called partnerships spanning supply chains and demand chains may not be effectively or fully mined for opportunities to the degree they could be, or should be. New formats for resource chain collaboration is a key frontier. Trust is a factor, every day. Tom Stallkamp, Jordan Lewis and others appeal to our most hopeful frontiers for business trust.

Investors have a lot to say about the nature and direction of a company. They influence strategic and operating initiatives, M&A moves, resource investments, reporting and operating criteria. They may play a direct role in governance, or they may swipe targets from the cover of broad public ownership. In private companies, the same general dynamic exists, along with compliance issues, albeit in a different format.

Observers in the trade and in media usually have a few things to say about a company's strategic agenda. They often have the luxury of watching from a safe distance, safe from risks that surround the direction, integration and execution of the strategic agenda. They can be quite obtuse, and they can be armchair quarterbacks, shouting from the bleachers and cheap seats. Outside observers can be allies in the strategic agenda.

When we stand back and think about all the people and entities who are involved, directly and indirectly with a company's strategy, it becomes clear that the multi-lateral interests of these audiences shape the strategic agenda. That makes engagement an important consideration for everyone. We are not posturing about strategic security, that is another issue.

SPECIAL ISSUES AND CONCERNS

The everyday affairs of business involve many interfaces with the company's strategic agenda. The growth, performance and change issues that guide a company's agenda can be approached in terms of many special challenges and situations. Over the next few pages, we will explore five special situations and concerns that can demand extra consideration in the strategic agenda. These areas of interest include:

1. QUALITY AND LEAN MANAGEMENT

Generating economic and competitive edge...
this includes Lean, Six Sigma and related disciplines

2. CATEGORY MANAGEMENT AND CHANGE

Mapping essential market space advantage...
this includes brand systems and market networks

3. PRODUCT AND SERVICE DEVELOPMENT

Constructing strong product and service solutions...
this includes planned innovation and extension

4. MERGERS, ACQUISITIONS AND VENTURES

Embarking on external growth and change avenues...
this includes joint ventures and operating plans

5. BUSINESS SCALE AND SCOPE CHANGE

Connecting the ideas that shape business models...
this includes shifts in core and/or edge strategy

In each of these areas, special issues shape the organizational risks and options for growth, performance and change. In each case, special issues and concerns form what must be addressed in the strategic agenda, shaping strategy direction, integration and execution. The following subject matter and discussions serve as thought starters and plan guideposts for the strategy leadership and management agenda. The questions posed are intended to stimulate thoughts and debates that help refine the company's strategic agenda. Our partners work in each of these areas to help companies guide the effective direction, integration and execution of business strategy. Our basic approach for addressing these special issues and concerns is the same.

1. QUALITY AND LEAN MANAGEMENT

Quality and operational efficiency are hallmarks in competitive edge and advantage. Quality management disciplines have evolved a great deal in the last half century. Lean principles and methods have combined with quality practices to shape product and process design, core operations, customer relationships and the approach to supply and demand chain management. Agility is part of the quality and lean picture in more and more companies, and speed is part of the formula in adaptive and extended enterprises.

Strategy Agenda

Quality and lean management shape operating costs, margins and capital resources. Special issues and concerns in quality and lean management relate to and through each aspect of the company's strategic agenda.

Strategy Direction

Quality and lean management choices are significant issues at the strategy direction front door. These choices reflect key commitments to a particular business model and definition, and they force certain commitments and investments. They also help define the cultural and structure engagement that will be required for ongoing success and evolution. Here are two key questions that need to be addressed...

> What must be the impact of quality and lean management on growth, performance and change to be considered a success in the near-term, and in the more sustainable long-term picture of the business? Explain, explore and expand...

> As marketplace and organizational conditions evolve, how will various quality and lean management efforts contribute to the value of the company? Can these degrade strategic and economic value in any way? Explain, explore and expand...

230

Strategy Integration

Operating efficiency is clearly a substantial front in the strategy agenda, often posing integration challenges. Quality and lean initiatives are rich with resource issues and priority concerns that span different processes, functions and systems of the organization. Cultural and structural issues of quality and lean strategy integration are also energized with technical relationships that determine success. Here are some questions that relate to tie the integration of quality and lean management precepts to the work of strategy integration...

> What processes, people and resources need to be connected to make quality and lean management possible in the company? What barriers exist? External resource options?

> What makes the quality and lean management system of the company more or less adaptable to changing business conditions, problems and opportunities? Incentives and constraints?

Strategy Execution

Quality and lean management initiatives come with their own set of execution issues. Process mechanics and measurement systems are clearly part of the execution mix. In addition, those responsible for execution need to exercise creative problem-solving and discovery as a matter of course. Otherwise, quality and lean initiatives can become stale and static, reducing the advantage and leverage they're supposed to provide to the organization. Here are some questions to consider at the execution front...

> What are the main execution elements that must be delivered in the quality and lean management time frame in order to contribute to successful outcomes?

> What could stand in the way of successful execution and how could the organization anticipate and adjust to barriers and opportunities in the strategy agenda?

DISCUSSION POINTS

Quality and lean management are unique initiatives. They require strategic thought and behavior at every level of the organization. As companies look at the value of quality and lean management, several things should stand out for consideration:

> How does the quality and lean management initiative relate to the natural goals of the company?

> How does the quality and lean story get conveyed across the organization to provide meaning and relevance?

> How does the quality and lean discipline match the structures, culture and resources of the company?

> How does the quality and lean challenge differ from the company's other strategic priorities and goals?

> How does the quality and lean management initiative relate to growth, performance and change themes?

Strategy leadership and management efforts in this area have been an important aspect of the strategy agenda for mature companies in evolving market categories. These efforts draw from accumulated knowledge about operations, market requirements, technology assets and market structure. In addition, they draw from knowledge about cross-industry practices and applications in other business settings. Strategy leadership and management in this area serves to get the broader organization prepared and resolved for operational efficiency, competitive advantage and business evolution.

Beyond the normal agenda for quality and lean management are some questions that relate to the natural limits of quality and lean. What happens when continuous improvement and innovation efforts face set boundaries? And, how does an obsession with quality and lean management impair a company's approach to change? These are questions that deserve serious contemplation. They are too important to be left in the hands and minds of process technicians. They are truly company-wide considerations, and they interface with business strategy in many areas, across the enterprise.

2. CATEGORY MANAGEMENT AND CHANGE

Companies develop, produce and deliver their offerings to customers in the context of served market categories. A category is defined by economic, customer and resource boundaries. Companies compete on the basis of their position in and around a market category. The more attractive the category in terms of growth, profit and asset dynamics, and the more dominant the company in terms of brand, system and process advantage … the more successful and sustainable the business. Category management and change is a strategic discipline that reflects on the technical, social and economic trends shaping the business. Categories are the business unit framers.

Strategy Agenda

Category management decisions shape everything from a company's revenue platforms to its resource platforms. Special issues and concerns in category management relate, as one would expect, to each and every aspect of the company's strategic agenda. Again, consider the framework that connects:

Strategy Direction

Category management and change issues are at the heart of the company's strategy direction, reflecting pure questions about business models and definitions. Once again, these business model elements include:

Category development and management issues are fundamental pivot points in strategy direction. They deal with course-setting and choice-making about the options for growth and change. These are the key compass-setters.

233

Category strategy is shaped by issues that focus on what a company can be. These issues also help define how the company elects to compete, how it focuses its efforts to protect and defend its position and how it evolves. Here are a couple of strategy management and leadership questions that need to be addressed along the way:

> What must be the impact of category management on growth, performance and change to be considered a success in the near-term, and in the more sustainable long-term picture of the business? Implications and risks? Discovery frontiers?

> As marketplace and organizational conditions evolve, how will category management and change efforts contribute to the value of the company? Can these degrade strategic and economic value in any way? Sector and competitive risks?

Strategy Integration

Dealing with market category focus and boundaries requires disciplined management and leadership at the integration level. Category management and change initiatives are often intertwined with processes, functional issues, resource issues and systems that can enable or confound progress.

Nowhere in the strategic agenda is effective collaboration more valuable than category management and change. Category development strategy is where business definitions and models are established and leveraged. This is germane to strategic positioning. Here are some questions that relate to the integration of category management and change:

> What processes, people and resources need to be connected to make category management possible and effective in the company? What barriers and boundaries exist? What about network leverage and external resource options?

> What makes the category management system of the company more or less adaptable to changing business conditions, problems and opportunities? Are there change and leverage mechanisms?

Strategy Execution

Category management and change issues bring about the possibilities of business evolution and breakthrough innovation. They confront the effectiveness of the customer-focused company. They put people in a position to discover and act upon opportunities for improvement and change. Category management choices will influence revenue, margins, capital and resources. Consider these execution questions for category management:

> What are the main execution elements that must
> be delivered in the category management time frame
> in order to contribute to successful outcomes?
> Who are the key players?

> What could stand in the way of successful execution and
> how could the organization anticipate and adjust
> to barriers and opportunities in the strategy agenda?
> Key hurdles? Technical or behavioral blocks?

DISCUSSION POINTS

Category management and change are significant matters in the strategic agenda of the organization. They embody business definition and the roadmap for business evolution. As we look at the meaning and relevance of these matters, we need to check on these questions:

> How does the category management and change initiative
> relate to the natural goals of the company?

> How does the category change story get conveyed across
> the organization to provide meaning and relevance?

> How does the category management discipline match
> the company's structures, culture and resources?

> How does the category change challenge differ from
> the company's other strategic priorities and goals?

> How does the category management initiative relate to
> company growth, performance and change themes?

Strategy leadership and management challenges in the category management arena have emerged as key discipline targets. The dynamics of technology, distribution channels, brand investment, supply chains, customer segments, solution development and market experience all have some bearing on category management and change. Stronger organizations draw knowledge and perspectives from outside metaphorical business experience. They become effective collaborators and they invest well in their entreship engines.

The Emergence of Category Strategy Discipline

For the most part, category development and management has been the domain of consumer goods companies whose demand chain relationships within their channels have reshaped how business is done. Brand management, pricing, product design, merchandising, product format, packaging and communication elements come together in the broader category development and management arena. In that arena, value propositions of competing brands joust for share of mind, shelf space, share of purse and everything else, up to and including consumer empathy. In our collaborative research on category strategy, we're discovering a new range of management and leadership themes as well as a new platform for managing consensus related to growth, performance and change. Category strategy applies at GE and Boeing, Volvo and Marine Max, Samsung, Intel and Lowes…everywhere.

Category managers live by the boundaries of the market spaces they choose to serve. Conquest and defense at market boundaries, as well as the development of new and/or different boundaries are critical aspects of category management and change. They're central to the strategic agenda, and the boundaries that get crossed represent new business frontiers to be settled. Think i-Pod and Honda Element, Eclipse Jet and energy bars.

Beyond the normal array of category management and change issues there are some questions that temper the strategic agenda. What happens when competitive realities alter the boundaries of a category? What happens when supply and demand chains evolve in ways that collapse a company's growth, performance and change prospects? These are huge issues for most companies, and they're deserving of broader and more disciplined strategy contemplation and review. Suppliers to Home Depot and Cabelas know this, as do winemakers, auto producers and service providers, investors, farm and agribusiness entities, builders, bankers and scientists.

3. PRODUCT AND SERVICE DEVELOPMENT

In most companies, new product and service contributions to the business portfolio are significant drivers of growth, performance and change. Revenue leverage and resource leverage are common objectives of product programs. More innovative product and service programs may serve as the basis for radical business change and competitive edge. The managerial disciplines used to guide product and service development help determine the strategic and economic impact of the program. The leadership practices that surround product and service development help shape the company's pace and caliber of growth and change. This is a key strategy frontier.

Strategy Agenda

Product planning and development shapes revenue patterns, margins and capital leverage. Special issues and concerns in product and service plans relate to each and every aspect of the company's strategic agenda, from direction to integration to execution.

It has become more and more popular to approach the market with customer solutions that blend products, information and service into some distinctive bundle. Beyond all the bluster and blather about solution planning is a basic premise about competitive advantage, and it goes something like this:

> Customers seek value in the tangible, relational and
> economic value of the solution sets their suppliers present.
> They need and seek better technical, social and economic
> impact from their providers.

That value must be real and responsive to real needs. If the prospective value proposition is unclear and noisy, or if the promise is not matched by the delivery of the promise, there is a problem for the customer as well as the company. Our research on value propositions suggests that most companies and customers have serious disconnects on this front, and that has to become one of our chief concerns in product and service strategy.

Strategy Direction

Product and service orientation is an essential part of the company's business definition. It defines key aspects of what the company provides to its customers, whether that is a component for a machine or a leisure time experience. When the company frames its strategic direction, its operations and its customer focus, these product and service portfolio guidelines are foundation ideas in its business strategy. Consider:

> What must be the impact of product development and management on growth, performance and change to be considered a success in the near-term, and in the more sustainable long-term picture of the business? Explain, explore and expand...Discover and rediscover...

> As marketplace and organizational conditions evolve, how will various product and service planning efforts contribute to the value of the company? Can these degrade strategic and economic value in any way? Explain, explore and expand...

Strategy Integration

The integration issues in product planning and development are the subject of a great deal of **collaborative tension**. To succeed in strategy integration, organizations and their partners, up and down the supply and demand chain, must deal with conceptual premises, performance criteria, design integration, customer interests, economic parameters, sourcing interfaces and a host of value management considerations. Most companies have creative and process disciplines that help guide those elements. And, most companies have concerns about the application and efficacy of these processes. Consider these questions in reference to product and service development:

> What processes, people and resources need to be connected to make stronger product and service planning possible? What barriers exist? What resource chains are in play?

> What makes the product and service planning system of the company more or less adaptable to changing business conditions, problems and opportunities? What drives change?

Strategy Execution

Product and service development involves venture and risk factor management. Programs involving product and service line extensions to existing product platforms are relatively simple. Programs that tackle breakthrough products are taking risks and making stakes at an entirely different level. From the conception of new ideas to compliance details and design nuances, the execution issues are critical. And, more often today, strategy execution will cross the boundaries of the organization with partners. Consider these questions:

> What are the main execution elements that must be delivered in the product and service planning time frame in order to contribute to successful outcomes?

> What could stand in the way of successful execution and how could the organization anticipate and adjust to barriers and opportunities in the strategy agenda?

DISCUSSION POINTS

Product and service development involve tough strategic initiatives. They require a unique blend of creative and critical thought, and a very special balance of strategic management and leadership. Companies can approach their product and service development agenda with the following process and practice considerations:

> How does the product and service planning initiative relate to the natural goals of the company?

> How does the product planning story get conveyed across the organization to provide meaning and relevance?

> How does the product planning discipline match the structures, culture and resources of the company?

> How does the product planning challenge differ from the company's other strategic priorities and goals?

> How does the product planning management plan relate to growth, performance and change themes?

The empirical research on product planning and development suggests that companies face significant challenges across the strategy agenda. Direction in product planning and development connects a company's attention and resources on key bets; focusing on the wrong projects can lead to disaster. Integration is much harder than it looks; few programs come together on target, and few meet their concept-to-breakeven calendar objectives. Finally, execution in product and service strategy reflects the paradox of discipline; the procedures and processes used to guide and control plans can retard and destroy outcomes. These play upon the randomness and practical chances of development programs and development progress.

The intangibles that go with effective strategy in product planning and development are critical. One of those intangibles is the cultural resolve to connect design research with category planning and resource planning. Focused entreship and leadership and management assets invested in these areas dictate whether a company has prolific development programs or processes that actually stifle progressive new business development.

Successful Product and Service Development

There are plenty of recipes for product development success and while every company faces different circumstances and prospects, our product and service development research points to four common considerations of successful business advancement programs...

> **Entreship Practice...** bureaucrats are not entrepreneurs and entrepreneurs have special disciplines and habits.

> **Flexible Processes...** good discipline is important but complex development systems choke a lot of high-potential projects.

> **Resource Leverage...** hard and soft capital and time are the key resources for product planning and development.

> **Venture Approach...** managing risk and choice is a venture portfolio practice. Trust it, and treat it as such.

There are many ways to enhance product and service development success conditions. A *blending of ambiguity and clarity* in the work of product and service development is often part of the strategic approach.

4. MERGERS, ACQUISITIONS & VENTURES

In the growth, performance and change strategies of many companies are merger and acquisition schemes and new venture programs. These are related to the extent that they force inter-organizational action. They're also related in terms of the entreship issues that come together to balance ideas, investments and risks. For a host of reasons, the common record on merger and acquisition success is a little rough. M&A adventures often fail to deliver on the targets established by stakeholders. Ventures of different types have muddy success records. That is why they are called ventures; they involve risk and choice, and these collide under the pressure for success.

Strategy Agenda

Ventures and M&A programs can have a transformative impact on a company's revenue, margin and capital foundations. Special issues and concerns in these external growth and change avenues relate to the agenda:

As we look at this broader pathway for business growth, performance enhancement and change, we could also explore the redevelopment issues of the enterprise. Deals are done and ventures are launched for different reasons, and here are some of the most common themes and intentions:

Access to or expansion of markets, customers

Access to or leverage of technology resources

Enhancement of capital platforms and foundations

Access to knowledge, talent, cultural assets

Staging for near-term and long-term change

There are other themes and logics, and these are not necessarily distinct from organic growth and change prerogatives. Deals made for dumb reasons are legion, and the strategy filters of companies do not always work. Deals get too far down the road when their logics disappear.

Strategy Direction

When external growth and change alternatives are directed into the agenda and choices of the company, executives and boards are making some big assumptions about the definition of the barriers and the dynamics of the organization. These often involve commitments to competitive edge, diversification, business model evolution, or some other significant move. Again, we need to address two questions:

> What must be the impact of external development programs on growth, performance and change to be considered a success in the near-term, and in the more sustainable long-term picture of the business? Explain, explore, expand...

> As marketplace and organizational conditions evolve, how will various external development strategies contribute to the value of the company? Can they degrade strategic and economic value in any way? Explain, explore, expand...

Strategy Integration

Most of the big stories about M&A integration define the challenges of putting two or more companies together in ways that create new strategic and economic value. The realities of integration range from information systems to operating processes to cultural networks to resource alignment to marketing practices to policies. In every new venture, the watchword is new. New ways and means, new organizations and systems, new agenda values, new paths and approaches to customers, resources and collaboration. The emergent nature of new ventures involves some ambiguity and some vulnerability. Discovery is part of M&A practice, in uncharted waters. For effective M&A integration, consider these questions:

> What processes, people and resources need to be connected to make external development programs possible in the company? What barriers exist? How is power dispersed? What's new?

> What makes the external development system of the company more or less adaptable to changing business conditions, problems and opportunities? Who holds the compass? What's new?

Strategy Execution

External growth and change programs come with specific and unique execution concerns. Very often, the assumptions used by the planners at the front end of a deal are not exactly in sync with the realities of program execution. A dynamic environment opens the gates for adjustment and adaptation, and by nature, the need to be prepared and resolved. New ventures are tricky execution fronts as well. Time is often the first victim of the venture execution process as the tactical and resource issues of venture development mount. Here are those two simple questions we need to ask and answer in the scheme of external and organic development:

> What are the main execution elements that must be delivered in the external development time frame in order to contribute to successful outcomes? Are the right skillsets in order? And, are the right players in the game?

> What could stand in the way of successful execution and how could the organization anticipate and adjust to barriers and opportunities in the strategy agenda? Time, resources?

DISCUSSION POINTS

External business growth and change strategy, whether via M&A programs or venture programs, imparts a challenging set of themes. The glory and hoopla of putting together even a small M&A deal or venture, all too often overshadow the targeted, grubby work that makes or breaks the endeavor. Beyond the front page hype are these issues:

> How does the external business development initiative relate to the natural goals of the company?

> How does the M&A venture story get conveyed across the organizations to provide meaning and relevance?

> How does the external growth discipline match the structures, culture and resources of the company?

> How does the external change challenge differ from the company's other strategic priorities and goals?

> How does the M&A or venture management initiative relate to growth, performance and change themes?

The very life of a company can be changed in dramatic ways in short time spans through external growth and change moves. This is true not only at the Cisco and GE level, but also with smaller, middle-market companies. Venture management drives a great deal of the innovation that emerges in technical and non-technical companies. Ventures can reshape a company's resources, its market base, its economic platform and its benchstrength. Internal venture activity can redefine corporate soft assets that engender growth, performance and change. Mixing internal and external ventures is a unique and powerful zone for collaborative new business development.

Venture and M&A strategies present other challenges for managers and leaders throughout the organization. These impact business models and definitions. They temper organizational culture and competence. They shape category and brand assets. They add to the context of how a company competes and sustains itself in the context of a changing technical, social and economic environment. In essence, in ways that test culture, they alter the meaning and presence of an organization. Business models are reshaped by organic and external development, structure, resource and strategy platforms. The character of a company evolves with these elements.

External Growth and Change Strategy

Groups including the Association for Corporate Growth and the National Association of Corporate Directors have more than casual interests in the success of M&A and venture work. Significant mergers can impact industry structure and the attractiveness of market categories. New business ventures can alter the competitive landscape of a category as well as the rules and norms that govern market activity. Collaborative ventures between and among partner companies can spread business risks and drive innovation energy, thus shaping cycle times and value creation. External growth and change strategy impacts the relevance of organic growth and change.

Finally, one cannot underestimate the power to create or destroy strategic and economic value through mergers, acquisitions and ventures. These entail big strategic and economic leverage. The knife cuts both ways. In our research on *Boards and Strategy*, we have focused on some of the challenges that are discovered on the road to external and organic growth, performance and change strategy. One thing is clear; effective prosecution of external growth and change strategy is a sure testament to the effective direction, integration and execution. Business success flows from an agenda.

5. BUSINESS SCALE AND SCOPE CHANGE

Most companies, at one point or another, will tackle key questions related to their own business scope and scale. This is always an interesting juncture because it forces the consideration of capability, opportunity and business transformation. It encourages the conversation about what a company stands for and where it should be headed. Scale and scope are key issues.

Beyond some often blind assumptions about company growth and change are some really important and perplexing issues. How a company defines its business relative to the categories it serves and the competitors it faces has a great deal of bearing on its prospects for profitable, capital-efficient growth. What is the right scope and scale of an enterprise? How does it evolve? Should one company become two, or three companies?

Strategy Agenda

Business scope and scale are definitive aspects of any company's strategic agenda. Scope frames what a company does. Scale frames the business entity along with mass and format. Beyond all the usual blather about scalability are deeper questions about business structure, culture, resources and strategy.

Business scope and scale issues also reflect upon the realities of market structure and competition. Much is written about strategic focus and scope and competitive orientation based on differentiation or other foundations. Nowhere in strategy management and leadership is the linkage of strategy direction, integration and execution more important. Nowhere are decision options more connected, or more susceptible to breakdowns.

The emergence of collaborative business models and net-centric constructs for business operations open many new pathways for business scope and scale. Consider Amazon, eBay, Oracle, Capella University, Lowes and a host of other entities that have morphed themselves and the categories they serve based on scope and scale moves. These are fundamental moves that precipitate many emergent issues in business scale and scope.

Strategy Direction

Business scale and scope choices may dictate the prospects for company success, both near-term and long-term. These choices reflect commitments to business models and resource platforms. They also impact a company's capacity to evolve over time. The options elected today may dictate other scale and scope options that are available to the company in the future. They may commit a company to an investment platform that enables competitive advantage and/or operational rigidness. Scale and scope alternatives may play out in new structures and resource networks, and new players could approach the business with competing net-centric models. Consider:

> What must be the impact of business scope and scale management on growth, performance and change to be considered a success in the near-term, and in the more sustainable long-term picture? Explore, explain, expand…

> As marketplace and organizational conditions evolve, how will various scope and scale management efforts contribute to the value of the company? Can they degrade strategic and economic value in any way? Explore, explain, expand…

Strategy Integration

Scale and scope concerns are prime integration concerns. They are often influenced by the scheme of resource deployment, the leverage of hard and soft capital, the attitude and competence of the organization, and the company's performance culture. As companies confront their options related to scope and scale, they must deal with fundamental assumptions about resource investment, business adaptiveness and the prospects for competing at the strategy integration level. Here are two questions that should emerge visibly in these conversations about business scale and scope:

> What processes, people and resources need to be connected to make scope and scale management possible in the company? What barriers exist? What about benchstrength?

> What makes the scope and scale management system of the company more or less adaptable to changing business conditions, problems and opportunities? Key resources?

246

Strategy Execution

Scale is typically about size and pace. Scope is usually discussed in terms of business model deployment. These have unique execution considerations. Companies can wrestle with execution problems that would present themselves at different business scale and scope parameters. What would be the execution premises for a $50 million business unit versus an $800 million business unit in the same market category? What are the operational and tactical trade-offs between these scale and scope alternatives? Here are some parallel questions that need to be in the mix:

> What are the main execution elements that must be delivered in the scope and scale management time frame in order to contribute to successful outcomes? Risks, implications?

> What could stand in the way of successful execution and how could the organization anticipate and adjust to barriers and opportunities in the strategy agenda? Leverage issues?

DISCUSSION POINTS

Scale and scope strategy issues present some fundamental themes for management and leadership contemplation. These help define what barriers to build and hold, and what barriers to change and perhaps divest for value rationale. Here are some questions that deserve conversation:

> How does the scope and scale business choice relate to the natural goals of the company?

> How does the scope and scale story get conveyed across the organization to provide meaning and relevance?

> How does the scope and scale discipline match the structures, culture and resources of the company?

> How does the scope and scale challenge differ from the company's other strategic priorities and goals?

> How does the scope and scale management initiative relate to growth, performance and change themes?

Scale and scope questions like these open the business discussion to new insights in most companies. They challenge the premises we hold and they pose new assumptions that expand our horizons. These are matters not just for the consideration of executives and people serving in governance. At the operating level, and the reaches of the organization, front-line and first-level people have unique insights about scope and scale. Too often, these people are not fully tapped for their experience. They have common sense about business scale and scope. They know the resource leverage triggers.

In addition to the obvious matters of scope and scale, we need to consider the energy and resource implications of scale and scope options. What about extended and adaptive enterprise concepts and collaboration in business development? How will resource chains reshape industries?

Adaptive and Extended Enterprise

The adaptive enterprise is one that is capable of bending and flexing to challenges and opportunities. It bends and flexes under stress, and it bends and flexes to reach stretch goals. It's prepared, responsive and resolved to deal with circumstances that may or may not be part of its normal course. The adaptive enterprise is stoked by the common challenges of survival, and the engines of entreship. It's also stoked by competition.

The extended enterprise is one that is structured to take advantage of assets, resources and markets that are outside the formal operating scheme of entity. Collaborative supply chain and demand chain systems are common extended enterprise themes. Outsourcing of everything from admin work to innovation is common in the lexicon of the extended enterprise. External networks enable business success and evolution.

Business scale and scope options are multiplied for the company that entertains extended and adaptive enterprise concepts. Under the right kind of leadership and management schemes, extended and adaptive companies have more avenues for discovery, more channels for learning, and more vehicles for credible, applicable experience in growth and change.

We need to consider new ways of putting together business models of dynamic scope and scale. Finally, how can we help our business units act big when they're small or small when they're big? These are matters that deserve deeper thought and active, deliberate debate at all levels.

A CULTURAL VIEW OF STRATEGY

From growth and revenue leverage to margin and profit leverage, more companies have credible opportunities to create new business value. Do successful companies have cultural biases for business success and evolution? The answer is yes, but the issue is framed by leadership and management ideas that engage people in the strategic agenda at every level, and in every corner of the enterprise. Cultural and subcultural foundations of business success advance some key responsibilities for the people of the organization...

> How does the organization share its awareness of the realities of the marketplace and the enterprise itself?
>
> How deeply and prospectively do people understand the real strategic purpose and agenda of the company?
>
> How do people become engaged in the work that goes with the strategic agenda, regardless of its challenges?

The culture and subcultures of a company of people who are truly and deeply prepared and resolved are built on foundations of **trust**. Trust lives in the realm of strategy direction, integration and execution. Another element of trust is a kind of **restlessness** that questions the possibilities of the company, the possibilities for business growth, performance and change. This opens the doors of the organization to the paradox of its strategic agenda which is the desire for clarity versus the prospects for change. A company's cultures and subcultures can embrace both clarity and ambiguity, but not without a little **tension**. That tension supports conversations and active learning, the kind taught as strategic change leadership at Michigan State University.

TENSION AND BALANCE

The best intentions and principles of an organization are matched against the business realities that lie ahead. The natural goals of business provide a crucible of tension, balance and strategic thought. How do we balance the convergent ideas of financial performance, competition advantage, customer connection, and corporate stewardship? These ideas are made for those great conversations that fuel strategic thought and behavior. Conversations that spike interest, constructive argument and focused debate are catalysts for productive thinking about the strategy agenda.

BUSINESS SUCCESS DESERVED

David McCullough noted the keen connections of foresight and strategic readiness in his book, *1776*. The tensions between George Washington and the Continental Congress gained a sense of balance and resolve when, through collective leadership and resolve, the young country determined that its *success would have to be deserved*. Many believe that providence played a significant role in this strategic deservedness. Historians do not ignore the technical, social and economic hurdles that were encountered.

The notion of *business success that is deserved* is something that we can mark as a principle-centered idea that steels the hearts and minds of the company that is prepared and resolved with a vision of and for the success of the company...a sense of the value created by doing whatever it takes to drive forward...a business model that is relevant to the marketplace it serves...a match of business challenges and convictions...a blend of management and leadership assets that are dedicated to that success of the business enterprise. These are ideological and purposeful themes.

OPEN TO POSSIBILITY AND THREAT

The strategic agenda is clearly not a guarantee of business success. As McCullough and others have expressed, courage mixes with destiny. And the outcomes we achieve are, most often, the outcomes we truly deserve.

Successful companies practice for possibilities and threats, challenges and options, situations and prospects. They are alert to confrontations, issues and consequences. They have a creative and analytic sense of the emergent forks in the road. They breed awareness in their people, and they engineer powerful practices of communication throughout the organization. They're open. Open to ideas and risks. Open to discerning arguments, tough debate and thoughtful review. Open to sometimes crazy points of view that nudge the status quo. Open to the pre-conditions of change. Open to destiny, perhaps.

Openness is an organizational quality and discipline of the company that is truly prepared and resolved. *Openness begets openness.* It feeds on the integrity of the organization and its people and it grows in the soul of the culture and subculture of the organization over time. In openness, we're seeking possibility and choices, shaped by the kind of trust that powers ongoing discovery and creative thought that is always engaged.

250

BECOMING PREPARED AND RESOLVED

A company's strategic agenda should be addressed as an evolving work in progress. Ideas and goals mix with business conditions to set the frame for business growth, performance and change. Through the work that is outlined in the applications we've presented in this section, it's clear that companies have the obligation to test their thoughts and behaviors against some pragmatic questions. These questions guide planning and decision-making answers.

This approach to the strategic agenda is optimistic by nature, and we advocate for a constructive and optimistic point of view that can be empowered in the managerial and leadership fiber of the company. Effective organizations are thoughtful and discerning organizations. They hold their people to account for sound practice and good foresight. They challenge themselves with clear principles and ideas that reach out into the emerging business frontiers that could shape company survival and/or company success. They accept adversity for what it really is and what it brings — a set of conditions to operate with. Nothing more and nothing less, opportunities to survive, succeed and evolve. Opportunities to think and behave wisely. Opportunities to evolve.

Effective, evolving companies are more prepared and more resolved to succeed in a dynamic, complex business environment. To every person in your organization, the strategic agenda that brings together the issues of direction, integration and execution is relevant. The agenda makes things meaningful and personal. It establishes the critical foundations for people at every level and reach of the organization to become prepared and resolved for sustained business success. The task of all leaders and managers is to make the agenda real and relevant for everyone in the organization.

EPILOGUE

The journey of business is interesting. Companies realize their success in the context of dynamic and complex business conditions. They accomplish their goals in the context of opportunities and challenges that shape the journey. They earn their position by virtue of the competitive edge and moves they muster. They adapt and respond, for better…and sometimes for worse.

Throughout this book, my intent has been to explore the many facets of strategic thought and behavior. Those ideas inform and impact the choices a company makes as it establishes direction. They shape the company's approach to resource and asset integration. And they have a huge impact on the way people engage in the execution of ideas, programs and action plans. Strategic thought and behavior is in the culture of successful organizations, and it gathers its stride when it's dispersed throughout the enterprise.

Every company faces survival and success frontiers. When I reflect on the companies we have attended to over the past twenty-five years, two very simple things stand out. First, positive management and leadership practices open up and frame opportunities for meaningful growth, performance and change. Second, every business is part of a system or network of strategic value, and that network is constantly evolving. These are basic themes that season the meaning and relevance of strategy throughout the company.

THE JOURNEY OF BUSINESS STRATEGY

The way a company approaches strategic direction, integration and execution says a lot about its constitution and culture. My sense of business strategy today and tomorrow is based on the need to address a number of tasks and prerogatives. These are the keynote themes of *Prepared and Resolved*.

The **practice of strategy is a thoughtful and meaningful approach to focusing on business results.** One could get caught up in the mantra rather than the real and relevant meaning of strategy, and that is a significant trap for a lot of organizations. So, here are two fundamental questions:

> What about your strategy is relevant to the entire organization as a matter of survival and success? And, how is this conveyed in your culture and across the subcultures of the company?

> What about your strategic agenda is meaningful to the organization in terms that inspire people to think and behave in their best manner, with full engagement?

Getting beyond the buzz words and strategy blather is key. Our studies of effective organizations clearly show the power of pursuing the meaning and **relevance of strategy** beyond the documents, beyond the declared plans. Effective organizations bake strategic thought and behavior into their practices, cultures, resources and structures. Strategy shows in the values and actions of people. It shows in open, receptive views about business growth, performance and change. It shows in action patterns.

Another keynote involves **recasting the everyday work of leadership and management into every corner of the organization.** Strategy is not some mystic stuff for senior executives and staff workers. Instead, strategy is a kind of circulatory system that conveys ideas and engages or disturbs the **hearts and minds of people at every level of the organization.** This is more than strategy charades and cheerleading. It's more than slogans and charters and mission statements and posters. Strategy is the agenda for business success.

My general views of management and leadership are based on the reality that people learn how to contribute to business success through work framed by their company's strategy. **Leadership capability and management competence are learned assets, built through the strategic agenda.** The organization must put these learning avenues in perspective.

The benchstrength of an organization is expressed in management and leadership assets that enable the sound pursuit of the agenda. Benchstrength must match the strategic agenda, and it must accrue through the everyday experiences of strategy direction, integration and execution.

A company that is *focused on business results* learns the cause-and-effect elements of *business growth, performance and change.* People learn to connect strategy direction, integration and execution in their everyday work. Lacking such a strategic agenda, and lacking the *principles and practices* of strategic leadership and management, the prospects for business success would be clouded. Focus is critical.

The disconnects between strategy direction, integration and execution are hazards for every organization. *The desire for perfect alignment of strategy, resources, structure and company prospects is nice.* But in the real world, *it's harder than it looks.* The strategic agenda provides order.

Most firms compete in business sectors with *considerable forces of change on every front – technical, market, social and economic.* And as a result, they live with the reality that their agenda of strategy direction, integration and execution is, at best, a complex and dynamic scheme. There will be disconnects; that's just reality. That is why we need an organization that is discerning about strategy in general, thoughtful and prospective, and thoughtful about the principles, purpose and intent of the company. Anything less is just not complete, not sufficient. The real world for every company is that in which challenges and opportunities pose themselves in different ways, stacking near-term and long-term choices to be addressed wisely by leaders and managers. It all starts with *awareness and perspective.*

Strategy is an energy source for your organization and it should come as no surprise that energy is conveyed in different ways, both positive and negative. Our studies show that senior management is typically more satisfied with company strategy than are the troops who are charged with the everyday work of integration and execution. This is a reflection of many things. More than anything else, it suggests that many people are not often engaged in strategic thought and behavior or the strategic agenda. If they were, energy and engagement would be positive, at every level, in every corner of the company and across the company's borders. Energy and engagement are huge cultural issues in companies today. Business success is powered by energy and engagement in the strategic agenda.

The cultures and subcultures of an organization are inspired by different strategies, for different reasons. Consider the stuff that inspires the research scientists and account sales people of a pharma company. Or, the stuff that product engineers dream about versus the daily work of plant accountants. Strategy is relevant to each of these people, but in different ways. Senior managers must pause to recognize the diversity of answers to the questions posed by individuals at every level of the organization; *what's in this for me and what is my role? What's my personal stake?*

My sense of the business world is that your answers to the big questions on *strategy relevance must address the natural goals of business* in realistic and personal ways. Here are some checkpoints to consider:

> How does your strategy address
> **financial performance**, and what are the
> implications for every individual and group?

> How does your strategy address
> **competitive advantage**, and what are the
> implications for every individual and group?

> How does your strategy address
> **customer connections**, and what are the
> implications for every individual and group?

> How does your strategy address
> **corporate stewardship**, and what are the
> implications for every individual and group?

If you are to engage and inspire your people to live and breathe the strategic agenda – their strategy – you will need to get them in the game. If they don't get the game plan, the purpose, the relevance and meaning of your strategy agenda, no amount of blind faith or hope will engage employees or suppliers or investors in their world. Think about the strategic agenda in terms of exchange and engagement. What does an organization exchange with itself to earn the commitment of its people to the elements of its strategic agenda? Ask this question of the troops who work in your organization, and those who advise your company in governance. What matters, and what counts? How do these criteria translate to people across the organization?

ONTO THE FRONTIER

When Lewis and Clark set forth on their grand journey across America, there was some angst and some risk. Those concerns paled in comparison to the adventure itself, and the purpose of the leaders. Such a journey out onto the frontiers of a business are really not much different. Some focus, some direction, some risk, some challenge, some doubt, some possibility.

Strategy is the agenda for growth, performance and change. Your strategy provides meaning and purpose to the organization, and it informs individual thought and behavior at every level. When individuals and groups tackle problems and develop ideas, they are operating in the context of your strategy. If your strategy agenda is meaningful and relevant to the troops, and if it's in sync with the realities of your business, that is good. If your strategic agenda is without good foundations, if the communication and conveyance of your strategic agenda is fuzzy and wattless, and if your leadership and management are disengaged, that is bad. *Now then, consider these issues for followers; what do the troops deserve, what do they think and how do they behave? How do they approach the future?*

My intent in *Prepared and Resolved* is simple and humble. I want to share a set of ideas that help organizations address their unique challenges and prospects. I want to point to a general framework that transcends business convention and strategic planning practices, a framework that deals with the realities of business development and business evolution. My premise is that your people are tremendous assets, and under the right conditions, they will contribute their very best thoughts and behaviors to the success of the enterprise. Your task as business leaders and managers is to recognize those conditions, and to treat the company's strategic agenda properly.

Your conclusions here are important. Do you approach the realities of your business with a sense of prepared and resolved? Do you presume that your mission will be done? Do you engage your people in the cause-and-effect issues that power strategy direction, integration and execution? Are you confident that things will work out somehow? Here's to your success and here's to the people who are *prepared and resolved* to create strategic and economic value in their work. Work for the success you deserve.

RESEARCH NOTES

The research references for this book include empirical and academic studies of strategy and performance issues. These references date back to some of the original strategic impact studies of the 1970's, as well as organizational research from the 1960's. Some are current, reflecting work prepared in specific business disciplines including resource management, product development, economic value programs, enterprise structure, category management and marketing systems. This is not an academic book. Our references are intended to explore, expand upon and engage strategic thought and behavior. Our proprietary research citings are always expressed in general and qualitative ranges. And, there is always more to discover.

READING THEMES

There is a great body of business thought and literature that is germane to the strategic agenda framed in *Prepared and Resolved*. We are often asked to recommend books and articles on subjects related to the agenda for growth, performance and change, and my reponse changes like the seasons. See *www.dewarsloan.com* for current book selections and reviews. Here are some suggestions for lifelong students of the strategic agenda:

> Do a steady diet of three or four good periodicals such as *Business Week, Fast Company, Fortune* and *Business 2.0.*

> Explore books in your discipline that are substantive, relevant, provocative and exploratory – not simplistic.

> Do a routine diet of topical searching on the web for important subjects that are relevant to your business.

Reading and sharing ideas with your professional peers serves to shape your awareness, understanding and engagement. Some of our clients have work groups that get together to discuss general and specific subject matter that has common business threads. In our view, this is a great and valuable kind of continuing education. Business people in every age/experience cohort need to learn about new material and perspectives every day.

ABOUT THE AUTHOR

Daniel Wolf is Managing Director of Dewar Sloan, a consulting practice focused on business growth, performance and change. Previously, Wolf served in corporate positions charged with leading worldwide planning, business development, marketing systems and product development.

Wolf has more than 30 years of corporate and consulting experience, in service to a wide range of great companies including Bombardier, Stryker, Masterbrand, Allied Signal, Herman Miller, W.L.Gore, Fisher Scientific, Cascade, Kelly Services, Siemens, Ingersoll Rand, TORO, Global Device and a host of middle-market and emerging organizations.

Much of his work involves the evolution of company direction, organization and resources, always focused on business results. Wolf is a frequent speaker to corporate, professional and executive education groups, and some of his more recent presentation topics include:

Driving Strategy Deep into the Organization

Leading Collaboration and Development Efforts

Growth and Category Development Strategy

Wolf has written dozens of protocol guides, white papers and policy briefs on related subjects in management, and he is active in a research program that addresses the concerns that surround governance and management. He is completing the research work on a *Boards and Strategy* monograph which deals with governance practices and the strategic agenda. Together with his partners, Wolf is active in strategy development and governance services for private and public entities, and he is also working with a collaborative group to address emerging problems and challenges in category development strategy and related enterprise strategy issues.

The author can be contacted at dwolf@dewarsloan.com.

For speaking arrangements, visit www.preparedandresolved.com.

For research references, visit www.dewarsloan.com.

INDEX

V

value...

>creation. 45-49, 79, 113, 122, 180, 197

>degradation. 176-177

>edge. 59

>network. 253

>vale proposition. 97, 107

vision. 41, 68, 117

volition. 38-39, 194

VUCA factors. 63, 115

W

Ward, Ralph. 221

web-centric business. 34-106

What Counts — Key Metrics. 188

Wired. 20

who, what, how, when. 171

workforce development. 126

World War II. 125